Recent developments in corporate finance

Recent developments in corporate finance

Edited by

JEREMY EDWARDS, JULIAN FRANKS,
COLIN MAYER and
STEPHEN SCHAEFER

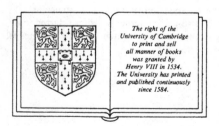

The right of the
University of Cambridge
to print and sell
all manner of books
was granted by
Henry VIII in 1534.
The University has printed
and published continuously
since 1584.

CAMBRIDGE UNIVERSITY PRESS

Cambridge
London   New York   New Rochelle
Melbourne   Sydney

CAMBRIDGE UNIVERSITY PRESS
Cambridge, New York, Melbourne, Madrid, Cape Town, Singapore,
São Paulo, Delhi, Dubai, Tokyo

Cambridge University Press
The Edinburgh Building, Cambridge CB2 8RU, UK

Published in the United States of America by Cambridge University Press, New York

www.cambridge.org
Information on this title: www.cambridge.org/9780521126397

First published 1986
This digitally printed version 2009

A catalogue record for this publication is available from the British Library

Library of Congress Cataloguing in Publication data

Recent developments in corporate finance.
1. Corporations–Finance.   I. Edwards, J. S. S.
(Jeremy S. S.)
HG4026.5.R43   1986   658.1′5   86–8241

ISBN 978-0-521-32964-4 Hardback
ISBN 978-0-521-12639-7 Paperback

Contents

FINANCIAL MARKETS

ISSUES IN CORPORATE FINANCE

Contents

INTERNATIONAL FINANCE

Tables

Figures

Preface

In this volume we are publishing the proceedings of the Economic and Social Research Council/Centre for Economic Policy Research conference 'Recent Developments in Corporate Finance, Investment and Taxation' held in Wadham College, Oxford and the Institute of Economics and Statistics, Oxford on 2–6 September 1985.

We would like to express our appreciation to the authors and discussants whose contributions are published here for their participation in the conference and readiness to help in the preparation of this volume. We also wish to thank the other participants in the conference, whose names are listed below, for their contributions to the discussion which made the conference one of great value.

We would like to thank the Economic and Social Research Council for providing financial support for the conference. We are also grateful to Drexel Burnham Lambert Ltd for making a financial contribution to the conference. The quality of this manuscript, and the speed with which it was published, owe much to the efforts of the technical editor, Michael Keen of the University of Essex. Finally we would like to thank Monica Allen and Wendy Thompson of the CEPR and Elaine Le Fevre and Rachel Swain of the London Business School for their major contributions to the organisation of the conference.

JEREMY EDWARDS
JULIAN FRANKS
COLIN MAYER
STEPHEN SCHAEFER

Contributors

Editors

Jeremy Edwards *St John's College, Cambridge*
Julian Franks *London Business School*
Colin Mayer *St Anne's College, Oxford*
Stephen Schaefer *London Business School*

Authors

Julian Alworth *Bank for International Settlements*
Luca Anderlini *Wolfson College, Cambridge*
Paul Asquith *Harvard Business School*
Ian Cooper *London Business School*
Richard Green *Carnegie-Mellon University*
Robert Heinkel *University of British Columbia*
Evi Kaplanis *London Business School*
David Mullins Jr *Harvard Business School*
Eduardo Schwartz *University of British Columbia*
Joseph Stiglitz *Princeton University and Bell Communications Research*
Lawrence Summers *Harvard University*
Eli Talmor *Tel-Aviv University*
Andrew Weiss *Columbia University and Bell Communications Research*

Discussants

Richard Brealey *London Business School*
Steven Fries *St Edmund Hall, Oxford*
Oliver Hart *Massachusetts Institute of Technology*
David Webb *London School of Economics*

Other participants

Alan Auerbach *University of Pennsylvania*
Sudipto Bhattacharya *Berkeley, California*
Willard Carleton *University of Arizona*
Chris Gilbert   *Wadham College, Oxford*
Paul Grout *University of Birmingham*
Martin Hellwig *University of Bonn*
Christopher Higson *Kingston Polytechnic*
Stewart Hodges *Warwick University*
John Kay *Institute for Fiscal Studies*
Michael Keen *Essex University*
John King *Institute for Fiscal Studies*
Mervyn King *London School of Economics*
Yoram Landskroner *Hebrew University of Jerusalem*
Saman Majd *The Wharton School*
Oliveira Marques *Porto, Portugal*
Anthony Neuburger *London Business School*
Stephen Nickell *Institute of Economics and Statistics, Oxford*
Archie Pitts *University of East Anglia*
Jim Poterba *Massachusetts Institute of Technology*
Abraham Ravid *State University of New Jersey*
Artur Raviv *Northwestern University*
Ailsa Roell *London School of Economics*
Janette Rutterford *London School of Economics*
Cornelius Schilbred *Norwegian School of Economics and Business Admin.*
Myron Scholes *Stanford University*
Jay Shanken *Berkeley, California*
Geert-Jan Schijndel *Tilburg University*
Theo Vermaelen *Universiteit Leuven*

Introduction

JEREMY EDWARDS, JULIAN FRANKS,
COLIN MAYER and STEPHEN SCHAEFER

Over the past decade there have been several significant developments in the field of financial economics. These have spanned a diverse range of topics from the empirical evaluation of financial markets to the theoretical description of specific features of financial arrangements. They have involved people working in a number of areas of economics including theoretical micro-economics, industrial, labour and public economics, as well as those who could be more conventionally classified as financial economists. Much of the research has been undertaken in the United States but a significant proportion is now being performed in other countries, in particular in Europe, Israel and Japan. With such important developments in finance occurring in a number of different areas of economics and parts of the world it seemed an opportune moment at which to bring together some of the leading participants in the field.

Wadham College, Oxford and the Institute of Economics and Statistics in Oxford were hosts in the first week of September 1985 to an international conference on "Recent Developments in Corporate Finance, Investment and Taxation". There were forty-five participants from eight countries. One of the major objectives of the conference was to encourage participation by young scholars and approximately a quarter of the authors of the papers and participants at the conference could be appropriately described as having recently entered the field. The conference was organized by the Centre for Economic Policy Research in collaboration with the London Business School. It was financed by the Economic and Social Research Council with additional support from Drexel Burnham Lambert. Of the seventeen papers presented at the conference eight are reproduced in this volume. The papers reflected the diverse range of developments in financial economics and general categorizations of the papers are not easy to come by. There were, however, a few themes that stood out as being common to several of the presentations: in particular, imperfections in financial

1

markets and the role of taxation in influencing the behaviour of investors and companies were discussed by many of the authors.

One aspect of perfect capital markets that has received increasing attention from economists is the assumption of complete information available to all participants. It is an assumption that is, of course, fundamental to the traditional descriptions of market economies as well as the asset pricing models of financial economics. While the importance of the assumption has been appreciated for a long time it is only recently that its validity in financial markets has been brought into serious question. More significantly the last few years have seen a proliferation of models that examine the effects of relaxing this assumption in specific circumstances. It is clear that while many fascinating models now abound we have as yet only seen the tip of a very sizeable iceberg that will shape future developments in financial economics.

Some of the models of imperfect information provide a new way of analysing issues that have been of long standing concern to economists. An example of this is the question of whether banks and other financial institutions can be expected to restrict the amount of credit available to potential borrowers – credit rationing. In the absence of externally imposed constraints on banks' freedom to set interest rates and in the absence of information available to banks on the relative credit worthiness of different borrowers, the question arises as to why banks should not raise interest rates to the point at which the market for loans clears. The answer that Stiglitz and Weiss provided in their now seminal 1981 paper was that a rise in interest rates may *reduce* the average return to banks on their loans. The reason for this is that if banks cannot establish the quality of their borrowers then a rise in interest rates may result in a worsening in the average quality of borrowers, as reflected in the riskiness of projects being undertaken (adverse selection) and/or a particular group of borrowers choosing more risky projects (moral hazard). As a consequence, the interest rate which maximizes banks' profitability is not necessarily the one that clears the market for loans.

Stiglitz and Weiss noted that collateral may be used to diminish the problems created by adverse selection and moral hazard. They argued, however, that collateral requirements may in themselves exacerbate problems by concentrating the market for loans among relatively wealthy individuals whose degree of risk aversion is comparatively low and who therefore choose risky projects. Thus neither an increase in interest rates nor an increase in collateral requirements necessarily raises bank profitability and the resulting equilibrium is one in which banks might ration credit to some borrowers.

A number of authors subsequently objected that while Stiglitz and Weiss had considered the effect of raising either interest rates or collateral requirements they had not analysed the simultaneous use of both instruments. Bester (1985), for example, has argued that interest rates and collateral can together be used to distinguish high and low risk borrowers. Low risk borrowers require a smaller reduction in interest rates for a certain increase in collateral requirements than high risk borrowers to maintain a given level of utility. This difference in marginal rates of substitution between low and high risk borrowers establishes a separating equilibrium in which interest rates will be set to clear the market for loans.

In their paper in this volume Stiglitz and Weiss demonstrate that relaxing the constraints on instruments to include the use of collateral alongside interest rates in fact broadens the range of possible equilibria. Pooling, partially separating, and completely separating equilibria may all be observed either with or without rationing. Furthermore the rationing may affect some or all classes of borrowers – a result that stands in contrast with their 1981 paper in which only one group was rationed. The reason that the additional instrument does not eliminate credit rationing is that banks continue to have only imperfect information about their borrowers. So long as this is the case then a further broadening of the class of instruments to include, for example, the partial financing of projects through equity capital will not ensure that all desired borrowing is fulfilled.

Information asymmetries may be a feature of not only the lending but also the deposit side of the banking sector. Banks play a fundamental role in an economy of transforming illiquid assets into liquid deposits. The demand for liquidity as described by Diamond and Dybvig (1983) comes from consumer uncertainty about their demand requirements in particular periods. Lack of observability of consumer demand type (as reflected in the periods in which requirements fall due) prevents consumers from insuring against this uncertainty. Instead bank deposits permit consumers to meet demand requirements as they arise. One equilibrium thus involves banks in providing liquidity for uncertain consumption requirements. Another, however, takes the form of investors withdrawing their deposits in the expectation that withdrawals by other depositors may prevent the bank meeting future obligations. As Diamond and Dybvig note, these bank runs may in no way reflect a deficiency in the financial state of banks but may merely be triggered by the anticipation that other depositors are about to withdraw. Furthermore, as Diamond and Dybvig observe, 'a demand deposit contract which is not subject to runs provides no liquidity services' (1983, p. 409).

A number of methods of discouraging bank runs have been suggested. Most obviously banks could suspend the right of depositors to convert their assets. Diamond and Dybvig suggest that if banks know the 'normal' demand for withdrawals in any period then suspension of convertibility can eliminate the risk of runs at no cost to consumption activities. However, Anderlini notes in the paper in this volume that this desirable feature of suspension of convertibility is not robust to generalizations of the preference function of consumers. Suspension cannot be used to rule out the possibility that consumers' withdrawal demands will exceed their consumption levels. The avoidance of untruthful equilibria has to find a resolution in one of the other methods that have been suggested for avoiding runs, namely deposit insurance schemes and lender of last resort facilities. In addition, Anderlini demonstrates that even in the absence of bank runs, a more complex description of consumer preferences prevents the banking system from achieving the optimal allocation that would be associated with complete markets in the presence of full observability.

Banks are not, of course, the only financial institutions in which problems of asymmetries of information arise. There are a number of unresolved questions about the new equity issuing practices of firms. One concerns the widely observed practice of underwriting new issues even in cases in which the issues takes the form of a rights offering and could therefore be priced at substantial discount with no detriment to existing shareholders. Both Marsh (1982) in the UK and Smith (1977) in the US have noted that the cost of underwriting an issue significantly exceeds the value of the service that is being provided in the form of a put option to sell to the underwriter if the issue is not fully subscribed. The deep discount rights issue could therefore have been expected to replace the underwritten offering.

Heinkel and Schwartz, however, suggest that this 'apparent mispricing' may be better comprehended when viewing the new issue decision through the lens of asymmetric information. The Heinkel and Schwartz paper is in the tradition of asymmetric information models in which managers have superior information about the quality of their firm than their investors and use some costly technique of signalling this information to their investors. Such models have been used to try to provide a resolution for another major paradox in finance, namely why do companies pay dividends to their shareholders? (Bhattacharya (1979), John and Williams (1985) and Miller and Rock (1985).) In the Heinkel and Schwartz model, managers' choice of new issue techniques conveys information to investors about firm quality: fully underwritten general cash offerings versus rights offerings, standby (underwritten) versus uninsured rights offerings. The information approach may help to explain not only when underwritten offerings may be chosen in preference to rights issues but also why rights issues may be underwritten and not set at arbitrarily low exercise prices. What the literature on signalling has not yet succeeded in doing is in choosing between the range of alternative instruments that may be available for conveying information to shareholders. In the absence of a description of the relative costs of signals it is difficult to analyse the optimality properties of different instruments in isolation.

A possibly related paradox surrounding new equity issues concerns the apparent importance that managers attach to the timing of new issues. Taggart (1977) and Marsh (1979) have observed that stock price movements bear heavily on the decision to issue new equity. In the case of Marsh's study there was evidence that both general market movement in share prices and movements in the firm's stock price relative to the market influence the timing decision. Asquith and Mullins in this volume provide further evidence on both these timing effects.

The reason that these observations present something of a paradox is that the cost of making a new equity issue should be unrelated to the price of the company's equity. If the share price accurately reflects the value of the firm's future earnings stream then the cost of the issue to existing shareholders will be unaffected by whether a large number of new shares are issued at a low share price or a few shares are issued at a high share price to raise a certain amount of equity capital. If the managers of the issuing firm have reason to believe that the firm is undervalued then they can benefit existing shareholders merely by making an announcement to that effect independently of making a new issue. However, evidence reported by Asquith and Mullins that share prices decline subsequent to new issues may help to explain the concern with timing. For if, as Asquith and Mullins suggest, the extent to which share price declines is related to previous share price movements, then managers may be acting in existing shareholders' interests by restricting new issues to periods of favourable share price changes. One explanation that is suggested for the share price decline on announcement of an issue is the negative information associated with the event.

The question of how share prices respond at the time of new equity issues is one aspect of the more general debate on market efficiency. Until comparatively recently there were few dissenting voices to the thesis that financial markets price assets appropriately in relation to available information and respond quickly to the arrival of new information. There are two parts to this assertion. First, if asset prices did not incorporate all available information then profitable opportunities should exist and with their exploitation such anomalies would be eliminated. Secondly, despite a wealth of empirical analysis very few contradictions to the efficiency hypothesis have been uncovered and where they have been observed the suspicion remains that they may reflect an inaccuracy in the theory of asset pricing that has been employed in the tests not a refutation of an efficient market. Such is the status of the efficient market hypothesis that it is widely cited as being the best documented empirical statement in economics.

A challenge to the efficient market hypothesis thus threatens the basis of much theoretical and empirical financial economics. But over the last few years a number of apparent inconsistencies with efficient markets have been recorded which are still to find an adequate explanation in traditional models. Modigliani and Cohn (1979) suggest that underpricing of equity prices may reflect inflation illusion on the part of investors. Shiller (1979, 1981a and 1981b) has documented the excess volatility of both bond and stock prices in relation to the underlying value of the assets. Ohlson and Penman (1985) have recorded a remarkable increase in the volatility of share prices subsequent to a stock split. Uncovering pricing anomalies has suddenly become an acceptable and fashionable pastime. However, none of the empirical observations of anomalies address the first argument mentioned above that deviations from efficiency should give rise to profitable opportunities. In this respect the article by Summers in this volume is of particular interest. He asserts that many of the tests economists have employed in analysing the efficiency hypothesis are very weak in rejecting the null hypothesis of efficiency. This comes from the fact that quite significant deviations from efficiency may only give rise to minute model misspecifications that can readily be swamped by the smallest amount of noise in the data or underlying processes. As a consequence powers of detecting model misspecifications are very weak and Summers notes that something like 5000 years of data would be required to have a 50 per cent chance of rejecting efficiency, even in cases in which market valuations may differ by more than 30 per cent from the rational expectation of the present value of future cash flows. Not only may this help to resolve the apparent contradiction between Shiller's findings of inefficiency using volatility measures and previous tests but it also may explain the failure to exploit profitable opportunities. For, as Summers argues, if economists lack the tools with which to establish deviations from efficiency, how should investors be expected to uncover profitable investments?

The efficiency property of markets can be viewed in the light of investors' portfolio choices. In the absence of transaction costs portfolio models suggest that all investors will hold all non-redundant assets in the market. In the Capital Asset Pricing Model (CAPM) with homogeneous expectations and common opportunity sets all investors will hold the market portfolio and the risk free asset or a zero-beta portfolio. Yet empirical studies of asset holdings have found that individuals allocate their wealth among a small number of assets. Blume and Friend (1975) found that 34 per cent of equity investors held only one stock and 70 per cent held three or fewer. King and Leape (1984) found that half of a 1978 survey of wealthy American householders held fewer than eight of the thirty-six assets considered.

An obvious explanation for this observation is that significant transaction costs are present. Brennan (1975), Goldsmith (1976), and Maysher (1979) have all demonstrated that the presence of fixed transaction costs can cause investors to restrict their holdings of available assets. One area in which transaction costs might be expected to be particularly relevant is international investment. Extending the portfolio model in an international context investors should hold the world market portfolio of risky assets. But exchange controls, withholding taxes, safe custody fees, risks of expropriation and lack of familiarity with overseas markets all give rise to costs of cross border investment that will discourage international diversification. Since the empirical measurement of at least some of these costs is difficult, a direct test of portfolio models in an international context is not readily forthcoming. Instead Cooper and Kaplanis in this volume work back from a CAPM to derive the implied shadow prices of international investing and compare these with known observable transaction costs. As in the domestic context, their results suggest that in some cases measurable costs can only account for a small proportion of total implicit costs.

Taxes represent a sizeable proportion of the observable costs in Cooper and Kaplanis' exercise. For countries that operate Double Taxation Relief (DTR) schemes the net costs associated with withholding taxes are determined by the relative rates of taxation that investors pay on investment income domestically and overseas. For example, if the withholding tax rate on overseas income is lower than a UK investor's domestic income tax rate then the tax liability is limited to the domestic income tax rate. But if the withholding rate is in excess of the domestic income rate then the withholding rate becomes the appropriate tax price. These considerations are not just relevant to investor portfolio allocations but also to the investment location decisions of multinational corporations. Deadweight costs on portfolio investment imply that the cost of capital for an overseas investment in real assets is lower than that for domestic investment. This does not imply an incentive to locate investments overseas for there may also be deadweight costs to real investment overseas. In the context of multinational investments tax complications are compounded by the relevance of domestic and foreign corporate tax considerations. As King (1974, 1977) demonstrated in analysing financing and investment decisions of firms, account has to be taken of the interactions of corporate with personal taxation. In a domestic context alone these factors can become quite complex to analyse. In an international setting these problems are exacerbated by differences in national tax systems and DTR provisions. To date most economists have, as a consequence, found descriptions of international tax arrangements virtually impenetrable. The great merit of Alworth's paper in this volume is that it describes a scheme of extending King's neat categorization of domestic tax systems to an international context. For the first time economists now have a coherent framework within which they can assess the effects of different systems of taxation and DTR on the international financing and investment decisions of firms. The paper should therefore be of wide practical application.

While great strides were made in the 1970's in incorporating relevant features of tax systems in financial and investment analyses, it is only recently that careful account has been taken of one important feature of corporate tax systems. This is the asymmetrical treatment of corporate profits and losses: profits are subject to taxation, losses have to be carried forward (or back) against future (or past) profits. With declining profitability in the early 1970s and again at the beginning of the 1980s this asymmetrical feature of corporation tax has become of considerable practical relevance. It affects the value of tax shields to investment and debt finance (DeAngelo and Masulis (1980), Cordes and Sheffrin (1983)), it encourages a variety of tax transfer activities (Cooper and Franks (1983)) and it influences the firm's financing (Mayer (1986)) and investment (Auerbach (1984), Green and Talmor (1985)) decisions. The paper by Green and Talmor in this volume focuses on the last of these. It notes that the asymmetric treatment of profits and losses can be viewed as a call option on the firm's earnings at the corporate tax rate, exerciseable at the level of profits at which tax allowances are just extinguished. It demonstrates that the effect of the asymmetry on the scale of investment chosen by a firm is dependent on the type of deductions being claimed. Deductions which depend on investment, for example depreciation allowances, distort investment decisions (in relation to a symmetric tax system) in the opposite direction to fixed deductions (for example, interest payments and losses carried forward from previous periods). In general the overall effect of the asymmetry is ambiguous. In a multiperiod context an analysis of the asymmetric treatment of taxation is complicated by the provision to carry forward and back losses. Majd and Myers (1985) use a simulation analysis to exploit the call option analogy in a multiperiod model and find that the scale of distortions to the investment decision can be very sizeable. They are led to conclude that asymmetries are a feature of the tax system to which future investigators will have to pay close attention if they are to provide accurate recommendations on capital budgeting and tax policy.

This book illustrates the diverse range of new issues that are beginning to emerge in financial economics. Some look to be of fundamental significance. Others may prove to be less enduring but are at least of much current interest, Observing the direction that future research takes should make the next few years a fascinating period for the study of financial economics.

REFERENCES

Auerbach, A. J. (1984). 'The Dynamic Effects of Tax Law Asymmetries.' National Bureau of Economic Research Working Paper No. 1152.

Bester, H. (1985). 'Screening Versus Rationing in Credit Markets with Imperfect Information.' *American Economic Review*, 75, 850–855.

Bhattacharya, S. (1979). 'Imperfection Information, Dividend Policy and the "Bird in the Hand Fallacy".' *Bell Journal of Economics*, 10, 259–270.

Blume, M. E. and I. Friend (1975). 'The Asset Structure of Individual Portfolios and Some Implications for Utility Functions.' *Journal of Finance*, 30, 585–603.

Brennan, M. J. (1975). 'The Optimal Number of Securities in a Risky Asset Portfolio when there are Fixed Costs of Transacting: Theory and Some Empirical Results.' *Journal of Financial and Quantitative Analysis*, 10, 488–496.

Cooper, I. and J. Franks (1983). 'The Interaction of Financing and Investment Decisions When the Firm has Unused Tax Credits.' *Journal of Finance*, 38, 571–583.

Cordes, J. J. and S. M. Sheffrin (1983). 'Estimating the Tax Advantage of Corporate Debt.' *Journal of Finance*, 38, 95–105.

De Angelo, H. and R. W. Masulis (1980). 'Optimal Capital Structure under Corporate and Personal Taxation.' *Journal of Financial Economics*, 8, 3–30.

Diamond, D. W. and P. H. Dybvig (1983). 'Bank Runs, Deposit Insurance and Liquidity.' *Journal of Political Economy*, 91, 401–419.

Goldsmith, D. (1976). 'Transactions Costs and the Theory of Portfolio Selection.' *Journal of Finance*, 31, 1127–1139.

Green, R. and E. Talmor (1985). 'The Structure and Incentive Effects of Corporate Tax Liabilities.' *Journal of Finance*, 40, 1095–1114.

John, K. and J. Williams (1985). 'Dividends, Dilution and Taxes: A Signalling Equilibrium.' *Journal of Finance*, 40, 1053–1070.

King, M. A. (1974). 'Taxation and the Cost of Capital.' *Review of Economic Studies*, 41, 21–35.

King, M. A. (1977). *Public Policy and the Corporation*. Chapman and Hall, London.

King, M. A. and J. I. Leape (1984). 'Household Portfolio Composition and the Life Cycle.' NBER Working Paper.

Majd, S. and S. C. Myers (1985). 'Valuing the Government's Tax Claim on Risky Corporate Assets.' NBER Working Paper.

Marsh, P. R. (1979). 'Equity Rights Issues and the Efficiency of the U.K. Stock Market.' *Journal of Finance*, 34, 839–862.

Marsh, P. R. (1982). 'The Choice Between Equity and Debt: An Empirical Study.' *Journal of Finance*, 37, 121–144.

Mayer, C. (1986). 'Corporation Tax, Finance and the Cost of Capital.' *Review of Economic Studies*, 53, 93–112.

Maysher, J. (1979). 'Transactions Costs in a Model of Capital Market Equilibrium.' *Journal of Political Economy*, 87, 678–700.

10   **Jeremy Edwards et al.**

Miller, M. H. and K. Rock (1985). 'Dividend Policy under Asymmetric Information.' *Journal of Finance*, **40**, 1031–1051.

Modigliani, F. and R. Cohn (1979). 'Inflation, Rational Valuation and the Market.' *Financial Analysts Journal*, **35**, 3–23.

Ohlson, J. A. and S. H. Penman (1985). 'Volatility Increase Subsequent to Stock Splits: An Empirical Aberration.' *Journal of Financial Economics*, **14**, 251–266.

Shiller, R. (1979). 'The Volatility of Long-Term Interest Rates and Expectations Models of the Term Structure.' *Journal of Political Economy*, **87**, 1190–1219.

Shiller, R. (1981a). 'Do Stock Prices Move Too Much to be Justified by Subsequent Changes in Dividends?' *American Economic Review*, **71**, 421–436.

Shiller, R. (1981b). 'The Use of Volatility Measures in Assessing Market Efficiency.' *Journal of Finance*, **36**, 291–304.

Smith, C. W. Jr (1977). 'Alternative Methods for Raising Capital: Rights Versus Underwritten Offerings.' *Journal of Financial Economics*, **5**, 309–328.

Stiglitz, J. E. and A. Weiss (1981). 'Credit Rationing in Markets with Imperfect Information.' *American Economic Review*, **71**, 393–410.

Taggart, R. A. Jr (1977). 'A Model of Corporate Financing Decisions.' *Journal of Finance*, **32**, 1467–1484.

FINANCIAL MARKETS

1 Do we really know that financial markets are efficient?

LAWRENCE H. SUMMERS*

I Introduction

The proposition that securities markets are efficient forms the basis for most research in financial economics. A voluminous literature has developed supporting this hypothesis. Jensen (1978) calls it the best established empirical fact in economics.[1] Indeed, apparent anomalies such as the discounts on closed end mutual funds and the success of trading rules based on earnings announcements are treated as indications of the failures of models specifying equilibrium returns, rather than as evidence against the hypothesis of market efficiency.[2] Recently the Efficient Markets Hypothesis and the notions connected with it have provided the basis for a great deal of research in macro-economics. This research has typically assumed that asset prices are in some sense rationally related to economic realities.

Despite the widespread allegiance to the notion of market efficiency a number of authors have suggested that certain asset prices are not rationally related to economic realities. Modigliani and Cohn (1979) suggest that the stock market is very substantially undervalued because of inflation illusion. A similar claim regarding bond prices is put forward in Summers (1983). Brainard, Shoven and Weiss (1980) found that the then low level of the stock market could not be rationally related to economic realities. Shiller (1979 and 1981a) concludes that both bond and stock prices are far more volatile than can be justified on the basis of real economic events. Arrow (1982) has suggested that psychological models of 'irrational decision making' of the type suggested by Tversky and Kahneman (1981) can help to explain behaviour in speculative markets. These types of claims are frequently dismissed because they are premised on inefficiencies and hence imply the presence of exploitable excess profit opportunities.

This paper argues that the strength of existing evidence confirming the hypothesis of market efficiency has been vastly exaggerated. It

13

demonstrates that the types of statistical tests which have been used to date have essentially no power against at least one interesting alternative hypothesis to market efficiency. Thus the inability of these tests to reject the hypothesis of market efficiency does not mean that they provide evidence in favor of its acceptance. In particular, the data in conjunction with current methods provide no evidence against the view that financial market prices deviate widely and frequently from rational valuations. The same considerations which make deviations from efficiency difficult to isolate statistically make it unlikely that they will be arbitraged away or eliminated by speculative trading. Thus the results here call into question the theoretical as well as empirical underpinnings of the Efficient Markets Hypothesis. While none of the analysis in this paper demonstrates that securities markets are inefficient, it does imply that belief in the Efficient Markets Hypothesis is a shared act of faith, with little in the way of theoretical or empirical support.

Section II distinguishes alternative concepts of market efficiency and lays out the formulation used here. Tests of market efficiency in its weak and strong forms are considered in Section III. The implications of the results for our understanding of speculative markets are discussed in the final section.

II Defining market efficiency

The notion of market efficiency has been defined in many ways. Fama (1976) presents a thorough discussion of both theoretical issues and empirical tests of this proposition. In the development below, I shall consider the evolution of the price of a single security. It can easily be taken to represent an entire portfolio. It is assumed that the required expected rate of return on the security is equal to a constant, r, which is known with certainty. As has frequently been observed, standard tests of market efficiency are really joint tests of efficiency and a model specifying expected returns. The assumption made here that the ex ante return is known and constant makes it possible to focus only on the test of market efficiency.[3]

Assume that the security in question yields a sequence of cash flows, D_t. These may be thought of as dividends if the security is a stock, or coupons if the security is a bond. If the security has a finite maturity T, then D_T may be taken to represent its liquidation value, and all subsequent values of D_t may be taken to equal zero. One statement of the hypothesis of market efficiency holds that

$$P_t = P_t^* = E\left[\left(\sum_{s=t}^{\infty} \frac{D_s}{(1+r)^{s-t}}\right)\Big|\Omega_t\right] \tag{1}$$

where Ω_t represents the set of information available to market participants at time t. This is not the form in which the hypothesis is usually tested. Equation (1) is mathematically equivalent to the statement that, for all t

$$P_t = E\left(\frac{P_{t+1}}{1+r}\right) + E(D_t) \tag{2}$$

or the equivalent statement that

$$E(R_t) = E\left(\frac{P_{t+1}}{P_t} - 1 + \frac{(1+r)D_t}{P_t}\right) = r \tag{3}$$

where the information set in equations (2) and (3) is taken to be Ω_t. Note that once a transversality condition is imposed on the difference equation (3), it implies equation (1).[4]

Equation (3) also implies that

$$R_t = r + e_t \tag{4}$$

where e_t is serially uncorrelated and orthogonal to any element of Ω_t. Market efficiency is normally tested by adding regressors drawn from Ω_t to (4) and testing the hypothesis that their coefficients equal zero, and/or testing the hypothesis that e_t follows a white noise process.[5] The former represent tests of 'semi-strong' efficiency while the latter are tests of 'weak' efficiency. A vast literature, summarized in Fama (1976), has with few exceptions been unable to reject the hypothesis of market efficiency at least for common stocks. This has led to its widespread acceptance as a scientific fact.

III Tests of market efficiency

The inability of a body of data to reject a scientific theory does not mean that the tests prove, demonstrate or even support its validity. As students of elementary statistics are constantly reminded, failure to reject a hypothesis is not equivalent to its acceptance. This principle applies to all scientific theories, not just those that are stated statistically. Experiments can falsify a theory by contradicting one of its implications. But the verification of one of its predictions cannot be taken to prove or establish a theory.[6]

How then do we evaluate the strength of the evidence supporting a hypothesis? Clearly we do not simply count the number of implications of a hypothesis which are validated. We give more weight to the verification of some implications than to the verification of others. For example, almost everyone would agree that findings that excess returns cannot be predicted using past data on sunspots provides less support for the hypothesis of market efficiency than do demonstrations that excess returns are not serially correlated. This is because we find it much easier to imagine alternative models in which returns are serially correlated than we do alternative models in which sunspots can help predict returns. The point here is that the usefulness of any test of a hypothesis depends on its ability to discriminate between the hypothesis and other plausible formulations. The validity of evidence purporting to demonstrate or support a hypothesis cannot sensibly be evaluated in a vacuum. Below I examine the usefulness of standard tests of market efficiency according to this criterion.

Evaluation of any test of a theory requires specification of an alternative hypothesis. A natural specification of an alternative hypothesis to market efficiency holds that

$$p_t = p_t^* + u_t$$
$$\tilde{u}_t = \alpha u_{t-1} + v_t \tag{5}$$

where lower-case letters indicate logarithms and u_t and v_t represent random shocks. This hypothesis implies that market valuations differ from the rational expectation of the present value of future cash flows by a multiplicative factor approximately equal to $(1 + u_t)$. The deviations are assumed to follow a first-order autoregressive process. It seems reasonable to suppose that deviations tend to persist so that $0 \leqslant \alpha \leqslant 1$. The assumption that u_t follows an AR process is made for ease of exposition and does not affect any of the substantive points at issue. For simplicity, it is assumed that u_t and v_t are uncorrelated with e_t at all frequencies.

Many, though not all, of the plausible senses in which markets might be inefficient are captured by this specification. It clearly captures Keynes's (1936) notion that markets are sometimes driven by animal spirits unrelated to economic realities. It also is consistent with the experimental evidence of Tversky and Kahneman (1981) that subjects overreact to new information in making probabilistic judgements. The formulation considered here captures Robert Shiller's suggestion that financial markets display excess volatility and overreact to new information (Shiller (1979, 1981a and 1981b)). One deviation from standard notions of market efficiency which does not take this form is Blanchard and Watson's (1982) suggestion of intermittent rational speculative bubbles.[7]

Adopting the approximation that $\log(1 + u_t) = u_t$, and that $\text{Div}_t/P_t \simeq \text{Div}_t/P_t^*$, equations (3), (4) and (5) imply that excess returns $Z_t = (R_t - r)$ follow an ARMA (1,1) process.[8] That is[9]

$$Z_t = \alpha Z_{t-1} + e_t - \alpha e_{t-1} + v_t - v_{t-1} \tag{6}$$

Granger and Newbold (1978) show that since Z_t can be expressed as the sum of an ARMA (1,1) process and white noise, ARMA (0,0), it can be

Table 1.1 *Theoretical autocorrelation of excess return assuming market inefficiency*

	α				
	.75	.9	.95	.99	.995
σ_e^2/σ_u^2:					
1.00	−.042	−.008	−.003	.000	.000
.5	−.062	−.014	−.004	.000	.000
.25	−.083	−.022	−.007	.000	.000
.1	−.104	−.033	−.012	−.001	.000
.05	−.113	−.040	−.017	−.001	.000
.01	−.122	−.048	−.023	−.003	−.001

Note: Calculations are based on Equation (7b).

represented as an ARMA (1,1) process. Equation (6) can be used to calculate the variance and the autocorrelations of Z_t. These calculations yield

$$\sigma_z^2 = 2(1-\alpha)\sigma_u^2 + \sigma_e^2 \tag{7a}$$

$$\rho_k = \frac{-\alpha^{k-1}(1-\alpha)^2\sigma_u^2}{2(1-\alpha)\sigma_u^2 + \sigma_e^2} \tag{7b}$$

where ρ_k denotes the kth-order autocorrelation. Note that the model predicts that the Z_t should display negative serial correlation. When excess returns are positive, some part is on average spurious, due to a shock v_t. As prices revert to fundamental values, negative excess returns result.

Weak form tests of market efficiency

At this point the power of 'weak form tests' of market efficiency can be evaluated. These tests involve evaluating the hypothesis that the $\rho_k = 0$. Table 1.1 presents the theoretical first order autocorrelation for various parameter combinations. In all cases, the parameters are chosen to accord with the observed variance in stock market returns. Note that (7b) implies that all subsequent autocorrelations are smaller in absolute value. In order to get a feeling for the magnitudes involved, it is useful to consider a concrete example. Suppose one is interested in testing market efficiency using aggregate data on monthly stock market returns over a 50-year period. With 600 observations, the estimated autocorrelations have a standard error of $1/\sqrt{597} \simeq .042$ on the null hypothesis of zero autocorrelation. This calculation leads to an overstatement of the power of tests because it counterfactually assumes a constant variance of excess returns and the normality of e_t. Suppose that $\sigma_u^2 = .08$ so that the standard deviation of the market's error in valuation is close to 30 percent, and that $\alpha = .98$. This implies that it takes about three years for the market to eliminate half of any valuation error u_t. These assumptions along with the observation that $\sigma_z^2 \simeq .004$ imply, using (7a), that $\sigma_e^2 \simeq .001$.[10] Equation (7b) implies that the theoretically expected value of ρ_1 is $-.008$. Thus, in this example, the data lack the power to reject the hypothesis of market efficiency even though market valuations frequently differ from the rational expectation of the present value of future cash flows by more than 30 percent.[11] In order to have a 50 percent chance of rejecting the null hypothesis it would be necessary to have data for just over 5000 years. Note also that in this example three-fourths of variance in excess returns is due to valuation errors u_t, rather than genuine information e_t. Even if $\sigma_u^2 = .10$, so that all the variance in market returns is spurious, and $\sigma_e^2 = 0$, the theoretical value of ρ_1 is only $-.01$, so that deviations from efficiency could not be detected. If, as is plausible, the serial correlation in valuation errors is greater, the power of standard tests is even lower.

Note that these results have implications for testing efficiency in other markets. Take, for example, the proposition that long-term bond yields represent the rational expectation of average short-term yields. As is widely understood, this is equivalent to the proposition that no predictable excess returns can be earned in the long-term bond market.[12] This is frequently tested in a manner which parallels the tests described here. It is instructive to note that if interest rates average 10 percent, and long-term bonds are approximated as consols, a 30 percent valuation error implies a deviation of 300 basis points between the yield on long-term instruments and the rational expectation of average future short-term rates. Thus, the results in this paper also suggest that evidence purporting to demonstrate the validity of the 'expectations' theory of the term structure of interest rates using long term bonds is not very powerful.

Two plausible objections might be lodged against this discussion. It might be that data at higher frequencies would yield more powerful tests. Further, the discussion so far has focused only on tests for first-order autocorrelation. Suppose one had daily rather than monthly data on excess returns over a 50-year period. It is true that one could then estimate daily autocorrelations much more accurately. In fact, the standard error would be approximately $1/\sqrt{(50.250)} \simeq .009$. However, if α was .98 using monthly data, it would be approximately .9990 using daily data so that the theoretical autocorrelation under the assumptions made earlier would be $-.0005$. Thus, the power of the data to reject inefficiencies of the type considered here is not enhanced by obtaining more frequent observations. Given the nature of the inefficiency being considered – persistent miscalculations – this should not be surprising.

As has been noted, the model predicts that the first-order autocorrelation should exceed those at higher orders. Thus, the remarks above apply to tests of other individual autocorrelation coefficients. Sometimes, however, a joint test of the hypothesis of zero autocorrelations at all orders is performed. The Box–Pierce Q statistic is normally used for this purpose. This statistic is computed as

$$Q = \sum_{k=1}^{m} \rho_k^2 \tag{9}$$

and is distributed as χ^2 with m degrees of freedom under the null hypothesis. In the example considered here, using monthly data, the theoretically expected value of Q is .29 for $m = 10$, .49 for $m = 20$, and .61 for $m = 30$ compared to critical values at the five percent level of 18.3, 31.4, and 43.8, respectively. To state the conclusion more dramatically, in order to have a 50 percent chance of rejecting the hypothesis of market efficiency, assuming 30 autocorrelations are used to form the Q-statistic, one would have to have approximately 1200 years worth of monthly data.

These results have implications for tests of market efficiency which go beyond the examination of serial correlation in excess returns. It has frequently been noted that one is unable to reject the hypothesis that excess returns follow a white noise process after a jump, following significant events such as stock splits and dividend announcements. The preceding discussion makes clear that this provides essentially no evidence against the hypothesis that the market either systematically over- or under-reacts to these announcements. In neither case would significant serial correlation be observed.

Tests of semi-strong efficiency

In closing the last section on weak-form tests we considered one type of test for semi-strong efficiency – examining the profitability of strategies of buying or selling following certain types of announcements. Here we consider a different type of test. Equation (5) implies that expected excess returns should be negative when $p_t > p_t^*$ and positive when $p_t < p_t^*$. This reflects the assumed tendency of market prices to return towards the rational expectation of the present value of future cash flows. The key question is whether these expected excess returns are large enough to be detectable.

In practice any effort used to test efficiency in this way runs into the problem that p_t^* is unobservable. This problem is assumed away so that the hypothetical tests considered here have far more power than any test that could actually be devised. Under the assumptions that have been made so far, it is easy to see that

$$E(Z_t) = -(1-\alpha)u_t = (1-\alpha)(p_t^* - p_t) \qquad (10)$$

In the example considered above with $\alpha = .98$, and $\sigma_u = .28$, (10) implies that when the market was undervalued by one standard deviation, the expected excess monthly return would be $(.02)(.28) = .0056$. This contrasts with a standard deviation of monthly returns of .06.

How much data would it take for these excess returns to be discernible statistically? Suppose that the regression equation

$$Z_t = a + b(p_t^* - p_t) + \eta_t \qquad (11)$$

is estimated. Equation (10) implies that $E(\hat{b}) = (1-\alpha)$. The standard error of $\hat{b}$ can be calculated from the expression

$$\sigma_{\hat{b}}^2 = \frac{\sigma_\eta^2}{n\sigma_u^2} \qquad (12)$$

In the example considered above one can calculate that $\sigma_{\hat{b}} \simeq .01$. This implies that the hypothesis of market efficiency would not be rejected at the five percent level, with probability of one-half.[13] If $\alpha = .99$, the probability of rejecting the null hypothesis is less than one-sixth. Of course this discussion vastly overstates the power of any test that could actually be performed. In addition to the problem of measuring p_t^*, there are the problems of non-normality in the residuals, and the problem of measuring expected returns. These factors combine to suggest that tests of semi-strong efficiency do not have much more power against the type of inefficiency considered here, than do tests on serial correlation properties of excess returns.

IV Implications and conclusions

The preceding analysis suggests that certain types of inefficiency in market valuations are not likely to be detected using standard methods. This means the evidence found in many studies that the hypothesis of efficiency cannot be rejected should not lead us to conclude that market prices represent rational valuations. Rather, we must face the fact that our tests have relatively little power against certain types of market inefficiency. In particular, the hypothesis that market valuations include large persistent errors is as consistent with the available empirical evidence as is the hypothesis of market efficiency. These are exactly the sort of errors in valuation one would expect to see if market valuations involved inflation illusion or were moved by fads as some have suggested.

The weakness of the empirical evidence verifying the hypothesis that securities markets are efficient would not be bothersome if the hypothesis rested on firm theoretical foundations, and if there were no contrary empirical evidence. Unfortunately, neither of these conditions is satisfied in practice.

The standard theoretical argument is that unless securities are priced efficiently, there will be opportunities to earn excess returns. Speculators will take advantage of these opportunities arbitraging away any inefficiencies in the pricing of securities. This argument does not explain how speculators become aware of profit opportunities. The same problems of identification described here which confront financial economists also plague 'would be' speculators. If the large persistent valuation errors considered here leave no statistically discernible trace in the historical patterns of returns, it is hard to see how speculators could become aware of them. Moreover, cautious speculators may be persuaded by the same arguments used by economists to suggest that apparent inefficiencies are not present. There is another logically separate point to be made here as well. Even if inefficiencies of the type considered here could be conclusively identified, the excess returns to trying to exploit them would be small and uncertain.

These inferences are supported by a cursory examination of the activities of actual speculators. A vast amount of speculative activity is directed at exploiting riskless arbitrage opportunities through triangular trades and the like. Traders engaged in this activity often are reluctant to hold naked positions for as long as ten minutes and typically admit to being completely oblivious to market fundamentals. Most risky speculation occurs in markets such as commodity futures, where the nature of traded securities ensures that valuation errors cannot persist. In commodity markets for example, the futures price must ultimately draw close to the spot price as the contract date is approached. Very little professional speculation appears to take place in markets like the stock market which have an indefinite horizon. The principal exception to this assertion is the activities of risk arbitrageurs who trade takeover candidates. Here again, the major uncertainty has a short horizon.[14]

While tests of the type considered have little power to detect inefficiencies, other forms of evidence suggest that valuation errors are pervasive. In markets where the horizon is short and so very persistent valuation errors are impossible, inefficiencies are frequently detected. For example, almost every examination has concluded that forward prices are not efficient predictors of future spot prices in the foreign exchange market (see Meese and Rogoff (1982) for a recent example). Other evidence comes from an examination of the relation between market valuations and fundamentals. A classic example is provided by the discounts on closed end funds. Corporations whose only assets are easily valued marketable securities sell at a substantial discount relative to the value of their assets. Observed patterns of takeover suggests that the same is true of many other corporations whose assets are less easily valued. A different kind of observation suggesting the incompleteness of current theories is the enormous trading volume observed on speculative markets. This is difficult to account for on the view that market valuations are rational expectations of rational calculations performed by market participants.

The foregoing discussion suggests that a more catholic approach should be taken to explaining the behavior of speculative markets. It may be possible to develop alternative models of pricing based on the observed experimental responses of persons to risky environments. These models may have testable implications differing from those of standard formulations. More modestly, it may be possible to explain how valuation errors once made can persist, by formalizing the notions of speculator learning discussed above. Finally, the analysis here suggests the importance of developing tests which have some power against the type of alternative hypotheses we considered. These might focus on the aftermath of apparently irrational market responses.

NOTES

* I am grateful to Fischer Black, Zvi Griliches, Jim Pesando and Jim Poterba for clarifying discussions, but remain responsible for any errors.
1 Similar assertions are very common in the finance literature. While doubts along the lines of the discussion here appear to be part of an oral tradition, the only reference I could find is Shiller (1981b).
2 For examples, see the recent issue of the *Journal of Financial Economics* devoted to anomalies in the Efficient Market Hypothesis (Jensen *et al.* (1978)).
3 Since the discussion here assumes that the model generating expected returns is known with certainty, it will overestimate the power of available statistical tests. Recent theoretical work such as that of Lucas (1978) suggests that the particular model of ex ante returns considered here cannot be derived rigorously. This is immaterial for the points at issue here. What is crucial is that the discussion is carried on assuming full knowledge of the model characterizing ex ante returns.
4 The transversality condition serves to rule out speculative bubbles.
5 Abel and Mishkin (1980) and Jones and Roley (1982) show that other standard tests of efficiency are essentially equivalent to those described in this paragraph.
6 A discussion of what it means to establish evidence in favor of a scientific hypothesis may be found in Hempel (1965).
7 Olivier Blanchard has pointed out to me that if $\alpha = 1 + r$ equation (5) will characterize a speculative bubble. In this case however, market valuations will come to diverge arbitrarily far from fundamental valuations.

8 These approximations are necessary in order to obtain simple analytic expressions. Monte-Carlo results confirm that these approximations are innocuous. Shiller (1981b) presents an example similar to the one here in his defense of volatility tests.

9 This can be seen as follows. With the approximations assumed here

$$R_t = (\text{Div}_t/P_t^*) + p_{t+1} - p_t$$
$$= (\text{Div}_t/P_t^*) + p_{t+1}^* - p_t^* + u_{t+1} - u_t$$

where the last equality is implied by equation (5). This can be written, using (3) and (4) as

$$R_t = r + e_t + u_{t+1} - u_t$$

Combining this last equation with equation (5) yields equation (6).

10 This estimate for σ_z^2 is consistent with the 20 percent annual standard deviation of market returns reported by Ibbotsen and Sinquefield (1976, 1979).

11 A more formal procedure would calculate the distribution of the test statistic (ρ_k/σ_k) under the alternative hypothesis. It should be obvious that carrying out this procedure would support the assertions in the text.

12 See Jones and Roley (1982).

13 There is one-half chance that $\hat{b} < E(\hat{b}) = .02$. In these cases the null hypothesis of efficiency will be accepted.

14 The argument here that the rational expectations assumption is untenable in settings where it is difficult to estimate structural parameters without extremely long time series is similar to that made in a macro-economic context by Benjamin Friedman (1979).

REFERENCES

Abel, A. and F. Mishkin (1980). 'A Unified Framework for Testing Rationality, Market Efficiency and the Short Run Neutrality of Monetary Policy.' Unpublished.

Arrow, K. J. (1982). 'Risk Perception in Psychology and Economics.' Economic Inquiry, 1–9.

Blanchard, O. and M. Watson (1982). 'Bubbles, Rational Expectations and Financial Markets.' NBER Working Paper No. 945

Brainard, W. C., J. B. Shoven and L. Weiss (1980). 'The Financial Valuation of the Return on Capital.' Brooking Papers on Economic Activity, 2, 453–502.

Fama, E. (1976). Foundations of Finance. Basic Books, New York.

Friedman, B. (1979). 'Optimal Expectations and the Extreme Information Assumptions of Rational Expectations Macro Models.' Journal of Monetary Economics, 23–41.

Granger, C. W. and P. Newbold (1977). Forecasting Economic Time Series. Academic Press, New York.

Hempel, C. (1965). Aspects of Scientific Explanation.

Ibbotsen, R. G. and R. A. Sinquefield (1976). 'Stocks, Bonds, Bills and Inflation: Year-by-Year Historical Returns (1926–1974).' Journal of Business, 11–47 (and update, 1979).

Jensen, M. C. *et al*. (1978). 'Symposium on Some Anomalous Evidence Regarding Market Efficiency.' *Journal of Financial Economics*, 93–330.

Jones, D. and V. V. Roley (1982). 'Rational Expectations, the Expectations Hypothesis, and Treasury Bill Yields: An Econometric Analysis.' Unpublished. Unpublished.

Keynes, J. M. (1936). *The General Theory of Employment, Interest and Money.*

Lucas, R. E. (1978). 'Asset Prices in an Exchange Economy.' *Econometrica*, 1429–1445.

Meese and Rogoff (1981). 'Exchange Rate Models of the 1970s: Are Any Fit to Survive?' Unpublished.

Modigliani, F. and R. Cohn (1979). 'Inflation, Rational Valuation and the Market.' *Financial Analysts Journal*, 24–44.

Shiller, R. (1979). 'The Volatility of Long-Term Interest Rates and Expectations Models of the Term Structure.' *Journal of Political Economy*, 1190–1219.

Shiller, R. (1981a). 'Do Stock Prices Move Too Much to be Justified by Subsequent Changes in Dividends?' *American Economic Review*, 421–436.

Shiller, R. (1981b). 'The Use of Volatility Measures in Assessing Market Efficiency.' *Journal of Finance*, 291–304.

Summers, L. H. (1983). 'The Non-Adjustment of Nominal Interest Rates: A Study of the Fisher Effect.' In J. Tobin (ed) *Macroeconomics, Prices, and Quantities: Essays in Honour of Arthur M. Okun.* Basil Blackwell, Oxford.

Tversky, A. and D. Kahneman (1981). 'The Framing of Decisions and the Psychology of Choice.' *Science*, 453–458.

COMMENT   RICHARD A. BREALEY

It is perhaps a sign of the subject's maturity that the 1980's have been a period of questioning some of our most cherished finance theories. In particular, we have become less confident about the power of the classic empirical analyses of the 1960's.

In the case of market efficiency tests there have been several reasons for these doubts. First, there has been a certain amount of anomalous evidence suggesting either persistent discrepancies from model equilibrium returns (e.g. the size effect) or temporary discrepancies during the days or weeks surrounding an event date.[1] Second, particularly in the case of semi-strong form tests we have become more aware of their lack of power. For example, the ratio of noise to signal grows so rapidly that it is unlikely that we could detect any prolonged impact of an event. Moreover, the plausible effect of a particular event is frequently so small that we stand little chance of distinguishing the market's reaction.

Yet despite these cautions, I suspect that most of us believe that speculative markets are to a close approximation efficient (whatever that may mean)[2] and rather than simply treating apparent anomalies as disequilibria, our first reaction is to *assume* that markets are well-functioning and question our models of equilibrium. Professor Summers' paper accords with the current mood of questioning. But his concerns are somewhat different. He does not dispute that *returns* may approximate equilibrium returns but points out that such results may be consistent with large but persistent disequilibrium in *prices*.

In the absence of a general equilibrium model, some boundary conditions are needed to define a unique set of equilibrium asset prices. Thus the price of the legendary tin of sardines that is used only in trading can differ by a scalar without affecting the equilibrium set of returns. Similarly, unless we take account of the industrial uses of gold, the equilibrium price of gold is unique only to a scalar.

For some assets such as common stocks whose cash flows extend over a prolonged period there may be a unique equilibrium but the actual price may differ substantially from this value with only a slight effect on returns. For example, one of the intriguing aspects of the British gilt market is that there are six different perpetual gilts that have on occasion offered significantly different yields. It is possible that these differences are a consequence of minor differences in terms such as the call provisions, but suppose for the sake of argument that they reflect disequilibrium prices. The differences in yields are sufficiently persistent, the cash flow sufficiently low and the noise sufficiently large that the differences have a negligible effect on holding period returns and the gains from any trading rule are unlikely to compensate for trading costs.

This appears to be the main source of Professor Summers' concern. A similar point, I remember, was made by John Treynor in a discussion of Keynes' beauty contest analogy. Treynor pointed out that in Keynes' world investors would always have the incentive to realise a higher expected cash flow per dollar of investment by buying the undervalued securities but that, when the duration of the cash flows is long, the returns gain from such strategies was liable to be very small.

Professor Summers illustrates his point nicely by supposing that prices may wander from, but nevertheless tend to revert to, 'intrinsic value'. Again there is some precedent for this model. The broad motivation is similar to Cootner's (1962) suggestion that the costs of the informed trader could result in reflecting price barriers and the development of the ARIMA model is reminiscent of a discussion by Granger and Morgenstern (1970).

It is very difficult to quarrel with Summers' basic point that persistent price disequilibrium may exist in markets with long horizons and yet not show up in returns. The message is an important and salutory one but we should not jump to the conclusion that existing empirical tests of market efficiency are economically uninteresting. For all its flaws the empirical evidence on security returns has exerted an appropriate and profound effect on the behaviour of financial managers. For example, in his book *The Money Game* Adam Smith described the activities in the late 1960's of the Winfield Kids, youthful gunslingers each managing several hundred million dollars of assets. I remember meeting one of the Winfield Kids at a broker's lunch in New York and boasting that we estimated that the fund for which I worked had mean excess returns of around 1/2 per cent per annum. His lip curled in a fine disdain and he replied that if he could not beat the market by 25 per cent every year he would shoot himself. My point is not to deplore that kid's fate but to point out that tests of strong form efficiency, while not as powerful as we would like, have nevertheless justifiably changed prevalent views of the gains from professional investment management. I suspect that most of us can think of similar ways that weak or semi-strong form tests have had important implications for financial behaviour.

Subject to this caveat I have so far no problems with Summers' argument. However, his assessment of the implications and possible solutions is much more contentious. It is to these issues that I would now like to turn.

(1) First, Summers argues that, even if large pricing errors could be conclusively identified, the excess returns from trying to exploit these errors would be small and uncertain. This he suggests is confirmed by a cursory examination of the activities of actual speculators. 'A vast amount of speculative activity is directed at exploiting riskless arbitrage opportunities' and most risky speculation is in assets like commodity futures rather than in markets like the stock market which have an infinite horizon. Leaving aside the issue of how far riskless arbitrage is speculative, I have three problems with this view:

(i) One man's cursory examination is probably no better than another's but I am far from convinced that 'very little speculation' occurs in markets with infinite horizons. For example, annual equity turnover on the NYSE (purchases plus sales) is about 50 percent of the market value of listed stocks. Do we really believe that these are largely liquidity-motivated trades or that they are for the purpose of rebalancing risk? And do we believe that the huge volume of spot currency transactions is undertaken largely in connection with trade?

(ii) Second, while some analysts in speculative markets may estimate equilibrium prices, many others accept the market price as an equilibrium price conditional on the market's information set and focus on predicting the marginal effect on security prices of new information. Thus, if I have superior information on Russian gold production or South African mining costs, I may be relatively relaxed that I cannot estimate a unique equilibrium value for gold and I can be fairly confident that when my information becomes public the price will adjust.[3]

(iii) Third, while Summers has shown that persistent mispricing *may* exist and give rise to negligible excess returns, it is of course an empirical issue whether such mispricing *does* occur. Wells Fargo has claimed that differences between stock prices and the value estimated from their discounted dividend model are eliminated very rapidly. Brennan and Schwartz (1982) also report that differences between actual bond prices and equilibrium prices estimated from a two factor pricing model likewise disappear quickly. Of course, these apparent anomalies may simply reflect data errors, model defects etc., but my point is that if we believe that substantial pricing errors do occur, then such evidence as exists would suggest that they are not persistent.

(2) Summers claims that while traditional tests have little power to detect inefficiencies, other forms of evidence suggest that valuation errors are pervasive. For example, he suggests that in markets where horizons are short and persistent valuation errors impossible, inefficiencies are frequently detected and he cites the evidence that forward exchange prices are not efficient predictors of spot prices. Such a claim is not consistent with Summers' earlier statements on the problem of measuring efficiency and it places more faith in the expectations hypothesis as a theory of equilibrium in forward markets than I suspect most of us would be prepared to accept.[4] Summers also suggests that other evidence comes from an examination of the relationship between market valuations and fundamentals. In particular, he cites the example of discounts on closed end funds. However, in this case Summers places considerable reliance on the assumption that the equilibrium value of closed end funds and the value of the underlying assets is identical. But we know that there are many reasons that this need not be so. For example, management fees are often a proportion of the value of the fund and, therefore, *ceteris paribus* we should expect the fund value to differ from asset value by the discounted value of this growing stream of fees.

(3) Summers also states that the enormous trading volume observed on speculative markets suggests the incompleteness of current theories and that it is difficult to account for on the view that market valuations are rational expectations of rational calculations performed by market participants. In one sense Summers is clearly right. Very little attention has been paid to the costs of acquiring and acting on information and we would expect that returns to speculators would need to compensate for these costs.[5] However, I find it difficult to reconcile Summers' statement here with his earlier claim that speculators are aware of the difficulties of capitalising on persistent disequilibrium and therefore very little speculation occurs in markets like the stock market. Nor can I see that speculative trading *per se* is evidence that market valuations do not reflect rational calculations

performed by participants. Indeed to take Summers' earlier example of the large volume of arbitrage activity, it is precisely those rational estimates of (partial) equilibrium that are the cause of the trading activity.

(4) While much of Professor Summers' paper is nihilistic, I have already noted that he does suggest two possible paths to salvation.

(i) The first is to focus on assets with short horizons. I find this unconvincing for a reason that I noted above. If, as Summers argues elsewhere, market efficiency is limited by the ability of speculators to detect inefficiencies, then the degree of mispricing will simply decline in inverse proportion to the power of the test. If this is not the source of the inefficiency, then we cannot make general statements on measurability unless we can model the friction. For example, Summers' hypothesis suggests that, if efficiency is indeed a function of the asset's horizon, then the opening of futures markets could substantially improve efficiency and result in a significant adjustment in prices. However, this is certainly not an inevitable consequence and it depends on the nature of the friction.

(ii) Professor Summers' second (hinted) solution is to work with a variable other than return. It has become fashionable in empirical work to scale price by previous price (i.e. to calculate returns) rather than to scale by some other variable. There is, I believe, some danger that we become locked into a particular methodology. For example, if we wish to understand equilibrium in the market for perpetual gilts we may do much better to focus on the differences in yield rather than on the much more noisy returns data (though again this will not help Professor Summers if efficiency is limited by our ability to measure inefficiency). Similarly, the interesting variable in closed end funds is the price relative to asset value. Or, to take a somewhat different example, we have evidence that returns have been a function of market capitalisation, but we cannot be sure whether this is a permanent feature or simply an ex post phenomenon that stems from an unexpectedly high level of profitability by small firms. If the observed differences in past performance do indeed reflect permanent and substantial differences in expected returns, then this should show up in measurable differences in the market valuation of these stocks. Twenty or thirty years ago it was common to analyse the effect on price of dividend yield or capital structure or size by focussing on the relationships between P/E and the variable in question. And despite the problems involved in these studies I would take Professor Summers' paper as a reminder that in many of these cases we should be cautious about focussing our attention solely on the return variable rather than on other scaled measures of price.

Let me sum up. I think few would disagree with Professor Summers' principal contention that empirical tests of efficiency are tests for disequilibrium returns and are at best very weak tests for disequilibrium prices. And, while such a view is not entirely novel, it has not to my knowledge been expressed so directly or succinctly. I have more difficulty with the elaborating discussion, much of which is arguable, confusing and contradictory. It is never dull.

NOTES

1 See Jensen *et al.* (1978).
2 For a discussion of possible definitions of market efficiency see Latham (1985).
3 Of course, if I cannot put a unique value on the security, I cannot do so on the new information either. But at least I can forecast the direction of the adjustment and may be able to put bounds on its magnitude.
4 Even if we were prepared to accept that market participants were risk neutral, we would still be left with the problem that with Jensen's inequality forward exchange rates cannot *in general* represent expected spot prices.
5 See Grossman and Stiglitz (1980).

REFERENCES

Brennan, M. J. and E. S. Schwartz (1982). 'Bond Pricing and Market Efficiency.' *Financial Analysts Journal*, 3–10.

Cootner, P. H. (1962). 'Stock Prices: Random Walks vs Finite Markov Chains.' *Industrial Management Review*, 24–45.

Granger, C. W. J. and O. Morgenstern (1970). *Predictability of Stock Market Prices*. Heath Lexington, Lexington Mass.

Grossman, S. and J. E. Stiglitz (1980). 'The Impossibility of Informationally Efficient Markets.' *American Economic Review*, 393–428.

Jensen, M. C. *et al.* (1978). 'Symposium on Some Anomalous Evidence Regarding Market Efficiency.' *Journal of Financial Economics*, 93–330.

Latham, M. (1985). 'Defining Capital Market Efficiency.' Finance Working Paper No. 150, University of California, Berkeley.

ISSUES IN CORPORATE FINANCE

2 Precommitment to equity financing choices in a world of asymmetric information

ROBERT HEINKEL and
EDUARDO SCHWARTZ*

I Introduction

Firms seeking new equity funds have several alternatives: a fully underwritten general cash offer, an uninsured rights offer or a standby rights offer, among others. In practice we observe all alternatives being used; some firms, however, constrain their financing choice to a preemptive rights offer with a charter provision. One possible explanation for this precommitment is the concern for control by a large shareholder. Hanson and Pinkerton (1982) offer empirical evidence for this explanation.

In the absence of concerns about control it is unclear as to why firms would voluntarily constrain future equity financing choices by precommiting to the use of rights offers. The issue is further complicated by the empirical findings of Bhagat (1983), who reports a significant negative price reaction to the elimination of the preemptive rights charter provision.

In this paper we develop a model based on asymmetric information with rational, value maximizing behavior that offers a possible justification for the precommitment to rights offers and is consistent with Bhagat's (1983) empirical findings.

In our model firms are assumed to have better information about future prospects (quality) than do investors. The act of precommiting to the use of rights offers serves as a signal to investors about firm quality: only higher quality firms are willing to sacrifice flexibility in their future equity financing choices. In this world removal of the charter provision requiring preemptive rights is a negative signal, resulting in a negative price reaction at the announcement. Firms removing the charter provision do so rationally since maintaining the provision would result in higher expected future costs.

The simplest model that captures the essential elements upon which we wish to focus consists of three dates: 0, 1 and 2. At time zero firms have limited information about their future opportunities (quality) while

33

investors have no such information; at this date firms decide whether to precommit to a rights offer at date one or not and their decision serves as a signal to investors. At time one firms receive better information about their quality and must choose an equity financing vehicle; firms that precommited at time zero must use a rights offer, while those that did not choose either a rights offer or a fully underwritten offer, providing an additional signal to investors. The sale of equity through a fully underwritten offering is completed at time one. Time two is the maturity date of the rights issued by those firms choosing a right offer at time one. By date two investors and firms are assumed to have symmetric information (that which the firms knew at date one).

The possible financing choices have associated with them different costs incurred at different times; these costs will be detailed in Section II. In making their decisions firms are assumed to maximize the current stock price at the time the decision is made, net of expected future costs. One way to induce this objective is by an appropriately designed wage schedule linking the manager's wage to stock price at each date. In essence, we assume firms do not maximize current benefits while ignoring future costs.

This model results in a partially revealing, sequential, rational expectations equilibrium in which investors correctly price securities based upon the signals given by managers' actions, and managers, by maximizing stock price net of expected future costs, truthfully reveal their information to investors.

The model shows an equilibrium in which higher quality firms precommit at time zero to a rights offer and lower quality firms do not. In addition, optimal equity financing choices for those firms not precommited are characterized by higher quality firms using rights offers and lower quality firms using an underwritten offer.

Section II develops the equilibrium equity financing choices of firms at time one. This stage of the sequential equilibrium is based upon the model of Heinkel and Schwartz (1985). In the spirit of dynamic programming, Section III derives the equilibrium precommitment decision at time zero, given optimal equity financing choices at time one. Section IV concludes the paper.

II Equilibrium equity financing choices

Following Heinkel and Schwartz (1985), we assume that a heterogeneous group of firms is selling new equity through one of three alternatives: a standby rights offer, an uninsured rights offer or a fully underwritten offer. The firms are assumed to differ by a parameter t in the distribution of date two (terminal) stock price $(P):g(P;t)$. Firms are assumed to know their quality parameter t at date one, while investors cannot distinguish among firms; investors do know that quality is distributed across the population according to the hyperbolic population density

$$n(t) = k/t, \qquad t \in [t_a, t_b] \tag{1}$$

Different equity financing alternatives involve different costs. In a standby rights offer an investment banker insures the success of a rights issue with a maturity date at time two. To properly price this guarantee the banker investigates the firm, at cost C per share, to determine the firm's quality parameter t. Assuming, for simplicity, risk neutral valuation, a zero interest rate and a competitive investment banker, the net proceeds to a type t firm employing a standby rights offer is $V(t) - C$ where $V(t)$, the true value of a type t firm, is

$$V(t) = \int_0^\infty Pg(P;t)dP \tag{2}$$

A firm using an uninsured rights offer with rights maturing at time two runs the risk of failing to raise the equity financing. The rights issue will fail if the terminal stock price P, is less than the subscription price S of the right. In this case we assume that the firm incurs a fixed failure cost of F per share. Thus the expected failure cost per share of an uninsured rights offer is

$$F\int_0^S g(P;t)dP$$

Since this cost function depends upon S and t, we hypothesize that the subscription price is used as a signal of quality and that investors determine a firm's current share value based upon the chosen subscription price: $V(S)$ is the investors' inference schedule of stock value excluding expected failure costs. Therefore, the date one share price of a type t firm using an uninsured rights offer is

$$V(S) - F\int_0^S g(P;t)dP \tag{3}$$

In equilibrium the firm's optimal choice of a subscription price, $S^*(t)$, is obtained by maximizing (3); the first order condition is

$$\frac{dV(S^*)}{dS^*} - Fg(S^*;t) = 0 \tag{4}$$

This $S^*(t)$ will fully reveal firm type to investors, so that investors correctly value the firm's shares:

$$V(S^*(t)) = V(t) \tag{5}$$

Combining equation (4) with the total differential of (5) provides the differential equation relating the equilibrium subscription price to firm type:

$$\dot{F}g(S^*; t)\frac{dS^*}{dt} = \frac{dV(t)}{dt} \tag{6}$$

Applying the solution to differential equation (6) to expression (3) provides the equilibrium net proceeds to a type t firm using an uninsured rights offer with a subscription price of $S^*(t)$, $W(t)$:[1]

$$W(t) = V(S^*(t)) - F\int_0^{S^*(t)} g(P; t)dP \tag{7}$$

Finally, firms may employ the services of a competitive, uninformed underwriter to immediately (at date one) sell their shares at a fixed underwriting cost of U per share. Since the underwriter cannot distinguish among firm types, the net proceeds to all firms using the underwriter will be the same. If all firms of type t and lower use the underwriter the correct offer price is the average price, $A(t)$:

$$A(t) = \frac{\int_{t_a}^t n(x)V(x)dx}{\int_{t_a}^t n(x)dx} \tag{8}$$

Thus the net proceeds per share to each firm type $t \in [t_a, t)$ using the uninformed underwriter are $A(t) - U$.

Using a normally distributed terminal stock price we derive a rational expectations equilibrium in which there exists a type $\hat{t}$ and a type t^* defined by

$$\begin{aligned} W(\hat{t}) &= V(\hat{t}) - C \\ W(t^*) &= A(t^*) - U \end{aligned} \tag{9}$$

such that:

(i) Firm types $t > \hat{t}$ optimally employ a standby rights offer and receive net proceeds per share of $V(t) - C$;

(ii) Firm types $t^* \leqslant t \leqslant \hat{t}$ optimally employ an uninsured rights offer, signaling their quality t through the subscription price $S^*(t)$ of the rights offer, being correctly priced at $W(t)$;

(iii) Firm types $t < t^*$ optimally choose the uninformed underwriter and receive net proceeds of $A(t^*) - U$, independent of t.

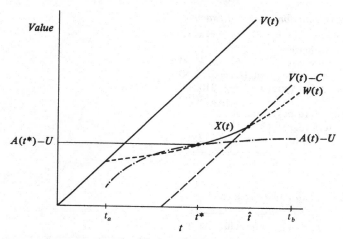

Figure 2.1 Values of equilibrium financing choices

Figure 2.1 illustrates the equilibrium.

We assume that the quality parameter t is the mean of the normal distribution of terminal stock prices:

$$g(P; t) = \frac{1}{\sigma\sqrt{2\pi}} \exp\left(\frac{(P^* - t)^2}{2\sigma^2}\right) \tag{10}$$

where σ is the standard deviation of the distribution.

The true value of firm type t, from equation (2), is[2]

$$V(t) = t \tag{11}$$

and the differential equation (6) becomes

$$\frac{dS^*}{dt} = \frac{\sigma(2\pi)^{1/2}}{F} \exp\left(\frac{-(S^* - t)^2}{2\sigma^2}\right) \tag{12}$$

This differential equation, subject to the boundary condition that the lowest possible quality firm t_a incur no signaling costs, $S^*(t_a) = 0$, has no closed form solution; we use numerical procedures to solve the equation.

In the case of normally distributed terminal stock price and hyperbolic population density, the average value of firm types t and lower, equation (8), is

$$A(t) = \frac{t - t_a}{\ln(t/t_a)} \tag{13}$$

Table 2.1. *Data for numerical example*

Investigation costs (C)	= \$ 12.00
Failure costs (F)	= \$ 35.00
Underwriting costs (U)	= \$ 2.50
Range of types t: $\quad t_a$	= \$100.00
t_b	= \$130.00
Standard deviation of terminal stock prices (σ)	= \$ 25.00

Table 2.2. *Equilibrium date one share values*

Firm type (t)	Date one share value $(X(t))$			
	Fully underwritten	Uninsured rights	Standby rights	Subscription price $(S^*(t))$
[100, 116.8]	105.68			
$t^* = 116.8$	105.68	105.68		104.94
117		105.78		105.34
117.5		106.03		106.34
118		106.29		107.32
$\hat{t} = 118.6$		106.60	106.60	
120			108.00	
130			118.00	

In summary, the net proceeds per share to firm type t depends upon the form of equity financing chosen, which in turn depends upon the firm type:[3]

$$
X(t) = \begin{cases}
t - C & \text{for } t > \hat{t} & \text{use standby rights offer} \\
W(t) & \text{for } t^* \leqslant t \leqslant \hat{t} & \text{use uninsured rights offer} \\
\dfrac{(t^* - t_a)}{\ln(t^*/t_a)} - U & \text{for } t < t^* & \text{use underwriter offer}
\end{cases} \tag{14}
$$

Table 2.1 contains the data used in a numerical example to illustrate an equilibrium set of equity financing choices at date one. Note that with a standard deviation of terminal stock price of \$25.00 the probability of a negative stock price for the lowest quality firm (with mean price equal to \$100.00) is essentially zero.

The equilibrium financing choices and date one share values are reported in Table 2.2. The lowest quality firm types $t \in [100, 116.8]$ employ an uninformed underwriter and receive net proceeds of $105.68 per share; investors are willing to pay $105.68 + $108.18 for the shares since this is the average value of the firms using the underwriter. Firm types $t \in [116.8, 118.6]$ utilize an uninsured rights offer, setting increasingly higher subscription prices to signal higher quality, resulting in higher share values. Finally, firm types t above 118.6 optimally choose a standby rights offer and pay the investigation costs to be correctly identified.

To demonstrate that this is an equilibrium consider the payoffs to a firm contemplating changing its equity financing choice. Firm type $t = 115$, optimally using the underwriter, receives net proceeds of $105.68; to credibly signal its type through an uninsured rights offer the firm would have had to set a subscription price of $101.27 resulting in a share price of $104.80 (which includes expected failure costs).[4] With investigation costs of $12 a standby rights offer would yield a share price of $103.00. Thus, firm type $t = 115$ has no reason to change its equity financing choice.

Firm type $t = 117$ optimally employs an uninsured rights offer using a subscription price of $105.34 resulting in a share price of $105.78. This payoff is preferred to the underwritten net proceeds of $105.68[5] and to the share price of $105.00 under a standby rights offer.

Firm type $t = 119$ optimally chooses a standby rights offer yielding a share price of $107.00, which is superior to $106.80 with an uninsured rights offer and $105.68 with the underwriter.

The example in Table 2.2 characterizes an equilibrium at date one in which all three equity financing vehicles are employed. Depending upon the relative costs of these vehicles there are possible equilibria in which only two or even one of these vehicles would be optimally employed.[6]

In this section we have developed an equilibrium at date one in which firms know their type, represented by the mean of the normal distribution of stock price at date two. In the following section we consider the problem at date zero and we assume that firms have only limited information about their type; we analyze the incentives of firms to signal this limited information at time zero by precommiting to a standby rights offer.

III The precommitment decision

At date zero firms anticipate both that they will be raising equity capital at date one and that they will have better information about their investment opportunities. Given limited information at date zero, the firms with more positive news have incentives to signal this news to investors. Since at date one the equilibrium involves optimal equity financing choices in which the highest quality firms choose a standby rights offer, we assume that the date zero signaling mechanism is to constrain the date one choice by precommitting at date zero to employ a standby rights offer at date one.

One possible manifestation of the precommitment act is the creation of corporate charter provision requiring the use of a preemptive rights offer. For simplicity we will assume that this is a standby rights offer. If a firm precommits to a standby rights offer at date zero we do not allow the firm to violate the precommitment at date one. This restriction at date one is consistent with significant costs and time delays in removing the charter provision. We do allow, however, amendments to the charter to remove or include the provision at time zero.

We choose a very simple date zero information structure to model the precommitment decision. Each firm will receive one of three signals $\{\mu_l, \mu_m, \mu_h\}$; the information partition is such that

firm type $t \in [t_a, t_l]$ receives signal μ_l

firm type $t \in (t_l, t_h)$ receives signal μ_m $\qquad (15)$

firm type $t \in [t_h, t_b]$ receives signal μ_h

For expositional purposes we assume, as shown in Figure 2.2,

$$
\begin{aligned}
t_a < t_l < t^* \\
\hat{t} < t_h < t_b
\end{aligned}
\qquad (16)
$$

This assumption implies that firms receiving signal μ_l know that their optimal date one equity financing choice is the underwritten offer and that firms receiving signal μ_h know that their optimal choice is a standby rights offer. On the other hand, firms receiving signal μ_m are uncertain as to their optimal financing choice at date one.

The above information structure at date zero allows us to derive an equilibrium in which firms receiving signal μ_h precommit to a standby

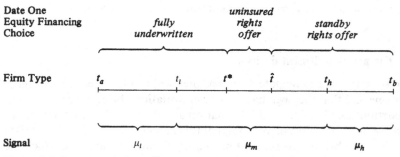

Figure 2.2 Date zero information partition

rights offer, while the others do not. Rational investors react to the precommitment decision by valuing higher those firms that precommit than those that do not. Similar equilibria are possible under more complex information structures; the simple one that we have chosen, however, is sufficient to accomplish our objective.[7]

For the precommitment signal by firms to be credible it is necessary that firms, besides considering time zero share value, must take into account the consequences of their precommitment decision on date one share value. Thus, as in Miller and Rock (1985), we essentially assume that the firm maximizes a weighted average of date zero and date one share prices. Such an objective function allows us to derive a signaling equilibrium in which lower quality firms (those that receive signals μ_l or μ_m at date zero), by not precommiting, are willing to accept a lower date zero value in order to maintain equity financing flexibility at date one.

To demonstrate the existence of the equilibrium described above, we conjecture that investors infer from a firm's act of precommiting to a standby rights offer that the firm received signal μ_h. Also, investors believe that signals μ_l or μ_m were received by firms that do not precommit. Thus the date zero share value, contingent on the signal of precommiting, is

$$Z_P = \frac{\int_{t_h}^{t_b} n(x)(V(x) - C)dx}{\int_{t_h}^{t_b} n(x)dx} \tag{17}$$

or, using equations (1) and (11),

$$Z_P = \frac{t_b - t_h}{\ln(t_b/t_h)} - C \tag{18}$$

Similarly, the date zero share value contingent on no precommitment is

$$Z_N = \frac{\int_{t_a}^{t_h} n(x)X(x)dx}{\int_{t_a}^{t_h} n(x)dx} \tag{19}$$

or, using equations (1) and (14),

$$Z_N = \left[(t^* - t_a) - U \ln(t^*/t_a) + \int_{t^*}^{\hat{t}} \frac{W(x)}{x} dx \right.$$
$$\left. + (t_h - \hat{t}) - C \ln(t_h/\hat{t}) \right] \Big/ \ln(t_h/t_a) \tag{20}$$

As mentioned above, we assume an objective function which is a weighted average of the date zero share value and the date one share value. Then, given the date zero valuations (18) and (20), we can describe the firm's multiperiod objective function, contingent upon the signal received, μ_i, $i =$

l, m, h and the precommitment decision, P or N:

$$Y_P(\mu_i) = \beta Z_P + (1-\beta)E[V(t) - C \,|\, \mu_i] \tag{21}$$

$$Y_N(\mu_i) = \beta Z_N + (1-\beta)E[X(t) \,|\, \mu_i] \tag{22}$$

where β is the intertemporal weighting factor and the expectation operator E is taken over t conditional upon the signal μ_i.

Note that $V(t) - C$ appears in the expectation in (21) because the firm is precommited to a standby rights offer at date one. Alternatively, by not precommitting the firm accepts a lower date zero share value, Z_N, in exchange for flexibility in date one equity financing, as represented by $X(t)$ in the expectation in (22).

In order to evaluate equations (21) and (22) we must specify the expectation terms for reach μ_i:

$$E[V(t) - C \,|\, \mu_h] = Z_P \tag{23}$$

$$E[V(t) - C \,|\, \mu_m] = \frac{t_h - t_l}{\ln(t_h/t_l)} - C \tag{24}$$

$$E[V(t) - C \,|\, \mu_l] = \frac{t_l - t_a}{\ln(t_l/t_a)} - C \tag{25}$$

$$E[X(t) \,|\, \mu_h] = Z_P \tag{26}$$

$$E[X(t) \,|\, \mu_m] = \left[\left(\frac{t^* - t_a}{\ln(t^*/t_a)} - U \right) \ln(t^*/t_l) \right.$$
$$\left. + \int_{t^*}^{\hat{t}} W(x)x \, dx + (t_h - \hat{t}) - C \cdot \ln(t_h/\hat{t}) \right] \Big/ \ln(t_h/t_l) \tag{27}$$

$$E[X(t) \,|\, \mu_l] = \frac{t^* - t_a}{\ln(t^*/t_a)} - U \tag{28}$$

For the date zero signaling equilibrium to be consistent with investors' conjectures, the date zero equilibrium payoffs must adhere to the inequalities shown in Table 2.3. In other words, the payoffs to firms receiving signals μ_l or μ_m should be higher under no precommitment, whereas the payoffs to firms receiving signal μ_h are higher under precommitment.

It is easy to show that

$$Y_P(\mu_h) = Z_P$$

and

$$Y_N(\mu_h) = \beta Z_N + (1-\beta)Z_P$$

Table 2.3. *Date zero equilibrium payoffs*

Signal	Action		
	Precommit		No precommit
μ_l	$Y_P(\mu_l)$	$<$	$Y_N(\mu_l)$
μ_m	$Y_P(\mu_m)$	$<$	$Y_N(\mu_m)$
μ_h	$Y_P(\mu_h)$	$>$	$Y_N(\mu_h)$

Table 2.4. *Date zero equilibrium payoffs and share values*

Signal	Action	
	Precommit	No precommit
μ_l	100.96	105.71
μ_m	105.61	105.75
μ_h	112.42	109.08

$$Z_N = 105.74$$
$$Z_P = 112.42$$
$$t_l = 103$$
$$t_h = 119$$
$$\beta = 0.50$$

Since $Z_P > Z_N$, it follows that

$$Y_P(\mu_h) > Y_N(\mu_h)$$

so that firms receiving signal μ_h always prefer to precommit at date zero.

The incentives of firms receiving signals μ_l or μ_m depend upon the parameters of the model. To demonstrate the existence of a sequential, rational expectations equilibrium we extend the numerical example introduced in the previous section.

Table 2.4 contains the date zero equilibrium payoffs and share values using parameter values of: $\beta = 0.5$, $t_l = 103.0$ and $t_h = 119.0$. As seen in this table the inequalities of Table 2.3 hold, so that no firm has an incentive to deviate from the behavior conjectured by investors. The share price of firms precommiting is $112.42, which is greater than $105.74 for those that do not.

Interestingly, firms receiving signal μ_m find it optimal to maintain financing flexibility by not precommiting at date zero in spite of the immediate loss in share value of $6.68, and the fact that some of these firms will at date one optimally choose a standby rights offer. The reason for this is, of course, that there are enough lower quality firms receiving signal μ_m so that the expected costs of losing flexibility are too high.

IV Summary and conclusions

In a sequential, rational expectations signaling model we have examined firms' potential incentives to restrict their future equity financing choices by precommiting to a preemptive rights offer. The resulting equilibrium is such that only the highest quality firms are willing to precommit.

In our three date model all firms are priced at the population average prior to any precommitment announcement by firms. Then, since the date zero share value with no precommitment is less than the date zero share value with precommitment, firms that remove the rights offer pre-commitment from the corporate charter will experience a reduction in share price. While there is no direct empirical evidence relating creation of a preemptive rights charter provision to share price reaction, Bhagat (1983) provides indirect evidence consistent with our model: firms removing the charter provision experience a negative abnormal stock price reaction. According to our model removal of the provision signals a deterioration of the firm's future prospects and makes future equity financing flexibility more desirable.

Two assumptions of the model deserve further elaboration. First, the information structure assumed to derive the equilibrium precommitment action in Section III is particularly simple. However, the results are easily generalizable to a larger number of partitions and to the location of the information partitions across firm quality types.

The second assumption is the multiperiod objective function. Firms are assumed to take into account future consequences when making their current decisions. This assumption is consistent with decision makers being concerned with the welfare of both current and future shareholders. A more complete model might attempt to endogenize the shareholders' choice of a wage schedule designed to induce the behavior obtained in our model by the assumption of a multiperiod objective function. Alternatively, this behavior might be obtained in a model explicitly designed to deal with managerial reputation.

NOTES

* Both authors, The University of British Columbia.
1 For a more detailed derivation, including second order conditions, see Heinkel and Schwartz (1985).
2 While the normal density allows for negative stock prices, this probability is negligible in the numerical example to follow.
3 For alternative equilibria and arguments concerning stability of the equilibrium, see Heinkel and Schwartz (1985).
4 Alternatively, if firm type $t = 115$ pretended to be a type $t = 116.8$ and mimicked that firm by using an uninsured rights offer with $S = S^*(116.8) = 104.94$, this would yield a net share value of \$104.76, which is lower than that received by using the underwriter (105.68).
5 This assumes investors do not recognize that firm type $t = 117$ is using the underwriter. If all firm types below $t = 117$ were to employ the underwriter, firm type $t = 117$ would still be worse off, receiving net proceeds of \$105.77.
6 For all possible cases, see Heinkel and Schwartz (1985).
7 For example, assuming $t^* < 116.9 = t_l$ and $t_h = 118.00 < \hat{t} = 118.6$ with the other data shown in Table 2.1 allows an equilibrium in which only firms receiving signal μ_h will precommit to a standby rights offer.

REFERENCES

Bhagat, S. (1983). 'The Effect of Pre-emptive Right Amendments on Shareholder Wealth.' *Journal of Financial Economics*, **12**, 289–310.
Hanson, R. and J. Pinkerton (1982). 'Direct Equity Financing: A Resolution of the Paradox.' *Journal of Finance*, **37**, 651–665.
Heinkel, R. and E. Schwartz (1985). 'Rights versus Underwritten Offerings: An Asymmetric Information Approach.' *Journal of Finance*, forthcoming.
Miller, M. and K. Rock (1985). 'Dividend Policy Under Asymmetric Information.' *Journal of Finance*, **40**, 1031–1051.

COMMENT STEVEN M. FRIES

The paper of Heinkel and Schwartz offers explanations for two phenomena. Firstly, a rationale for the co-existence of three issue techniques for equity offerings, insured and uninsured rights and underwritten offerings, is provided. Secondly, an explanation is proposed for some firms choosing to precommit to the use of one type of issue technique through the use of corporate charter provisions. Their explanation of the latter phenomenon is contingent upon their rationale for the former. Accordingly, my comments will be in two parts.

Choices of issue technique by firms

Given an asymmetry of information about future prospects (qualities) of firms, with firms possessing more precise information than investors, firms' choices of issue technique may be guided by a desire to signal their qualities to investors. In Heinkel and Schwartz's analysis, a firm can signal its quality to investors using either an uninsured or insured rights offering. Underwritten offerings, however, convey no signals about firms' qualities. The choices of issue technique by firms are thus two-fold decisions: whether or not to signal their qualities, and if they choose to do so whether insured or uninsured rights offerings are the lower cost signalling device.

Suppose that a firm uses uninsured rights for its equity offering. When setting a subscription price for the rights, the firm must assess the effect of this price on the probability of a failed issue because such a failure would impose certain costs upon the firm. Moreover, since the probability of a failed issue depends upon not only the subscription price but also the firm's quality, uninformed investors form a conjecture about the relationships between the firm's quality and the subscription price of its rights. Given that the conjecture of investors is fulfilled by the firm's choice of a subscription price, a lower subscription price is shown to signal a lower firm quality. Therefore, the firm also must assess the effect of its choice of subscription price on its market value. The trade-off between a higher market value and higher expected failure costs leads to an optimal subscription price.

For firms of relatively high quality, insured rights offerings may be a less costly signalling device than uninsured rights offerings. By seeking a stand-by underwriting agreement from an investment banker, the firm creates an incentive for the banker to become well informed about the firm's quality so that the agreement can be accurately valued. The terms of the standby agreement, the subscription price and the underwriting fee, thus can reveal information acquired by the underwriter. If the underwriting fee equals the option value of the agreement plus the underwriter's information costs, as it would in a competitive market, and as assumed by Heinkel and Schwartz, the signalling cost to the firm would equal the information cost. But the relationship between the firm and underwriter must be a bilateral monopoly if duplication of information costs is to be avoided. The solution to this bargaining problem, obviously, need not be the competitive outcome. Nevertheless, information plus bargaining costs for relatively high quality firms can be less than the dissipative signalling cost of an uninsured rights offering.

For relatively low quality firms, the cost of signalling, even using an uninsured rights offering, may exceed the benefits in terms of increased market values. In such an instance, Heinkel and Schwartz argue that a firm would seek a firm-commitment underwriting agreement from an investment banker. An underwriting agreement, in their analysis, is a commitment to purchase any equity offering at an appropriately set average price less a fixed spread. The underwriter then offers the issue to investors at the set price. The price choosen by the underwritern reflects the average quality of firms which select this issue technique, while the fixed spread compensates the underwriter for any expenses. Since investors know how firms' choices of issue technique are related to their qualities, investors can rationally infer the average value of underwritten issues. Investors are thus willing to purchase issues from an underwriter at the offering price.

In this analysis, an underwriter simply collects the spread between the price at which he buys and sells underwritten equity offerings. He performs no signalling or distribution function. The rationale for the existence of underwritten offerings is that they allow firms to avoid the expected failure costs of rights offerings.[1] But if an underwriter provides no services of value to firms, they may benefit from offering their securities directly to investors and accepting their valuation of the issue.

Suppose that firms have the option of selling their issues in a competitive market and that investors know the population density function of firms but not qualities of particular firms. Since investors also know the relationship between firms' choices of issue technique and their qualities, they can rationally infer the average value of direct offerings. Therefore the valuation schedule of direct offerings is $A(t)$ and everywhere dominates the valuation schedule of underwritten offerings, $A(t) - U$. By directly offering their issues to investors, firms receive an average valuation for their issues but avoid paying an underwriter's fee.

An alternative interpretation of Heinkel and Schwartz's underwritten offering valuation schedule may exist, however. Suppose that direct offerings are not feasible because a distribution or retailing function must be performed to locate investors for issues. An underwriter, or more correctly, an investment banker often provides this service in return for a fixed fee. In such a case, the investment banker is not involved in the pricing of an offering. Rather, the issue yields its market value. This issue technique is generally referred to as a best-efforts distribution. Therefore, $A(t) - U$ can be interpreted as the valuation schedule for best-efforts distributions where $A(t)$ is the market valuation of such offerings and U is the investment banker's compensation for his distribution efforts. To maintain consistency across issue techniques, the distribution costs imposed upon *ex ante* shareholders in rights offerings also should be included in the analysis.

Finally, a suggestion about how to incorporate firm-commitment underwritten offerings into the analysis of firms' choices of issue technique is offered. In its present form, the model's exogenously imposed information structure is somewhat peculiar. The underwriter can become fully informed about firms' qualities in insured rights offerings; however, in underwritten offerings, the underwriter cannot acquire this information even though he clearly would benefit from its acquisition. If an underwriter does become fully informed about firms in underwritten offerings, we could assume that the bargaining solution to the bilateral monopoly between a firm and underwriter would be the competitive outcome. This assumption would be consistent with Heinkel and Schwartz's treatment of stand-by underwriting agreements. Given these assumptions, the public offering price of an underwritten issue would convey the same information as the terms of a stand-by agreement and do so at the same expense.[2] Distribution costs then could be used to differentiate underwritten from insured rights offerings.

Precommitments to an issue technique

Firms that possess some knowledge of their future prospects prior to issuing securities may choose to convey this information before their planned equity offerings. For example, suppose that firms will not be issuing shares until next period but do have imprecise knowledge of their qualities. More specifically, the information possessed by each firm in the current period establishes a range of values in which its actual quality lies. In the next period each firm learns precisely its quality. Moreover, suppose that firms are concerned with both the present and next period's share prices. Given this objective, some firms may precommit to a particular issue technique, such as an insured rights offering, in the current period with the anticipated effect of increasing their present share prices. Precommitments in the current period convey information because of the separating equilibrium that will occur next period as firms choose among issue techniques. The cost of precommitments is the possibility of being constrained to use a sub-optimal issue technique in the second period when firms learn precisely their qualities.

Heinkel and Schwartz establish the existence of an initial period signalling equilibrium in which firms may choose to precommit to an insured rights offering. In the initial period, each firm receives a signal indicating that its actual quality lies in one of three ranges. The highest range is a subset of those firm qualities that correspond with the use of insured rights offering. They demonstrate that firms observing the highest signal convey this information by precommiting to an insured rights offerings. For firms receiving the lower signals, the expected second period costs of precommitment exceed the current period benefits; hence, they do not precommit. Therefore, the first period valuation of firms that precommit to insured rights offerings is the average value of those firms that receive the highest signal. Firms that do not precommit also receive an average valuation, but one derived from the distribution of firms that receive the lower signals.

Heinkel and Schwartz's analysis of the precommit decision follows logically from the separating equilibrium they derive for firms choosing among issue techniques. However, some reservations about this separating equilibrium have been registered, particularly with regard to their treatment of underwritten offerings. I have suggested that underwritten offerings are quite similar to insured rights offerings and that they would be used by firms of the relatively high quality. Lower quality firms would use direct offerings or best-efforts distributions. If this conjecture is true, the initial period signalling equilibrium must account for the use of underwritten offerings by relatively high quality firms.

Finally, Heinkel and Schwartz cite a study by Bhagat (1983) as providing indirect evidence consistent with their model. Precommitment to a rights offering, according to their model, would convey favourable information about a firm's quality; conversely, abandonment of such a precommitment would convey unfavourable information. Bhagat observed that firms removing corporate charter provisions that require the use of rights offerings experienced a negative abnormal stock price reaction. When arguing that this evidence is consistent with their model, Heinkel and Schwartz presume that alternative issue techniques to rights offerings are used only by relatively low quality firms. As was previously suggested, however, underwritten offerings may be used by firms of higher quality than those which use uninsured rights offerings. Therefore, Bhagat's evidence is consistent with their hypothesis if firms removing corporate charter provisions that require the use of rights offerings are expected to use direct offerings and best-efforts distributions rather than underwritten offerings.

NOTES

1 This rationale for the existence of underwritten offerings is found in Heinkel and Schwartz (1985).
2 The conveyance of information in negotiated underwritings is analysed by Fries (1985a) and (1985b).

REFERENCES

Bhagat, S. (1983). 'The Effect of Pre-emptive Right Amendments on Shareholder Wealth.' *Journal of Financial Economics*, **12**, 289–310.

Fries, S. (1985a). 'A Stochastic Production Economy with an Endogenous Underwriter of a Security Issue.' Mimeo.

Fries, S. (1985b). 'An Underwritten Security Issue, Information Acquisition, and Interests of *Ex Ante* Shareholders.' Mimeo.

Heinkel, R. and E. Schwartz (1985). 'Rights versus Underwritten Offerings: An Asymmetric Information Approach.' *Journal of Finance*, forthcoming.

3   Equity issues and offering dilution

PAUL ASQUITH and DAVID MULLINS Jr*

I Introduction and issues

This paper investigates the effect of equity issues on stock prices. An enduring anomaly in financial economics is the reliance of firms on internally generated funds as their chief source of equity financing and their corresponding reluctance to issue common stock (Donaldson (1961), Lintner (1960), Sametz (1964)). This behavior is less anomalous to financial practitioners. Financial executives, investment bankers, and many regulators argue that selling equity causes a firm's stock price to fall. Their view, labelled the price-pressure hypothesis by Scholes (1972), contends that an increase in the supply of shares causes a decline in a firm's stock price because the demand curve for shares is downward sloping. The implication is that each firm's shares are unique, and close substitutes do not exist. In addition, some proponents of this hypothesis argue that the price reduction is short-lived and that a post-offering increase in stock prices or 'sweetener' is necessary to market additional shares.

In contrast, the theoretical literature in finance assumes that the demand curve for a firm's shares is essentially horizontal. The prices of securities are determined solely by the risk and expected return associated with a security's future cash flows. Close substitutes for a firm's shares, e.g. securities with similar risk and return characteristics, are either directly available in the capital markets or they can be constructed through combinations of existing securities. Moreover, efficient capital markets rule out new issue price effects not based on changes in a security's expected cash flows. Thus with close substitutes, efficient capital markets, and fixed investment policies, the price of any firm's shares should be independent of the number of shares the firm, or any shareholder, chooses to sell. This view of equity financing is also not without challenge. There are also theoretical arguments, other than a downward sloping demand curve, for predicting a stock price decrease with equity issues. Chief among these are the effect of new equity issues on corporate capital structures and the role of stock issues as informative signals.

With tax advantages from debt financing, a new equity issue may reduce a firm's stock price if it reduces the firm's debt ratio (see Modigliani and Miller (1963), DeAngelo and Masulis (1980), and Masulis (1980a, 1980b and 1983)). In addition, an unanticipated reduction in financial leverage will make debt less risky resulting in a transfer of wealth from shareholders to bondholders (Galai and Masulis (1976)). Finally, a firm's choice of capital structure may convey management's expectations about the firm's prospects (Ross (1977)). Higher debt ratios are binding constraints on the firm and thus signal positive management expectations concerning future cash flows. In contrast, issuing new equity is a negative signal and may reduce a firm's stock price.

Others have theorized that equity issues serve as signals which communicate managers' superior information independent of capital structure considerations. In a world of asymmetric information managers and insiders have superior information compared to investors, and management's decision to issue equity conveys information about a firm's 'intrinsic' value. A stock price reduction is produced by rational investors hedging against the risk that, in selling stock, managers are using their superior information to benefit existing shareholders at the expense of new shareholders. A more benign interpretation is that the information available to managers is not favorable enough to preclude selling stock, and thus the decision to issue equity is a negative signal. Leland and Pyle (1977) hypothesize that, *ceteris paribus*, large equity issues by entrepreneurs to outside investors are a negative signal. In Miller and Rock's (1985) model of dividend policy, equity issues are equivalent to negative dividends and convey negative information concerning the firm's future earnings. In the Myers and Majluf (1984) model, when managers have superior information, issuing equity always reduces a firm's stock price.[1]

Several empirical studies investigate the price effects associated with the sale of seasoned equity. These studies examine both secondary distributions by shareholders and primary distributions by corporations. A secondary offering involves the sale of stock from a group of current shareholders. That is, the number of shares outstanding remains the same and the firm receives no proceeds from the sale. A primary offering consists of new shares issued by the firm which receives the proceeds.

Studies of secondary offerings include Scholes (1972), Kraus and Stoll (1972), and Dann, Mayers, and Raab (1977). The samples employed in these studies consist primarily of unregistered block trades.[2] Scholes and Kraus and Stoll find evidence of a permanent price reduction (of approximately 2%) with block trades. In addition, Kraus and Stoll find a small, temporary intra-day price decline which is substantially reversed by the end of the day. They attribute the decline to a price-pressure or distribution effect. Dann, Mayers, and Raab investigate this intra-day price decline and conclude that abnormal trading profits are possible (before transaction costs) if investors react within 15 minutes of the news of a block trade.

Despite this permanent price decline, Scholes concludes that the demand curve for firms' shares is essentially horizontal. This conclusion is based on the finding that the price reduction is not associated with the size of the distribution (as a percentage of the firm's total shares) and he argues that the decline is due to a discrete information effect.[3] Kraus and Stoll find that price declines are significantly related to the value of the distribution, but they can not determine whether this relationship was due to price-pressure or information.

Studies of unregistered secondary distributions provide only limited insight into the effect of large stock distributions by firms and investors. First, unregistered block trades are small compared with registered secondaries and primary issues.[4] Moreover, the conflicting findings concerning a size effect leave this important issue unresolved.

A number of studies have focused on primary issues of seasoned equity (Smith (1977), Logue and Jarrow (1978), Marsh (1979), and Hess and Frost (1982)).[5] These studies generally find a small price reduction in the period surrounding the equity issue. Marsh and Hess and Frost test and reject the hypothesis that the price decline is associated with the size of the issue. These two studies, however, focus on the issue date rather than the date that the offering is announced. This is because they are testing for a price-pressure effect on the issue date. These papers do not examine the possibility that a price decline would be anticipated by investors at the announcement date.

A recent unpublished study, Korwar (1983), does focus on the announcement day price effect of primary issues of seasoned equity.[6] Korwar's study of 424 equity issues finds a price decline of approximately 2.5% on announcement day. This study does not investigate the relationship between the size of the issue and the magnitude of the price reduction since it views equity issues from a capital structure perspective.[7]

Despite the literature reviewed above, the nature and magnitude of the impact of equity offerings on stock prices are unresolved issues. None of the previous studies employs a comprehensive sample of large primary and secondary offerings to examine the announcement day price effect and its relation to issue size.

The announcement day price effect predicted by the various theories can be grouped into three categories:

No Price Effect – consistent with the close substitutes/efficient markets hypotheses

Negative Price Effect – consistent with (1) a downward sloping demand curve for firms' shares leading to a permanent price reduction, (2) capital structure hypotheses based upon redistribution of firm value among classes of security holders, tax effects, and/or leverage-related information effects, (3) information effects associated with the sale of equity by informed sellers, both firms and investors, and (4) large transaction costs associated with equity issues.

Positive Price Effect – consistent with (1) a favorable information effect associated with investment, (2) a value enhancing reduction in financial leverage due, for example, to a reduction in the expected costs of financial distress and/or agency costs.

The first priority is to determine which of the predictions listed above is consistent with the data. A secondary priority is to investigate whether the size of the issue influences the price effect. A significant relation between issue size and the magnitude of the price effect would be expected in the latter two groups of hypotheses. For leverage-related hypotheses the size of the issue is related to the magnitude of the change in capital structure. For information-related hypotheses, the size of the issue should be a measure of the size of the informative signal. Consistent with Scholes' (1972) argument, the lack of relationship between the price effect and issue size is consistent with a horizontal demand curve for the firm's shares even if there is a non-zero average price effect due either to the release of a discrete quantum of information or to fixed transaction costs.

Distinguishing among the many hypotheses within any of the three categories is difficult, but some discrimination is possible. For example, secondary issues do not result in changes in corporate capital structure and their comparison with primary issues provides a testable capital structure hypothesis.[8] Differences in results for industrial firms and public utilities, and evidence on the timing of equity issues also provide insight into the factors responsible for price effects. Finally, examination of post announcement day stock returns should reveal any failures in semi-strong capital market efficiency such as temporary price-pressure around the issue date.

This paper examines the announcement day and issue day price effects of both primary and registered secondary issues of seasoned equity. The results demonstrate that equity issues reduce stock prices. For industrial issues, regression results indicate that the announcement day price reduction is significantly related to the size of the equity offering. Although the percentage reduction in equity value is small, the loss in firm value on announcement day is a substantial fraction of the proceeds of the stock issue. These results may explain why firms are reluctant to issue new equity.

The results presented in this paper confirm the finding of Taggart (1977) and Marsh (1979) that primary stock issues are more likely to occur after a rise in stock prices. However, the decision to issue equity appears to be related more to the performance of a firm's stock price relative to the market than to the performance of the market as a whole. Regression results for industrial issues indicate that the announcement day price reduction is inversely related to stock price performance in the year prior to the announcement. This finding provides an explanation for why firms tend to issue equity after a rise in stock prices. These results are also consistent with the suggestion by Myers and Majluf (1984) that the price reduction associated with equity issues varies through time and that firms respond by issuing equity when price reductions are relatively small.

The findings also indicate that primary stock offerings for public utilities are accompanied by price reductions. The price effects for utilities are smaller than those observed for industrial issues, and there is no relation between the timing of utility issues and stock price performance. One possible explanation is that differences in the announcement day price effects for industrial issues and utilities are due to a larger information content associated with industrial offerings.

Finally, the roughly similar price effects observed for primary issues by corporations and registered secondary distributions suggest that the price reduction is not related solely to tax effects or leverage-related information associated with a change in capital structure. The results are generally consistent with the hypothesis that equity sales by firms and knowledgeable investors are viewed by the market as unfavorable signals about a firm's current performance and future prospects. The results are also consistent with the price-pressure hypothesis that there is a downward sloping demand for a firm's shares.

II Data

This study analyzes 531 registered common stock offerings by utilities and industrial firms. These common stock offerings were chosen by examining *Moody's Industrial Manual* and *Moody's Public Utility Manual*. Industrial stock offerings were obtained by examining the common stock histories of each firm rated by Moody's or included in the full coverage or comprehensive coverage sections of *Moody's Industrial Manual*. Stock offerings by these firms are included in the sample used here if they met the following requirements:

(a) The stock offering took place between January 1963 and December 1981.

(b) The firm was listed on the ASE or NYSE at the time of the stock offering. Therefore, there are no initial offerings.

(c) The offering was public, underwritten, and registered with the SEC.

(d) The offering was for common stock only. No joint offerings of common stock and any other financing instrument are included.

(e) Firms with more than one class of voting common stock are excluded from the sample.

(f) The offering announcement was reported in the *Wall Street Journal.*

These requirements assure data availability on the Center for Research in Security Prices (CRSP) daily stock return file and a sample of common stock offerings uncontaminated by simultaneous offerings of other financial instruments or by merger bids.[9] The sample also covers a long time period and include only listed, well established firms to avoid initial offerings and small, thinly traded stocks. There are 266 common stock offerings by industrial firms in the sample.

Utility stock offerings were obtained by first examining the common stock histories of any utility both rated by Moody's and included in the full coverage section of *Moody's Public Utility Manual.* To be included in the sample of utility common stock offerings these offerings also had to meet the six requirements listed above. There are 265 utility common stock offerings in the sample used here.

The sample of common stock issues collected from Moody's was checked in the *Wall Street Journal Index* and the *Wall Street Journal* to make sure the offerings were for common stock only. In addition, several other data items were collected for each offering. First, the type of each offering (primary, secondary, or combination) was determined. A primary offering is for new shares of common stock which are added to the number of shares outstanding. A secondary offering is for the sale of securities owned by a present stockholder, and it does not change the number outstanding. A combination offering combines a primary and secondary offering. Where available, the type of offering was taken from the *Moody's Manuals* and in other instances from the *Wall Street Journal* article, the offering prospectus, or the firm's 10K report. The size of each offering, both announced and actual, was collected in a similar manner. The number of shares of stock currently outstanding for the firm was obtained from several sources including the *Wall Street Journal* article if it gave that information, the offering prospectus when it could be obtained, or the firm's 10K report.

In addition to this offering data, the percentage of the firm's stock owned by insiders and information about the firm's capital structure were obtained for as many firms as possible. Insider ownership percentages were collected from the *Value Line Investment Survey*, debt ratios were obtained from *Compustat*, and Moody ratings of senior and subordinated debt were collected from the *Moody's Industrial* and *Moody's Public Utility Manuals.* Finally, for the time period surrounding each stock offering in the sample, the performance of the value weighted market return and the S&P Index of 500 Stocks were also collected from the CRSP index files.

Table 3.1. *Announcement dates by year for industrial and utility common stock offerings*

| | Type of offering | | | | |
| | Industrial | | | | Utility |
Year	All	Primary	Secondary	Combustion	Primary[1]
1963	1	0	1	0	1
1964	1	0	0	1	2
1965	5	1	3	1	0
1966	5	2	3	0	1
1967	4	1	1	2	0
1968	6	3	0	3	2
1969	19	3	12	4	4
1970	16	9	2	5	6
1971	29	8	8	13	7
1972	36	6	24	6	14
1973	11	4	7	0	20
1974	7	3	3	1	13
1975	20	12	6	2	25
1976	23	13	7	3	24
1977	5	1	2	2	30
1978	12	6	4	2	31
1979	8	7	0	1	33
1980	39	32	1	6	35
1981	19	17	1	1	16
TOTAL	266	128	85	53	264

[1] Only one utility stock offering in the sample was not a primary offering. There was one secondary offering in 1967.

In summary, the sample used in this paper contains 531 common stock offerings over the period 1963–1981. The sample includes 266 industrial offerings and within this classification there are 128 primary offerings, 85 secondary offerings, and 53 combination offerings. The sample also includes 265 utility stock offerings during this period; all are primary offerings except for one secondary offering. The distribution of offerings by year and type are given in Table 3.1.

III Methodology

The stock market's reaction to equity offering announcements is measured using daily excess stock returns. These excess stock returns are estimated from the daily stock returns file provided by the CRSP. The daily excess return for any security is estimated by estimated by

$$XR_{it} = R_{it} - E(\tilde{R}_{it}) \tag{1}$$

where

t = the day measured relative to the event

XR_{it} = the excess return to security i for day t

R_{it} = the return on security i during day t

$E(\tilde{R}_{it})$ = the expected rate of return on security i for day t

$E(\tilde{R}_{it})$ is estimated by grouping annually all securities listed on the NYSE and the AMEX into ten equal control portfolios ranked according to their Scholes–Williams (1977) beta estimates. Each security is therefore assigned to one of ten portfolios. The observed return to the control portfolio to which security i is assigned is then used as the estimate of $E(\tilde{R}_{it})$. The CRSP daily returns file provides the observed returns for each security R_{it}. The excess return for each security, XR_{it}, is then calculated as the difference between the actual return to a security and the return to its control portfolio.

Average excess returns for each relative day are calculated by

$$XR_t = (1/N) \sum_{i=1}^{N} XR_{it} \tag{2}$$

where N is the number of securities with excess returns during day t. The cumulative excess returns for each security i, CER_i, are formed by summing average excess returns over event time as follows:

$$CER_{i,K,L} = \sum_{t=K}^{L} XR_{it} \tag{3}$$

where the $CER_{i,K,L}$ is for the period from t = day K until t = day L.

Average cumulative excess returns over the event time from day K until day L are calculated by

$$CER_{K,L} = (1/N) \sum_{i=1}^{N} CER_{i,K,L} \tag{4}$$

In particular, a two-day average excess return is generated for each equity offering announcement examined. A two-day excess return is necessary to capture the effect of an announcement due to its timing relative to the market's trading hours. Day $t = 0$ is the day the news of an announcement is published in the *Wall Street Journal*. In most cases, the news is announced on the previous day, $t = -1$, and reported the next day.

If an equity offering is announced before the market closes, then the market's response to the news actually predates the publication by one day. If the news is announced after the market closes, the market will respond the next day and the reaction is indeed on day 0. Thus in reality there is a two-day announcement 'day', $t = -1$ and $t = 0$. This two day return for firm i is $CER_{i, -1, 0}$ where

$$CER_{i, -1, 0} = XR_{i, -1} + XR_{i, 0} \tag{5}$$

and

$XR_{i, -1}$ = the excess return to security i on the day prior to a published announcement in the *Wall Street Journal*

$XR_{i, 0}$ = the excess return to security i on the day an announcement is published in the *Wall Street Journal*

Finally, t-statistics are calculated for $CER_{K,L}$ by

$$t(CER_{K,L}) = CER_{K,L}/S(CER_{K,L}) \tag{6}$$

where

$S(CER_{K,L})$ = the standard deviation of $CER_{K,L}$

$= (T \cdot \text{Var}(XR_t))^{1/2}$ with $T = K - L + 1$

The $\text{Var}(XR_t)$ is estimated over the period from 68 days before the announcement day until 21 days before the announcement day.[10] If $K = L$, $t(CER_{K,L})$ is equivalent to the t-statistic for XR_K.

IV Results

IV.1 Industrial offerings

IV.1.1 Announcement day effects

For industrial offerings the average excess returns surrounding the announcement day are reported in Table 3.2. Consistent with no information leakage before the announcement and semi-strong market efficiency, the excess returns for the total sample and all three subsamples are concentrated in the two day announcement period. The average two-day announcement period excess returns for the total sample is -2.7% with a t-statistic of -14.8. The average two-day excess return is -3.0% for primary offerings, -2.0% for secondary offerings, and -3.2% for combination offerings. All three average excess returns are statistically significant. These average announcement period returns are not the result

Table 3.2. *Average excess returns (XRET) and cumulative excess returns (CER) from 10 days before until 10 days after the announcement day of industrial equity offerings by type of offering in the period 1963–1981 (%)*

| Day | Type of offering | | | | | | | |
| | All | | Primary | | Secondary | | Combination | |
	XRET	CER	XRET	CER	XRET	CER	XRET	CER
−10	−0.1	−0.1	0.0	0.0	0.2	0.2	−0.6	−0.6
−9	0.0	−0.1	−0.1	−0.1	−0.1	0.3	0.1	−0.5
−8	0.1	0.0	0.1	0.0	0.1	0.4	0.2	0.3
−7	0.1	0.1	0.3	0.3	0.0	0.4	−0.4	−0.7
−6	−0.3	−0.2	−0.3	0.0	−0.3	0.1	−0.5	−1.2
−5	0.0	−0.2	−0.4	−0.4	0.3	0.4	0.4	−0.8
−4	0.0	−0.2	0.0	−0.4	0.0	0.4	0.1	−0.7
−3	0.1	−0.1	−0.2	−0.6	0.5	0.9	0.1	−0.6
−2	−0.4	−0.5	−0.3	−0.9	−0.1	0.8	−1.1	−1.7
−1	−1.8	−2.3	−2.3	−3.3	−1.0	−0.2	−1.8	−3.5
Announcement								
Day	−0.9	−3.2	−0.7	−3.9	−1.0	−1.2	−1.4	−5.9
+1	0.0	−3.2	−0.1	−4.0	0.0	−1.2	0.0	−5.9
+2	0.1	−3.1	0.0	−4.0	0.0	−1.2	0.2	−5.7
+3	0.2	−2.9	0.3	−3.7	0.2	−1.0	0.1	−5.6
+4	0.2	−2.7	0.1	−3.6	0.3	−0.7	−0.1	−5.7
+5	0.0	−2.7	0.1	−3.5	0.1	−0.6	−0.4	−6.1
+6	0.0	−2.7	−0.1	−3.6	0.3	−0.3	0.1	−6.0
+7	0.3	−2.4	0.1	−3.5	0.2	−0.1	1.2	−4.8
+8	0.0	−2.4	−0.1	−3.6	0.0	−0.1	0.2	−4.6
+9	0.1	−2.3	−0.1	−3.7	0.1	0.0	0.6	−4.0
+10	0.0	−2.3	0.2	−3.5	0.0	0.0	−0.3	−4.3
Two Day Announcement Return	−2.7		−3.0		−2.0		−3.2	
t-statistic	14.8		12.5		9.1		5.9	
N	266		128		85		53	

of a few outliers. Tables 3.3 and 3.4 illustrate that more than 80% of the industrial equity issues exhibit negative excess returns.

While price reductions on the order of 2% to 3% may appear small, Tables 3.3 and 3.4 provide additional insight into the magnitude of the price effect. For each of the subsamples, Tables 3.3 and 3.4 present distributions of the average reduction in aggregate equity value on announcement day as a percentage of the proceeds of the equity issue.

Table 3.3. *The announcement day offering dilution for industrial equity offerings, defined as the reduction in the value of the equity of a firm as a percentage of the planned value of a primary equity offering*

| Dilution % | Dilution of offering | | | |
| | 121 Primary | | 45 Combination | |
	N	Cumulative %	N	Cumulative %
$80 < \leqslant 100$	1	.8	2	4.4
$60 < \leqslant 80$	0	.8	0	4.4
$40 < \leqslant 60$	2	2.5	0	4.4
$30 < \leqslant 40$	0	2.5	0	4.4
$20 < \leqslant 30$	3	5.0	0	4.4
$10 < \leqslant 20$	7	10.7	1	6.7
$0 < \leqslant 10$	9	18.2	4	15.6
$-10 < \leqslant 0$	20	34.7	3	22.2
$-20 < \leqslant -10$	9	42.1	7	37.8
$-30 < \leqslant -20$	11	51.2	3	44.4
$-40 < \leqslant -30$	25	71.9	4	53.3
$-50 < \leqslant -40$	6	76.9	5	64.4
$-60 < \leqslant -50$	5	81.0	5	75.6
$-70 < \leqslant -60$	6	86.0	0	75.6
$-80 < \leqslant -70$	4	89.3	1	77.8
$-100 < \leqslant -80$	6	94.2	3	84.4
$-120 < \leqslant -100$	4	97.5	3	91.1
$-140 < \leqslant -120$	1	98.3	0	91.1
$-160 < \leqslant -140$	1	99.2	0	91.1
$-200 < \leqslant -160$	0	99.2	1	93.3
$\leqslant -200$	1	100.0	3	100.0
Average dilution	-31.0%		-53.2%	
Median dilution	-28.0%		-35.6%	

For primary issues we define the ratio of the change in the equity value of the firm to the proceeds of the issue as 'offering dilution'. A ratio of 0% means that on announcement day the equity value of the firm does not change. A ratio of -100% means that on announcement day, the equity value falls by an amount equal to the new equity raised in the issue. That is, with a -100% ratio, after the proceeds are received on issue date, equity value will be exactly equal to the pre-announcement equity value. This is 100% 'dilution' since the same common stock value is now divided by a larger number of shares, and the reduction in stock price is exactly proportional to the increase in shares outstanding.[11] Offering dilution between 0 and -100% will leave post-issue equity value greater than pre-

Table 3.4. *The announcement day offering dilution for industrial equity offerings, defined as the reduction in the value of the equity of a firm as a percentage of the planned value of a secondary equity offering*

Offering dilution %	Type of offering			
	82 Secondary		51 Combination	
	N	Cumulative %	N	Cumulative %
200 < ⩽ 300	3	3.7	0	0.0
150 < ⩽ 200	0	3.7	0	0.0
100 < ⩽ 150	3	7.3	0	0.0
60 < ⩽ 100	4	12.2	0	0.0
30 < ⩽ 60	1	13.4	2	3.9
20 < ⩽ 30	1	15.9	0	3.9
10 < ⩽ 20	1	17.1	1	5.9
0 < ⩽ 10	3	20.7	5	15.7
−10 < ⩽ 0	3	24.4	7	29.4
−20 < ⩽ −10	8	34.1	7	43.1
−30 < ⩽ −20	6	41.5	8	58.8
−40 < ⩽ −30	4	46.3	9	76.5
−50 < ⩽ −40	4	51.2	5	86.3
−60 < ⩽ −50	2	53.7	0	86.3
−80 < ⩽ −60	5	59.8	4	94.1
−100 < ⩽ −80	9	70.7	0	94.1
−150 < ⩽ −100	9	81.7	1	96.1
−200 < ⩽ −150	3	85.4	2	100.0
−300 < ⩽ −200	5	91.5	0	100.0
−400 < ⩽ −300	2	93.9	0	100.0
−500 < ⩽ −400	2	96.3	0	100.0
−600 < ⩽ −500	2	98.8	0	100.0
−700 < ⩽ −600	0	98.8	0	100.0
−800 < ⩽ −700	1	100.0	0	100.0
Average offering dilution	−77.6%		−31.1%	
Median offering dilution	−43.4%		−25.0%	

announcement equity value and will result in a stock price reduction which is less than proportional to the increase in shares.

Table 3.3 illustrates that primary stock issues (and the primary portion of combination issues) are highly dilutive in the sense defined above. On average the loss in firm value on announcement day is 31% of the funds raised in primary offerings. For example, to raise $100 million dollars in new equity, existing shareholders, on average, gave up $31 million in current market value. The median dilution is −28.0%. Almost 25% of the primary issues produce offering dilution greater than 50%, and 6% of the primary issues result in dilution greater than 100%. For the offerings with greater than 100% dilution, after the proceeds of the equity issue are received, equity value is actually lower than the equity value before the issue is announced. These results imply that a substantial portion of the proceeds of an equity issue, in effect, comes out of the pockets of old shareholders.

Table 3.4 reports the aggregate announcement day loss in equity value as a percentage of the proceeds of registered secondary issues and combination issues. An offering dilution ratio of -100% for secondary issues means that on announcement day the equity value falls by an amount equal to the amount being sold. This is identical to a -100% offering dilution for primary issues except that in a secondary distribution the firm does not receive the proceeds of the sale. The reduction in equity value associated with the announcement of a secondary distribution is, on average, a large fraction of the size of the issue. The average reduction in firm value is 78% of the proceeds of the sale, the median is -43.4%, and in almost 30% of the secondary issues, firm value fell by more than the proceeds of the sale.[12] The larger reductions observed for secondary distributions compared with primary offerings suggest that secondary issues may be viewed as relatively more pessimistic signals.

In interpreting these results an important issue is whether the price reductions associated with equity issues harm existing shareholders. If the price reductions are caused by negative signals, wouldn't the negative information eventually be released anyway?

Despite this argument, in most signalling models price reductions associated with equity issues are detrimental to shareholders. First, for shareholders who are consuming a portion of their wealth through time, postponing the release of negative information is beneficial (see Greenwald, Stiglitz and Weiss (1984)). Secondly, correctly priced 'good' firms which must issue equity to fund a positive net present value project incur the price reduction because they cannot convincingly distinguish themselves from 'bad' firms issuing equity to take advantage of overvaluation. Even though they will later be recognized as good firms, the harm has been done by selling equity at a low price to the detriment of 'old' shareholders and the benefit of 'new' shareholders. This is a classic adverse selection problem which harms existing shareholders both when 'good' firms issue equity and when they forego positive net present value projects rather than incur the equity issue price reduction (see Miller and Rock (1985) and Myers and Majluf (1984)). Finally, and perhaps most importantly, Myers and Majluf contend that the detrimental impact on 'good' firms can be avoided or minimized. Their reasoning is that the magnitude of the adverse selection problem varies through time. In time periods when the equity issue price reduction is small, firms can sell shares and invest in financial slack (cash reserves or unutilized debt capacity) thereby obviating the need to suffer a larger reduction later when funds are needed to finance worthwhile projects.

IV.1.2 Firm and stock market performance

The findings reported in Tables 3.5 and 3.6 explore the timing of equity sales. Table 3.5 focuses on the performance of sample firms' stock returns adjusted for the performance of the stock market as a whole. For all three subsamples, positive average cumulative excess returns are observed in the two years preceding the announcement of the issue. The average CERs for the period from two years until ten days preceding the issue are 40.4% for primary issues, 21.4% for secondaries, and 41.8% for combinations.[13] For all three subsamples the average cumulative excess returns in the two years following the equity issue are at first slightly positive then negative. Thus, firms and secondary issuers sell stock following a period in which the stock outperforms the market. Subsequent to the issue, superior performance ceases and average or below average performance is observed.

Table 3.6 provides insight into the timing of equity issues relative to the general level of stock prices, and these results are easily interpreted. For all three subsamples, market returns are positive in the two years preceding the announcement of the issue. Despite the fact that equity is sold following an increase in the general level of stock prices, the results in Table 3.6 reveal no ability by sellers to time the market. The general level of stock prices continues to rise in the two years following the equity issue. Therefore, the results in Tables 3.5 and 3.6 show pre-announcement market-adjusted returns exceeding post-announcement market-adjusted returns and no timing pattern for the general level of stock prices centered on the announcement date.[14]

IV.1.3 Issue size and price effects

The regression results presented in Table 3.7 provide additional insight into the price effects from equity issues for industrial firms. For all subsamples the two-day announcement period excess returns are regressed against a measure of the size of the issue (the planned proceeds of the offering divided by the pre-announcement value of the firm's equity) and against the cumulative excess return for the eleven months prior to the month of the announcement.[15]

Regressions for the total sample of industrial issues indicate that the announcement day excess return is inversely related to the size of equity issue and positively related to the CER in the year preceding the

Table 3.5. *Cumulative excess returns from 490 days before until 480 days after the announcement of industrial equity offerings in the period 1963–1981 (%)*

| Days | Type of offering | | | |
	All[1] $N = 189$	Primary $N = 80$	Secondary $N = 76$	Combination $N = 33$
−480	0.5	0.9	0.1	0.7
−440	3.1	3.8	2.6	2.4
−400	5.1	5.8	3.0	8.4
−360	7.4	9.0	3.8	10.8
−320	10.4	13.1	4.8	16.9
−280	10.5	12.2	5.3	18.2
−240	13.7	16.5	7.5	21.1
−200	16.5	18.7	11.1	23.8
−160	19.2	21.7	11.8	29.8
−120	24.4	28.5	15.3	35.4
−100	25.7	30.0	16.9	36.2
−80	27.8	33.5	17.5	37.8
−60	30.4	36.0	20.0	41.1
−40	31.0	37.7	20.3	41.7
−30	31.2	37.6	19.7	42.0
−20	32.5	39.5	20.2	43.5
−10	33.0	40.4	21.4	41.8
Announcement Day	29.7	35.5	20.2	37.8
+10	30.6	36.2	21.2	36.9
+20	30.5	35.6	20.8	40.5
+30	30.9	37.9	20.2	38.5
+40	30.8	37.1	21.1	38.1
+60	32.3	39.4	22.5	38.0
+80	32.4	39.0	23.0	38.0
+100	33.2	39.6	23.9	38.9
+120	33.0	40.0	22.8	39.7
+160	33.8	42.6	22.4	38.6
+200	33.2	41.1	23.0	37.5
+240	31.8	41.7	20.0	35.3
+280	29.1	38.9	16.8	33.8
+320	27.3	37.0	15.3	31.7
+360	27.1	36.0	14.0	35.3
+400	26.3	35.7	12.9	33.0
+440	25.6	34.7	13.4	30.9
+480	23.3	32.4	10.1	32.1

[1] There are less than 266 firms in the sample because not all firms had usable stock returns for the entire four year period.

Table 3.6. *Cumulative average value weighted market returns from 490 days before until 480 days after the announcement of industrial equity offerings in the period 1963–1981 (%)*

| Days | Type of offering | | | |
	All N = 189	Primary N = 80	Secondary N = 76	Combination N = 33
−480	−0.0	−0.4	0.0	0.6
−440	−0.5	−1.0	−0.3	0.5
−400	−0.4	−1.6	1.0	−0.9
−360	0.7	−0.4	3.4	−2.6
−320	1.3	−0.4	4.3	−1.5
−280	2.6	0.4	6.6	−1.3
−240	4.1	1.2	9.0	0.0
−200	4.5	2.2	8.7	0.6
−160	5.6	2.9	10.1	2.0
−120	6.6	2.90	11.8	3.3
−100	7.4	4.3	11.8	4.8
−80	8.7	6.0	12.1	7.6
−60	9.9	7.1	13.4	8.9
−40	12.0	9.4	15.0	11.3
−30	13.0	10.8	15.5	12.6
−20	13.5	11.6	15.6	13.1
−10	14.3	12.3	16.3	14.3
Announcement Day	14.6	12.7	16.8	14.2
+10	14.9	13.1	17.1	13.9
+20	15.3	13.2	17.6	14.9
+30	15.3	13.3	17.3	15.3
+40	15.0	13.2	16.9	15.2
+60	15.4	13.5	17.5	15.0
+80	15.4	13.5	17.5	14.9
+100	16.0	14.8	17.5	15.5
+120	16.3	15.1	17.7	16.0
+160	16.7	17.0	16.0	17.8
+200	18.9	19.6	17.2	20.9
+240	20.0	21.4	17.8	21.6
+280	21.4	23.0	18.5	24.1
+320	22.0	24.4	18.0	25.2
+360	23.0	25.3	19.2	25.6
+400	23.9	26.1	20.2	26.9
+440	23.5	26.0	19.7	26.1
+480	23.4	26.5	19.8	24.1

Table 3.7. *Estimated coefficients and t-statistics from regressing the two day excess returns for the announcement of an industrial equity offering on the size of the offering[1] and the previous eleven month cumulative excess return[2]*

Equation:	$\left(\dfrac{\text{Two day}}{\text{excess return}}\right) = \alpha + \beta_1(\text{Size}) + \beta_2\left(\dfrac{\text{Eleven}}{\text{month } CER}\right)$		
	α	β_1	β_2
All	$-.02217$	$-.07721$	$+.01466$
offerings	(-6.01)	(-2.95)	(2.05)
$N = 251$	$R^2 = .043$	$F = 5.51$	Significance of
			F-statistic $= .005$
Primary	$-.02516$	$-.08675$	$+.02807$
offerings	(-3.80)	(1.93)	(2.21)
$N = 121$	$R^2 = .057$	$F = 3.55$	Significance of
			F-statistic $= .032$
Secondary	$-.01410$	$-.21380$	$+.01740$
offerings	(-2.30)	(-1.80)	(1.23)
$N = 78$	$R^2 = .058$	$F = 2.29$	Significance of
			F-statistic $= .108$
Combination	$-.03477$	$+.00011$	$+.00610$
offerings	(-2.74)	(0.00)	(0.50)
$N = 48$	$R^2 = .006$	$F = 0.13$	Significance of
			F-statistic $= .881$

Notes: t-statistics in parentheses.
[1] The size of the offering is measured as the planned proceeds of the offering divided by the pre-announcement value of the firm's equity.
[2] The eleven months ending one month before the announcement of the offering.

announcement. For the sample of all industrial offerings, both coefficients are significant at the 5% level and the regression is significant at the 1% level. These results imply that, *ceteris paribus*, increasing the size of an equity issue by $100 million dollars, on average, results in an additional reduction of $7.7 million in firm value on announcement day. A one year pre-announcement *CER* of 50% is associated with an increase in the announcement day excess return of about 0.75%. Conversely, a larger announcement day price reduction is experienced by stocks that have performed poorly prior to the announcement. The regression constant illustrates that the announcement of a sample equity issue, independent of its size or the pre-announcement performance of its stock, is associated with a 2.2% price reduction.

For the subsample of primary industrial issues, the size coefficient is marginally larger than the corresponding coefficient for the total sample and the *CER* coefficient is double the total sample *CER* coefficient. Both coefficients are significant at the 10% level and the regression is significant at the 5% level. In the regression results for the sample of secondary issues, the size coefficient is significant at the 10% level but the *CER* coefficient does not meet standard significance criteria.[16]

Although the regression for secondary issues is not significant when both size and *CER* are included, it is significant at the 10% level when only size is considered. In the regressions reported in Table 3.7 the estimated size coefficient for secondary offerings is roughly double the size coefficient in the regressions on primary issues. While this suggests that secondary issues are received by the market as more unfavorable signals compared with primary issues, Chow tests on primary versus secondary regressions and *t*-tests on the differences in the estimated size coefficients for primaries and secondaries both fail to reveal statistically significant differences.

Regression results for combination issues are insignificant. This may be due to the mixing, in combination offers, of different price effects associated with primary and secondary issues. For all samples, regressions of announcement day excess returns against the pre-announcement market return and the level of general stock price indices are insignificant.[17]

The major implication of the regressions in Table 3.7 is that announcement day price reductions are significantly related to the size of equity issues. This finding is consistent with the strongly held belief by executives and investment bankers that large equity issues depress stock prices. However, this result does not distinguish between the price-pressure hypothesis and explanations based on asymmetric information since a size effect is consistent with both hypotheses.

The results reported in Table 3.7 together with those presented in Table 3.5 provide insight into the timing of equity issues. Firms tend to issue equity following an increase in stock prices, and after such a pre-announcement stock price increase the announcement day price reduction tends to be smaller. This is consistent with the contention by Myers and Majluf (1984) that firms time equity issues to minimize the adverse impact on stock prices.[18]

IV.1.4 The price-pressure, leverage and signalling hypotheses

An important issue is whether the negative market reaction to equity offerings is explained by associated changes in financial leverage. To test the importance of capital structure changes as an explanatory variable, additional regression analyses are performed using a measure of the change in sample firms' net debt ratio. Net debt is defined as total debt minus cash and cash equivalents, and the net debt ratio is net debt divided by net debt plus net worth. The change in net debt ratio is calculated as the difference between the ratio after the equity issue minus the average net debt ratio for the five years preceding the announcement of the offering.[19]

To examine the capital structure hypothesis, the two-day announcement perioid excess returns are regressed against the change in net debt ratio or primary issues, and for a sample including both primary issues and the primary component of combination offerings. The regression results presented in Table 3.8 indicate that the change in leverage coefficient is significant at the 10% level (using a one tail test) for both samples. However, this significance disappears when size is included as an explanatory variable in the regressions. The addition of a third explanatory variable, the CER in the year preceding the announcement, further reduces the size and significance of the coefficient of the change in leverage variable for both samples. Moreover, size and change in net debt ratio are highly collinear with a correlation coefficient of .35 for primary offerings and .28 for the sample including both primary and the primary component of combination offerings.

In an attempt to circumvent the collinearity problem, other leverage-related measures are investigated. The deviation of sample firms' pre-announcement capital structure from historical leverage is calculated as the difference between the net debt ratio prior to the announcement and the preceding five year average net debt ratio. This variable is not significant as the sole explanatory variable in a regression, nor is it significant when size and pre-announcement CER are included in a regression. Bond ratings are another proxy for the extent to which a firm's debt ratio is viewed as extreme. When used as a dummy variable in regressions, bond ratings, for both senior and subordinated debt, are not significant either alone or with size and pre-announcement CER included in the regression.

The collinearity between change in leverage and issue size makes it difficult to determine which variable is associated with the announcement day price reduction.[20] Furthermore, there are difficulties in associating equity issue price effects with changes in capital structure. First, most equity issues are a relatively small percentage of total capital. Even if the entire proceeds of the issue are used to repay debt, the impact on financial leverage and tax shields are not large relative to the magnitude of the reduction in equity value associated with stock issues. Secondly, changes in leverage induced by equity issues may be ephemeral. Finally, a leverage-related explanation of the price effects of primary equity issues cannot explain the

Table 3.8. *Estimated coefficients and t-statistics from regressing the two day excess returns for the announcement of an industrial equity offering on the change in net debt ratio,[1] the size of the offering[2] and the previous eleven month cumulative excess return[3]*

Equation:	$\left(\begin{array}{c}\text{Two day}\\\text{excess return}\end{array}\right) = \alpha + \beta_1\left(\begin{array}{c}\text{Change on}\\\text{net debt ratio}\end{array}\right) + \beta_2(\text{Size}) + \beta_3\left(\begin{array}{c}\text{Eleven}\\\text{month } CER\end{array}\right)$			
α	β_1	β_2	β_3
Primary offerings:			
−.02749	.02808	—	—
(−7.31)	(1.41)		
$N = 96$	$R^2 = .021$	$F = 1.98$	Significance of F-statistic = .163
−.01858	−.01784	−.07819	—
(−2.64)	(0.82)	(−1.52)	
$N = 90$	$R^2 = .048$	$F = 2.17$	Significance of F-statistic = .120
−.02338	.00814	−.10553	.03596
(−3.26)	(0.38)	(−2.05)	(2.36)
$N = 90$	$R^2 = .105$	$F = 3.37$	Significance of F-statistic = .022
Primary offerings plus primary component of combination offerings:			
−.02994	.02891	—	—
(−9.93)	(1.59)		
	$R^2 = .016$	$F = 2.54$	Significance of F-statistic = .143
−.01950	.02212	.08488	—
(−3.39)	(1.15)	(−1.97)	
$N = 140$	$R^2 = .048$	$F = 3.48$	Significance of F-statistic = .033
−.02223	.01949	−.08890	.01371
(−3.70)	(1.01)	(2.07)	(1.50)
$N = 140$	$R^2 = .064$	$F = 3.09$	Significance of F-statistic = .029

Notes: t-statistics in parentheses.
[1] Change in net debt ratio is calculated as the ratio after the equity issue minus the average net debt ratio for the five years preceding the announcement of the offering. Net debt is defined as total debt minus cash and cash equivalents, and the net ratio is net debt divided by net debt plus net worth.
[2] The size of the offering is measured as the planned proceeds of the offering divided by the pre-announcement value of the firm's equity.
[3] The eleven months ending one month before the announcement of the offering.

price effects of secondary distributions which do not affect corporate capital structures. As reported above, size is still an important explanatory variable in regressions on secondary distributions, while not surprisingly, all leverage-related variables exhibit no explanatory power in regression analyses of secondary offerings.

Since the price reduction for secondaries cannot be attributed to a change in leverage, is it likely that the similar market reaction to primary issues is caused by the change in leverage? It seems at least as likely that both phenomena are explained by investors' reaction to a negative signal concerning the firm's stock price, the announcement that informed sellers are selling a large block of stock.[21] If issue size is the true explanatory variable and change in leverage only a proxy for size, this provides an alternative explanation for the findings of other empirical tests of capital structure theory (e.g. Masulis (1980a, 1980b and 1983)) which are based on the analysis of the market's reaction to equity transactions (e.g. exchanges and repurchases).[22]

Thus, the findings of a significant announcement day price reduction and a significant size effect for both primary and secondary issues, as well as the regression analyses of leverage variables, argue against a pure capital structure explanation of the effects observed for primary issues. These results suggest instead that the price reductions are due to the information effects predicted by Miller and Rock (1985) and Myers and Majluf (1984). These theoretical analyses predict that price reductions are associated with the source and magnitude of financing rather than with changes in corporate capital structure. Our findings are also consistent with the price-pressure hypothesis. Finally, the reduction in firm value as a percentage of the proceeds appears too large to be explained by issue-related transactions costs.

IV.2 Public utility offerings

This study also investigates the effect on stock prices of equity issues by public utilities. The average announcement period excess returns for primary issues by public utilities appear in Table 3.9. The two-day announcement period excess return is only $-.9\%$ but the associated t-statistic is -7.8. Two-thirds of the equity issues are associated with negative announcement day returns. The mean dilution for public utilities reported in Table 3.10 is -12.3%, the median is -8.4% and only 2% of the issues produced dilution greater than -100%.

In contrast to the results for industrial issues, Table 3.11 shows that stock of public utility issuers underperforms the market on a risk-adjusted basis both in the two years preceding the announcement of the issue and in the

Table 3.9. *Average excess returns (XRET) and average cumulative excess returns (CER) from 10 days before until 10 days after the announcement day of primary equity offerings by utilities in the period 1963–1981* (%)

Day	XRET	CER	Day	XRET	CER
−10	0.0	0.0	+1	−0.1	−1.5
−9	−0.1	−0.1	+2	−0.2	−1.7
−8	0.1	0.0	+3	−0.0	−1.7
−7	−0.0	0.0	+4	−0.1	−1.8
−6	−0.1	−0.1	+5	−0.2	−2.0
−5	−0.1	−0.2	+6	−0.1	−2.1
−4	−0.1	−0.3	+7	−0.1	−2.2
−3	−0.1	−0.4	+8	0.2	−2.0
−2	−0.1	−0.5	+9	−0.1	−2.1
−1	−0.6	−1.1	+10	−0.0	−2.1
Announcement					
Day	−0.3	−1.4			
Two day					
announcement					
return		−0.9			
t-statistic		−7.8			
N		264			

subsequent two years.[23] This underperformance appears to be steady over the entire four years. Consistent with industrial issues, no ability to time the general level of stock prices can be detected in Table 3.11. Market returns are positive and roughly equal in magnitude in the 240 days preceding and following the announcement of primary issues by public utilities.

The results for primary issues by utilities differ from the findings for industrials in several respects. The percentage price-reduction on announcement day for utility issues, though statistically significant, is much smaller than the reduction associated with industrial issues. The offering dilution (the reduction in firm value as a percentage of the planned proceeds of the sale) is also smaller for utility issues. Also the positive one year *CER*s preceding industrial issues are replaced with negative stock market performance preceding utility issues. Finally, although not reported, regressions of announcement day excess returns against the planned size of the issue and the *CER* for the eleven months prior to the announcement are not significant for utilities. This is in contrast to industrial equity issues.

While these results document differences between utility issues and industrial issues, the reason for these differences is not apparent. The smaller reduction in firm value for utilities at announcement suggests that equity issues by utilities are more fully anticipated. This could be due to the

Table 3.10. *The announcement day offering dilution for utility equity offerings, defined as the reduction in the value of the equity of a firm as a percentage of the planned value of a primary equity offering*

Dilution %		Offerings 259 Primary offerings	
		N	Cumulative %
$100 <\ \leqslant$	150	1	.4
$80 <\ \leqslant$	100	2	.4
$60 <\ \leqslant$	80	0	.4
$40 <\ \leqslant$	60	6	2.7
$30 <\ \leqslant$	40	3	3.9
$20 <\ \leqslant$	30	6	6.2
$10 <\ \leqslant$	20	18	13.1
$0 <\ \leqslant$	10	50	32.4
$-10 <\ \leqslant$	0	56	54.1
$-20 <\ \leqslant$	-10	37	68.3
$-30 <\ \leqslant$	-20	32	80.7
$-40 <\ \leqslant$	-30	23	89.6
$-50 <\ \leqslant$	-40	8	92.7
$-60 <\ \leqslant$	-50	7	95.4
$-70 <\ \leqslant$	-60	1	95.8
$-80 <\ \leqslant$	-70	4	97.3
$-100 <\ \leqslant$	-80	2	98.1
$-120 <\ \leqslant$	-100	3	99.2
$-140 <\ \leqslant$	-120	0	99.2
$-150 <\ \leqslant$	-140	0	99.2
$-200 <\ \leqslant$	-150	2	100.0
	$\leqslant -200$	0	100.0
Average dilution		-12.3%	
Median dilution		-8.4%	

disclosure required by regulated firms and/or the fact that many utility issues are motivated by the necessity of making investments to service customer demand while simultaneously maintaining debt ratios within a range mandated by regulation.[24] Such a capital structure process would predict forthcoming equity offerings and would also imply that the change in leverage produced by an equity issue is temporary.

Another potential explanation is that the smaller announcement day affect is due to the fact that public utility industries are composed of relatively homogeneous firms.[25] Many sources of valuable inside information (research and development, the value of natural resources, etc.) are absent for most utilities. Key determinants of the value of utilities

Table 3.11. *Cumulative excess returns (CER) and cumulative average value weighted market returns from 490 days before until 480 days after the announcement of equity offerings by utilities in the period 1963–1981 (%)*

Days	CER N = 211	Market return N = 211	Days	CER N = 211	Market return N = 211
−480	0.0	−0.3	+10	−20.6	12.9
−440	−1.3	0.0	+290	−20.7	13.3
−400	−3.0	0.5	+30	−21.2	13.6
−360	−5.0	0.5	+40	−21.7	14.0
−320	−6.4	2.4	+60	−22.7	14.4
−280	−8.9	3.3	+80	−23.5	15.2
−240	−10.6	4.7	+100	−24.2	16.0
−200	−12.2	6.0	+120	−24.9	16.6
−160	−13.8	6.9	+160	−27.2	17.9
−120	−15.1	7.9	+200	−28.4	19.3
−100	−15.5	9.5	+240	−31.3	20.7
−80	−16.1	9.5	+280	−33.1	22.8
−60	−16.7	101.	+320	−35.0	24.6
−40	−17.9	10.9	+360	−38.0	26.1
−30	−18.3	11.3	+400	−39.8	27.3
−20	−18.2	11.5	+440	−41.2	28.8
−10	−18.6	11.9	+480	−43.1	30.3
Announcement Day					
	−20.0	12.4			

include cost structures, production technologies, and marketing demographics, that are relatively well known and intensively studied by security analysts. Nonetheless, even if utility equity issues are partially predicted and leverage changes are temporary, the average price-reduction associated with utility issues is highly significant.

IV.3 Issue day results

Finally, this study examines the issue day average excess returns for industrial and utility equity issues. The results, although not reported, are consistent with semi-strong capital market efficiency. Market prices at issue date already reflect the effects of the announcement, and no significant temporary price pressure effects are apparent around the issue date. The results suggest that a permanent reduction in firm value is associated with the announcement of an equity issue, and the subsequent execution of the sale takes place at the discounted stock price.

V Conclusions

The results of this study demonstrate that announcement of common equity offerings reduce stock prices. This finding is pervasive in that over 80% of the sample industrial issues are associated with negative announcement day excess returns. The average announcement day excess return for all industrial issues is -2.7% and is statistically significant. Though this price effect may appear small, the aggregate reduction in industrial firms' equity value as a percentage of the planned proceeds of a primary issue averages 31%. On average, registered secondary distributions of industrial stocks are accompanied by a reduction in firm value equal to 78% of the proceeds of the sale. This study also documents a timing pattern related to industrial issuers' market-adjusted stock price performance. During the two years prior to the issue, sample industrial firms' stock outperforms the market by an average of 33%. In the two years following the issue, the sample industrial firms on average underperform the market by 6%. No evidence of an ability to time the general level of stock prices is apparent in the data since positive market returns are observed in the two years preceding and following industrial equity issues.

Regression results for industrial issues indicate that the announcement day price reduction is significantly related to both the cumulative abnormal stock price performance during the eleven months prior to the month of the issue and to the size of the issue (as a percentage of total equity value of the firm). Better risk-adjusted stock price performance in the months prior to the issue is associated with smaller price reductions on announcement day. Larger equity issues are associated with larger announcement day price reductions. For secondary industrial issues, the negative effect of issue size is larger than for primary issues. However, for secondary issues no significant association is found between announcement day excess returns and abnormal stock returns in the months prior to the issue.

Primary equity issues by public utilities also are accompanied by negative excess returns on announcement day. Approximately two-thirds of the utility issues are associated with price reductions. The average announcement day excess return for utility issues is $-.9\%$ and is statistically significant. The average reduction in the sample firms' market value equals 12% of the proceeds of the issue. The results for utility issues reveal no evidence of timing patterns based on the market-adjusted performance of individual stocks or the performance of the market as a whole. In contrast to industrial issues, negative abnormal stock returns of roughly equal magnitude are observed in the year preceding and following public utility issues. Consistent with the results for industrial issues, positive market returns are exhibited in both the year preceding and the year following utility issues. For utility issues there is no relationship between the announcement day market reaction and issue size or the previous performance of the utility's stock. The differences between the results of industrial and utility issues might be explained by a larger information content associated with industrial issues. Finally, no significant excess returns are found in the days surrounding the issue date for industrial stocks and public utilities. This result is consistent with semi-strong capital market efficiency.

The similarity of the price effects for primary issues and registered secondary distributions suggests that the price reduction is not related solely to tax effects or to leverage-related information effects associated with a change in corporate capital structure. In addition, the reduction in firm value as a percentage of the proceeds of the sale appears too large to be explained by issue-related transactions costs in the case of primary issues where the firm bears those costs. The results are consistent both with the hypothesis that equity sales by corporations and informed investors are intepreted by the market as unfavorable signals about a firm's current performance and future prospects, and with the hypothesis that there is a downward sloping demand curve for a firm's shares. These hypotheses are not separable using tests presented in this study, and the design of tests to distinguish between these two hypotheses is an important task for future research.

The findings for primary issues also have important implications for corporate financial decisions. For example, the reduction in firm value associated with equity issues represents a substantial 'cost to false signalling' in dividend signalling models of the type developed by Bhattacharaya (1980). The finding of stock price reductions associated with external equity financing rationalizes a reluctance on the part of firms to issue equity. This is consistent both with the theoretical analysis presented by Myers and Majluf (1984) and with the empirical observation that firms rely on internally generated funds as the chief source of equity financing. The timing pattern associated with equity issues is also consistent with the Myers–Majluf argument that firms should time equity issues to minimize the attendant adverse stock price effects. Firms tend to issue equity following a rise in stock prices, and this is when the equity issue price reduction tends to be small. These results have important implications for financing policy. Moreover, the negative market reaction to external equity financing produces an interaction among major financial decisions: investment policy, capital structure policy, and dividend policy. The necessity of jointly determining financial policies is suggested by the constraint imposed by the negative market reaction to external equity financing, and this would lead to optimal financial decisions which differ from those predicated on the traditional assumption that a firm can always issue equity at the current stock price.

Finally, the findings for equity issues are related to empirical results for stock repurchases (e.g. Vermaelen (1981) and Dann (1981)) and dividends (e.g. Asquith and Mullins (1983)). Emerging from these empirical studies of equity cash flows is a theory of the firm based upon superior information possessed by managers *vis-à-vis* investors. These empirical studies are consistent with a view of the firm as a 'black box' where unanticipated equity cash flows communicate information to investors. Cash outflows (stock repurchases and increases in dividends) are viewed as positive signals accompanied by increases in stock prices. Conversely, if a firm requires cash inflows from the equity market (through equity issues or a reduction in dividends), this is interpreted as a negative signal resulting in a reduction in the stock price. While empirical studies have documented that stock prices and unanticipated equity cash flows are positively related, additional research is needed to develop a corresponding theoretical model which is both rigorous and comprehensive.

NOTES

* We wish to thank Robert F. Bruner, Larry Dann, Bruce C. Greenwald, Richard S. Kaplan, Richard Leftwich, Wayne Mikkelson, Jerold Warner, and especially Clifford W. Smith, Jr. We also wish to thank the participants in finance seminars at the Harvard Business School, the University of Rochester, the University of Chicago, Duke University and the University of North Carolina for helpful discussions and substantive suggestions. We also wish to thank Susan Chevoor for her assistance in data collection. Generous financial support was provided by the Division of Research, Harvard University Graduate School of Business Administration.

1 The latter two papers model the interaction of investment and financing, and in both managers may forego profitable investment projects because of the negative information impact of equity financing.

2 Block trades are not registered with the SEC. Registration is often used for very large secondary sales and is required if sellers have a control relationship with the firm. Registration statements include a prospectus, and the seller must wait for SEC approval before the sale. Unregistered block trades are announced on the day of the sale, and thus, unlike registered offerings, the announcement date and sale date coincide.

3 The price-pressure hypothesis is also rejected because of an assumption that price-pressure should be a temporary phenomenon. The failure of stock prices to recover within several weeks after the issue date leads him to conclude that the price reduction reflects a permanent revaluation of the firm's shares.

4 Unregistered block trades represented 79% of Scholes' (1972) sample. The median size (percentage of total shares of firm) of his sample was 1%. The mean was 2%, but 70% of his sample distributions were less than 2% of the firm's outstanding shares. The sample of registered secondary distributions used in this study averages about 5% of the outstanding shares while the sample of primary industrial distributions averages more than 12%.

5 The study by Smith (1977) included rights issues as well as general cash offers and Marsh's (1979) study focused exclusively on rights issues. We do not explore the difference in these alternative methods of issuing equity.

6 Several other unpublished papers have recently utilized announcement day price effects to investigate equity distribution. Mikkelson and Partch (1984) examine large block trades in secondary distributions and Hess and Bhagat (1983) examine new equity issues by utilities.

7 Korwar (1983) does analyze the magnitude of the change in leverage produced by the equity issue.

8 This assumes a homogeneous motivation for primary and secondary issue announcement day price effects. It is possible that the price effects for primary and secondary offerings are similar but the result of different explanations.

9 This does not eliminate all other sources of information. Almost all equity announcements simultaneously release other information by stating the purpose that the funds will be used for. This statement is often very general; e.g. used for general corporate purposes, to increase working capital, to pay off short-term debt, for general investment purposes, etc. Tests of differences in market reaction between these uses showed none and the results are not reported here.

10 This period was chosen because estimating the $\text{Var}(XR_t)$ over the event period may result in a higher or lower estimate than non-event periods. That is, the event may change $\text{Var}(XR_t)$ from that usually observed. The t-statistics were also run with

$$S(CER_{K,L}) = [T \cdot \text{Var}(XR_t) + 2(T-1)\,\text{Cov}(XR_t, XR_{t+1})]^{1/2}$$

The covariance term adjusts for possible first-order autocorrelation between the excess returns due to non-synchronous trading. The covariance term was found to be approximately equal to zero for all tests (out to 5 significant figures), and thus only t-statistics from the first method are reported.

11 From the shareholders' viewpoint, the effect of 100% dilution for a primary offering is equivalent to the firm's donating newly issued shares and receiving nothing in return.

12 It should be noted that secondary issues are substantially smaller (as a percentage of firm value) than primary issues. The ratio of the proceeds of the issue to the pre-announcement aggregate equity value is 12.5% for primary issues, 5.2% for secondaries and 16.5% for combination issues, on average.

13 These average CER's have t-statistics of 8.73, 4.90, and 5.62 respectively. The t-statistics were calculated using the technique mentioned above in footnote 10 where the $\text{Var}(XR_t)$ is estimated over the period from 490 days before the announcement day until 21 days before the announcement. Although this means the variance of XR_t is estimated over the same period as the CER, there is no reason to believe this period has a greater or lower variance than any other estimating period that could have been chosen.

14 See Hendriksson and Merton (1981) for a more sophisticated approach to estimating these two timing components.

15 This variable tests whether the announcement day price effects are related to the recent performance of the firm's stock. The CER is for the period -240 trading days until -20 trading days. Minus 20 days was chosen to eliminate the effect of any leakage of information in the period one month before the announcement of an equity issue.

16 The regression for secondary offerings excludes four outliers where the issue size is three standard deviations larger than the mean size of the secondary sample. The size of these four offerings are 47.5%, 28.8%, 18.2% and 17.1%. Two of these secondary offerings (28.8% and 17.1% in size) are for the same firm. These large offerings may contain additional information about control of the firm. Regression results for the complete sample do not differ substantially in either sign or significance from these reported above.

17 Other explanatory variables also tested but not significant include percentage of inside ownership and identity of the seller. Furthermore, all regressions with size as an explanatory variable were also estimated with the log of size as the explanatory variable, and the results do not differ in nature or significance from those reported.

18 Myers and Majluf (1984) argue that the equity issue price effect will be smaller if uncertainty is less and/or the asymmetry in information between insiders and outsiders is smaller. While the timing evidence cannot be interpreted unambiguously, it is not inconsistent with the Myers–Majluf argument. There are two potential explanations for the finding that the equity issue price effects are smaller following an increase in stock prices. First, an increase in stock prices tends to unleverage the firm's equity and thus reduce its volatility. In the Myers–Majluf analysis, a smaller price reduction is incurred when selling a less risky security, *ceteris paribus*. Secondly, one explanation for an increase in stock prices is that uncertainty has been resolved thereby reducing the risk of equity and possibly the magnitude of the asymmetry in information. Conversely, an increase in uncertainty would tend to reduce stock prices and result in larger equity issue price reductions. Finally, the finding of a firm-specific (rather than market wide) timing pattern is consistent with the Myers–Majluf argument.

19 Subtracting cash from debt adjusts for the negative financial leverage resulting from investments in cash. Also, in all regression analyses the change in leverage defined above (using the five year average net debt ratio) is superior both in R^2 and significance to an alternative measure, the change in net debt ratio from the year preceding the equity issue to the year following it.

20 Korwar's (1983) measure of change in leverage should also be a strong proxy for the size of the equity issue. In his analysis Korwar defines the change in leverage as a hypothetical post-issue debt ratio minus the debt ratio immediately prior to the equity issue. The hypothetical post-issue debt ratio is defined as the pre-issue ratio instantaneously adjusted to reflect the new equity offering. This change in leverage measure should clearly capture the size of the issue. Moreover, Korwar's regressions include both change in leverage and tax shield measures as explanatory variables. Change in leverage and tax shield variables may also be collinear, although Korwar does not report the correlation coefficient for these variables. Finally, Korwar presents several analyses which support an information explanation for the negative market reaction to equity issues. These include analyses of bond price reactions to equity issues and analyses of post-issue earnings performance. These findings are consistent with the interpretation that the size of the equity issue, rather than the change in leverage, is the driving force underlying the market's reaction.

21 The capital structure view of equity issues is deficient in another respect as well. It does not explain firms' reliance on internal equity funding and their reluctance to issue equity. Even the leverage-related information models (e.g. Ross (1977)) regard external equity and retained earnings as perfect substitutes. In contrast

the analyses by Miller and Rock (1985) and Myers and Majluf (1984) rationalize a reluctance to issue equity. In these papers, it is the source and magnitude of equity financing which is viewed as an informative signal, rather than the change in debt ratio. In both analyses firms may forego profitable investment projects because of the stock price effects of issuing equity.

22 Vermaelen (1981) also contends that the capital structure inferences drawn from studies of stock repurchases are inappropriate. Consistent with the reasoning outlined above, he argues that the market's reaction to stock repurchases is explained by their role as an informative signal, rather than their impact on debt ratios. This argument is also supported by Dann's (1981) study of stocks repurchased. Masulis (1983) includes 'information effects' related to changes in firm debt level as one possible explanation of his results.

23 The negative CER from 490 days before until 20 days before the announcement for utility firms has a t-statistic of -13.16 which is statistically significant. This is also in contrast to industrial firms where all three subsamples had positive and statistically significant $CER's$ in the two-year period to an equity issue announcement.

24 However, in the Miller–Rock (1985) model a forced equity issue may still be informative because it reveals information concerning a firm's current earnings. Nonetheless, little information would be released if regulation effectively forced disclosure of a utility's earnings. Forced investment and financing could conceivably resolve the information based conflict motivating the Myers–Majluf (1984) model. This would be true if regulation ensured that utility managers pursue all profitable investment projects even if they require external equity funding.

25 Consistent with this, advocates of the price-pressure effect might argue that, relative to industrial firms, there are many close substitutes for a given utility's shares, and this may account for the smaller price reduction associated with utility issues.

REFERENCES

Asquith, P. and D. W. Mullins Jr (1983). 'The Impact of Initiating Dividend Payments on Shareholders' Wealth.' *Journal of Business*, **56**, 77–96.

Bhattacharaya, S. (1980). 'Nondissipative Signaling Structures and Dividend Policy.' *Quarterly Journal of Economics*, **95**, 1–24.

Dann, L. (1981). 'Common Stock Repurchases: An Analysis of Returns to Bondholders and Stockholders.' *Journal of Financial Economics*, **9**, 113–138.

Dann, L., D. Mayers and R. Raab (1977). 'Trading Rules, Large Blocks, and the Speed of Adjustment.' *Journal of Financial Economics*, **4**, 3–22.

Dann, L. and W. Mikkelson (1984). 'Convertible Debt Issuance, Capital Structure Change and Financing-Related Information: Some New Evidence.' *Journal of Financial Economics*, **13**, 157–186.

DeAngelo, H. and R. Masulis (1980). 'Optimal Capital Structure under Corporate and Personal Taxation.' *Journal of Financial Economics*, **8**, 3–29.

Donaldson, G. (1961). 'Corporate Debt Capacity.' Division of Research, Graduate School of Business Administration, Harvard University, Boston, Mass.

Galai, D. and R. Masulis (1976). 'The Option Pricing Model and the Risk Factor of Stock.' *Journal of Financial Economics*, **3**, 53–82.

Greenwald, B., J. E. Stiglitz and A. Weiss (1984). 'Informational Imperfections in the Capital Market and Macroeconomic Fluctuations.' *American Economic Review*, **74**, 194–200.

Hendriksson, R. D. and R. C. Merton (1981). 'On Market Timing and Investment Performance, II: Statistical Procedures for Evaluating Forecasting Skills.' *Journal of Business*, **54**, 513–534.

Hess, A. C. and S. Bhagat (1983). 'A Test of the Price Pressure Hypothesis using Announcement Data.' Unpublished Working Paper, University of Washington, Seattle.

Hess, A. C. and P. A. Frost (1982). 'Tests for Price Effects of New Issues of Seasoned Securities.' *Journal of Finance*, **36**, 11–25.

Korwar, A. N. (1983). 'The Effect of New Issues of Equity: An Empirical Investigation.' Unpublished Working Paper, University of Iowa, Iowa City.

Kraus, A. and H. R. Stoll (1972). 'Price Impacts of Blocks Trading on the New York Stock Exchange.' *Journal of Finance*, **27**, 569–588.

Leland, H. and D. Pyle (1977). 'Information Asymmetries, Financial Structure, and Financial Intermediation.' *Journal of Finance*, **32**, 371–387.

Lintner, J. (1960). 'The Financing of Corporations.' In E. S. Mason (ed.), *The Corporation in Modern Society*. Harvard University Press, Cambridge, Mass.

Logue, D. E. and R. A. Jarrow (1978). 'Negotiation Versus Competitive Bidding in the Sale of Securities by Public Utilities.' *Financial Management*, **7**, 31–39.

Marsh, P. R. (1979). 'Equity Rights Issues and the Efficiency of the U.K. Stock Market.' *Journal of Finance*, **34**, 839–862.

Masulis, R. W. (1980a). 'The Effects of Capital Structure Change on Security Prices: A Study of Exchange Offers.' *Journal of Financial Economics*, **8**, 139–178.

Masulis, R. W. (1980b). 'Stock Repurchase by Tender Offer: An Analysis of the Causes of Common Stock Price Changes.' *Journal of Finance*, **35**, 305–311.

Masulis, R. W. (1983). 'The Impact of Capital Structure Change on Firm Value: Some Estimates.' *Journal of Finance*, **38**, 107–126.

Mikkelson, W. H. and M. M. Partch (1984). 'Stock Price Effects and Costs of Secondary Distributions.' Unpublished Working Paper, University of Chicago, Chicago.

Miller, M. H. and K. Rock (1985). 'Dividend Policy under Asymmetric Information.' *Journal of Finance*, **40**, 1031–1051.

Modigliani, F. and M. H. Miller (1963). 'Corporate Income Taxes and the Cost of Capital: A Correction.' *American Economic Review*, **53**, 433–443.

Myers, S. C. and N. S. Majluf (1984). 'Corporate Financing and Investment Decisions when Firms Have Information that Investors Do Not Have.' *Journal of Financial Economics*, **13**, 187–222.

Ross, S. (1977). 'The Determination of Financial Structure: The Incentive-Signalling Approach.' *Bell Journal of Economics*, **8**, 23–40.

Sametz, A. W. (1964). 'Trends in the Volume and Composition of Equity Financing.' *Journal of Finance*, **19**, 450–469.

Scholes, M. S. (1972). 'The Market for Securities: Substitution Versus Price Pressure and the Effects of Information on Share Prices.' *Journal of Business*, **45**, 179–211.

Scholes, M. and J. Williams (1977). 'Estimating Betas from Nonsynchronous Data.' *Journal of Financial Economics*, **5**, 309–328.

Smith, C. W. Jr (1977). 'Alternative Methods for Raising Capital: Rights Versus

Underwritten Offerings.' *Journal of Financial Economics*, **5**, 273–307.

Taggart, R. A. Jr (1977). 'A Model of Corporate Financing Decisions.' *Journal of Finance*, **32**, 1467–1484.

Vermaelen, T. (1981). 'Common Stock Repurchases and Market Signalling: An Empirical Study.' *Journal of Financial Economics*, **9**, 139–183.

4 Effects of asymmetric taxation on the scale of corporate investment

RICHARD C. GREEN and ELI TALMOR*

I Introduction

Corporations with losses in a given tax year typically receive less than a full offset, or rebate of their 'negative tax liability', from the government. While losses may be carried back or carried forward, and while some mechanisms exist for marketing unused losses, it seems unlikely that firms can plan on recovering the full present value of redundant tax shields.[1]

The structure of the tax code is an important determinant of the allocation of capital across the corporate and private sectors of the economy, across industries, and indeed across alternative activities within the firm. Thus, it is not surprising that the effects of the asymmetric treatment of gains and losses on corporate investment incentives have long been of concern to researchers in public economics and have drawn increasing attention in the finance literature.[2] As an approximate representation of the tax asymmetry, one may assume taxes are paid at a constant rate for positive earnings, and that the tax liability is zero when deductions, such as depreciation and interest payments, exceed cash flows from operations. In this situation the government's tax claim on the firm can be viewed as a call option on the cash flows. Several recent papers have exploited this analogy to value the firm's tax liability using contingent claims valuation methods.[3]

In a paper closely related to this one, Green and Talmor (1985) studied the effects of the option-like structure of the tax liability on the firm's choices over its mix of projects. That paper showed that the firm had incentives to underinvest in risky projects and to engage in conglomerate mergers, but it left the question of the firm's overall level of investment unresolved. It is to this issue that we turn our attention here. Specifically, for a given corporate tax rate, how does the existence of potentially redundant tax deductions affect the firm's chosen scale of investment? Does the asymmetric treatment of gains and losses provide an incentive or a disincentive to investment? How does the source of the deductions affect these incentives?

We employ a simple, one-period model to explore the dependence of the firm's scale of investment on the source and amount of tax deduction. Deductions which depend on the level of investment, such as depreciation, have different consequences than those which are fixed, such as loss carry-forwards from previous periods or interest deductions from outstanding debt. When deductions are generated by accounting depreciation alone, the optimal investment by the firm decreases, relative to its choice under symmetric taxation. When all deductions are due to interest expenses the reverse is true. If both are present there is an ambiguous relationship between investment levels under symmetric and asymmetric taxation. Considering these relationships in the context of our simple model may suggest guidelines for policy makers whose objectives are to influence corporate investment behavior through the tax code. While increases in allowable deductions generally work to increase investment by corporations, their marginal effects may be very different under symmetric and asymmetric taxation. For example, in our model, changes in 'fixed' deductions have no marginal impact on investment in a symmetric tax regime, but work to increase investment under asymmetric taxation in some situations. Our analysis also suggests a simple interpretation of Auerbach's (1984) result that investment may locally decrease as deductions increase, and extends his results to a global comparison.

Myers (1977) has suggested that when shareholders are free to maximize the value of their equity position, with debt already outstanding, a conflict of interest is created between bondholders and stockholders. This is due to the option-like structure of the equity claim. Myers shows that this conflict of interest can result in the firm failing to undertake profitable investments. By taking the promised payment on the debt claim as exogenous, our model captures the basic features of Myers's arguments. We can then analyze the relationship between effects of the 'tax option' and 'equity option' on the firm's scale. We show that for some capital structures the presence of the tax option increases the conflict of interest between bondholders and stockholders. This result is a direct analogue to the claim in Green and Taylor (1985) that the tax option may aggravate the 'asset substitution' problem discussed in Jensen and Meckling (1976).

The paper is organized as follows. Section II describes the model. In Section III the optimal level of investment is characterized and compared to the amount of investment under symmetric taxation. Section IV discusses the incentives associated with different sources of non-cash deductions, and Section V contains our analysis of the relationship between the equity and tax options. Section VI concludes the paper.

II A model of corporate investment

In this section we show that, in a simple one-period environment, the corporate tax liability assumes the form of a call option. The nonlinear nature of this claim affects the firm's incentives to undertake investment in the presence of uncertainty. Our purpose here is to make precise the nature and sources of these incentives in a very simple model. Thus we will make several assumptions to give the tax liability and the firm's objective function forms which are both tractable and capture the essential features of asymmetric treatment of gains and losses.

The structure of the model, and notation, employed here closely resemble Green and Talmor (1985). Consider a firm which chooses a level of investment I. These investments generate state-contingent cash flows, $X(I, \omega)$ for the firm, according to the production function:

$$X(I, \omega) = k(I)\theta(\omega) \tag{1}$$

The scale function $k(\cdot)$ is concave and twice differentiable in its argument. The random multiplicative shock $\theta(\omega)$ depends on ω, the state of the world, which is an elementary outcome from the universal set Ω. Since we are focusing here on the case of a single multiplicative shock for the firm as a whole, no generality will be lost when, later, we suppress the dependence on the state ω. We will assume that $k_i'(0) = \infty$, where a prime denotes the derivatives, and that $\theta(\omega) \in (0, \infty)$. Thus, negative earnings for the firm as a whole will be due, not to the shock itself but to real and/or accounting depreciation.

We will assume for the time being that the firm lasts for a single period. To raise the funds required for operation, the firm can issue debt and outside equity at the initial date. The debt claim is issued at a face value of B, with interest paid at rate r. We denote as α the fraction of equity sold to outsiders. The firm is allowed to depreciate a fraction ϕ of the amount of funds raised at the initial date over the current period, for tax-accounting purposes.

Taxes are introduced according to the 'interest-first' doctrine for treating taxes in bankruptcy, whereby partial payments to debtholders are credited first to interest and then to principal (see Baron (1975) and Talmor, Haugen and Barnea (1985)). The firm's tax deductions consist of its accounting depreciation, ϕI, and its interest expense, rB. Note that principal is not assumed to be deductible, except to the extent that the funds raised contribute to depreciation. We have also assumed that tax losses cannot be marketed or carried over.[4] Let τ represent the corporate tax rate. We can specify the cash flow to equityholders, X_E, and bondholders, X_B, as:

$$X_E = \max\{X - B(1+r) - \tau \max[X - \phi I - rB, 0], 0\} \tag{2}$$

$$X_B = \min\{X - \tau \max[X - \phi I - rB, 0], (1+r)B\}. \tag{3}$$

The sum of these cash flows represents the after tax cash flow of the firm,

$$X_E + X_B = X - \tau \max\{X - \phi I - rB, 0\}. \tag{4}$$

Finally, we assume that the firm's securities are traded in a capital market which is sufficiently complete to 'span', or uniquely value, them. Zero-arbitrage conditions in these markets will imply that this valuation is linear (see Ross (1978)). Let $\rho(\omega)$ be the positive price of a state-contingent-claim implied by the prices of marketed assets. Because we are dealing with a 'single-project' firm, we need concern ourselves here only with the implicit prices of pure 'Arrow-Debreu' securities for the events associated with the technological shock for the firm. Let $p(\theta) = \int_{\Omega(\theta)} \rho(\omega)d\omega$ where $\Omega(\theta) = \{\omega : \theta(\omega) = \theta\}$. The firm's investment and financing problem can now be written as:

P1:

$$\max_{I,B,\alpha,r} (1-\alpha) \int_0^\infty p(\theta) \max[k(I)\theta - B(1+r)$$
$$-\tau \max\{k(I)\theta - \phi I - rB, 0\}, d\theta \tag{5}$$

$$\text{s.t. } I \leqslant B + E \tag{6}$$

$$B = \int_0^\infty p(\theta) \min[k(I)\theta - \tau \max\{k(I)\theta - \phi I - rB, 0\}, (1+r)B]d\theta \tag{7}$$

$$E = \int_0^\infty p(\theta)\alpha \max[k(I)\theta - B(1+r) - \tau \max\{k(I)\theta - \phi I - rB, 0\}, 0]d\theta \tag{8}$$

In this problem, the firm's management simultaneously chooses investment and financing policies which maximize the value of the initial shareholders claim. Note that equation (7) constrains the firm to issue the bonds at par. Without this constraint, the optimal solution would trivially involve a fixed payment consisting entirely of 'interest', which is tax deductible, and no 'principal'. Equation (6) is the flow of funds constraint. It states that the total amount invested must not exceed the combined values of the debt and outside equity. Equations (7) and (8) express these values as a function of I, the investment undertaken by the firm. The assumption that this variable is observable, and chosen simultaneously with the firm's financing policies, ensures that no conflict of interest arises between bondholders and shareholders concerning investment choice. As a result, the investment level which solves P1 will maximize the Net Present Value (NPV) of the firm's after tax cash flows, given the optimal choices of the financial variables, B, α, and r. This follows from the envelope theorem, and is a standard result in corporation finance.[5] In the context of a model very similar to this one, Green and Talmor (1985, Lemma 1), demonstrate that the investment level which maximizes the wealth of initial shareholders also solves the following problem:

P2:

$$\max_{I} \int_0^\infty p(\theta)k(I)\theta d\theta - I - \tau \int_0^\infty p(\theta) \max\{k(I)\theta - \phi I - rB, 0\}d\theta$$

$$= V[k(I)\theta] - \tau V[\max\{k(I)\theta - \phi I - rB, 0\}] - I \tag{9}$$

where r and B are the optimizing choices from P1.

From (9) it is apparent that the value of the government's claim is proportional to the value of a call option on the firm's cash flow. The exercise price on this option is the firm's total deductions, $\phi I + rB$. The effect of the asymmetry is to cut off certain states of the world from the tax claim. The behavior of the firm's real earnings, $k(I)\theta$, over these states will determine whether this increases or reduces the firm's tax burden at the margin. This, in turn, will determine the optimal investment level. One more assumption is needed before proceeding. To characterize the optimal policies with first-order conditions, expression (9) must be differentiable with respect to I. The function $\max\{\cdot, \cdot\}$ has a kink where the two arguments are equal. However, the *value* of such a claim, which is an integral taken over it, will be differentiable so long as the point of non-differentiability has zero measure. This will be the case if the random component of earnings, θ, has a continuous joint density which we will assume to be the case.

III Investment decisions

To characterize the firm's investment decisions we will employ the first-order conditions for P2. The maximand in (9) is concave and our assumptions on the scale function $k(\cdot)$ ensure an interior solution, so the first-order conditions will be both necessary and sufficient. First, however, we need a benchmark or standard against which to evaluate the firm's decisions. As we are interested in the effects of asymmetric taxation, the logical choice for such a benchmark would seem to be the case of fully symmetric, or linear, taxation. This is not to say that symmetric taxes do not induce distortions of themselves. In a general equilibrium setting they will affect the structure of the valuation functional, here summarized by the function $p(\cdot)$, and may lead to allocations which are not Pareto optimal. In our partial equilibrium context, where we take the valuation functional as given, symmetric taxation will reduce investment relative to the no tax case. There is a sense, however, in which this penalty is uniform across types of firms, because the firm's objective function is linear in everything but the investment choice itself.

Under symmetric taxation the firm maximizes:

$$\int_0^\infty p(\theta)[k(I)\theta - \tau(k(I)\theta - \phi I - rB)]d\theta - I \tag{10}$$

Let $\hat{I}$ denote the investment scale that maximizes (10). The necessary and sufficient first-order condition for a maximum is:

$$k'(\hat{I})(1-\tau)\int_0^\infty p(\theta)\theta d\theta = 1 - \frac{\tau\phi}{1+r_f} \tag{11}$$

where r_f is the riskless rate of interest and we have used the fact that the value of a unit payoff in all states is $\int_0^\infty p(\theta)d\theta = 1/(1+r_f)$. Equation (11) states that the firm invests until the marginal scale product times the after-tax value of the random shock is equal to the cost of the last dollar invested. This cost is the dollar itself less the value of the contribution to the tax deduction. Note that the interest deductions, rB, do not appear in the first-order conditions. Under symmetric taxation tax deductions can be viewed as a lump sum transfer to the firm, paid in all states. In good states the firm reduces its taxes by that amount and in bad states it receives rebates, but the magnitude of the subsidy does not determine its marginal incentives except insofar as current investment increases deductions directly. Increased investment does, at the margin, directly increase depreciation. It increases interest deductions only indirectly as another policy variable in the budget constraint. This variable has already been chosen in an optimal fashion, obviating the need to consider these indirect increases in deductions.

Our intent here is not to literally mimic the tax code, but rather to summarize some of its essential features in a stylized way. Thus, one can interpret 'depreciation' as representing those deductions which depend directly on current investment levels and 'interest' as representing those which are independent of it. Under symmetric taxes they have very different incentive consequences. Depreciation matters but fixed deductions do not. These differences are also apparent under asymmetric taxation, although the relationship is more complicated.

The first-order condition which characterizes the maximization of (9) can be found by applying Liebnitz's rule. Let I^* be the maximizing choice. Then,

$$k'(I^*)\left[\int_0^\infty p(\theta)\theta d\theta - \tau\int_{\theta^*}^\infty p(\theta)\theta d\theta\right] = 1 - \tau\phi\int_{\theta^*}^\infty p(\theta)d\theta \tag{12}$$

where θ^* is the value for the shock term at which the tax liability becomes zero:

$$\theta^* \equiv \frac{\phi I^* + rB}{k(I^*)} \tag{13}$$

As in equation (11), the left-hand side of (12) represents the after-tax contribution of the last dollar invested to the present value of the firm's output. Unlike (11), however, the shock term contributes at the margin to the tax liability only over the interval $[\theta^*, \infty)$. Similarly, the right-hand side of (12) represents the marginal investment outlay less the increase in deductions through accounting depreciation. As the marginal project is only penalized for contributing to the tax liability on a subset of states, so it is only rewarded for adding to deductions in those states where they are used.

Comparing (11) and (12) we see that the only differences are due to the two components of the contribution to the tax liability. In (12) this contribution only matters over the upper portion of the distribution of the firm's output. The effect of the asymmetry on each term taken separately is clear, but together they have an ambiguous impact on the level of investment. Since $p(\theta) > 0$ and $\theta^* > 0$, $\tau \int_{\theta^*}^{\infty} p(\theta)\theta d\theta < \tau \int_{0}^{\infty} p(\theta)\theta d\theta$. Thus the factor multiplying $k'(\hat{I})$ is less than that multiplying $k'(I^*)$. Since $k'(\cdot)$ is decreasing this will tend to drive up investment in the asymmetric relative to the symmetric case. On the other side of the equations, however, $\tau \phi \int_{\theta^*}^{\infty} p(\theta)d\theta < \tau\phi/(1 + r_f)$, so the right-hand side of (12) is larger than that of (11) which implies less investment in the asymmetric case.

The interaction between these two effects can easily be seen by rearranging (12) and substituting from (11) as follows:

$$[k'(I^*) - k'(\hat{I})] \int_{0}^{\infty} p(\theta)\theta d\theta(1 - \tau) = -\tau \int_{0}^{\theta^*} p(\theta)[k'(I^*)\theta - \phi]d\theta \tag{14}$$

Here we use the fact that the integral over the interval $[\hat{\theta}, \infty)$ is the integral over all states less that over $[0, \hat{\theta}]$. The right-hand side of (14) values the marginal impact of the investment on the tax liability in the states which are 'chopped off' by the tax asymmetry. Whether $I^* > \hat{I}$ depends simply on whether this term is positive or negative. Where the magnitude and nature of the deductions is arbitrary, the sign of this term cannot be determined. The cut-off state, θ^*, may be either high or low, and the sign of the integrand for $\theta < \theta^*$ is undetermined.

Expression (14) also clarifies the source of the seemingly puzzling comparative statics result in Auerbach (1984) that investment may decrease as deductions increase, despite the fact that more 'income' is being sheltered. As we increase fixed deductions (for example, carry-forwards), we raise θ^*. The marginal impact of this on the right-hand side of (14) will be $-\tau p(\theta^*)(k'(I^*)\theta^* - \phi)$ which will be negative only if $k'(I^*)\theta^* > \phi$. If deductions are low, θ^* is small, and this term may be positive. The additional deductions obtained render depreciation redundant. The firm no longer needs depreciation to shelter its income in the state associated with θ^*. However, the contribution to depreciation is an important component of the value of the marginal investment. In those cases where the additional depreciation generated exceeds the value of the incremental cash flows provided, the marginal investment becomes a net loss, and I^* decreases. Auerbach's comparative statics shows that the change in investment is proportional (in our notation) to $k'(I^*)\theta^* - r$, where r is the riskless rate of interest. In his model deductible interest expense is directly proportional to current investment, and thus serves the same role as depreciation in our model.

Auerbach (1984) interprets this behavior as due to the unprofitability of the firm in the states where the new deductions shelter income. In his model $k'(I)\theta - r$ represents economic profit for the firm. Our use of accounting depreciation serves to focus attention more directly on the role of redundant deductions. The magnitude of ϕ has nothing to do with the real 'profitability' of the firm's technology. It simply measures the direct contribution of the marginal investment to tax shelters.

IV Depreciation versus interest deductions

In general the right-hand side of equation (14) is ambiguous in sign. Thus, the introduction of the tax asymmetry may cause the firm to either invest more or less relative to its policies under symmetric taxation. It depends simply on whether, when averaged over the lower portion of the firm's distribution, the marginal contributions to operating cash flow exceed the accounting depreciation rate. The 'weights' in this averaging are the positive state-prices. In the absence of more knowledge as to the source and magnitude of the deductions, the point at which the firm stops paying taxes, θ^*, is not sufficiently specified to sign this average. By looking at some cases where the magnitude of θ^* is restricted we can understand more about the incentive effects of different types of tax deductions under asymmetric taxation.

Case 1: Non-depreciable assets ($\phi = 0$)

The consequences in this situation are by now clear. With no depreciation, deductions provide tax shelters to the full extent of operating cash flows. In determining its investment policy, the firm looks upon asymmetric taxation as in effect a tax forgiveness over a portion of its distribution. By marginally increasing cash flows through investment in those states where $\theta < \theta^*$, the firm loses only taxes, not rebates, as in the symmetric case, or depreciation deductions, as when $\phi > 0$. The interest payments to debtholders, which contribute to the value of the firm's securities, are simply not taxed. The integrand on the right side of (14) will therefore be positive for every θ. Accordingly, when all deductions are due to interest expense, $k'(I^*) < k'(\hat{I})$, and there is overinvestment under asymmetric taxation relative to the symmetric case.

Case 2: All deductions from depreciation

When there are no debt related deductions, as for example with an all equity firm, we obtain the reverse of the result for Case 1. The state at which taxes are no longer paid solves $k(I^*)\theta^* - \phi I^* = 0$. Substituting this value into the integrand in (14) gives:

$$k'(I^*)\theta^* - \phi = k'(I^*)\frac{\phi I^*}{k(I^*)} - \phi$$

$$= \phi \frac{I^*}{k(I^*)}\left(k'(I^*) - \frac{k(I^*)}{I^*}\right) < 0 \tag{15}$$

the last inequality holds because of our assumption that the production function is concave. The average product will always exceed the marginal product. If $k'(I^*)\theta^* - \phi < 0$, then clearly $k'(I^*)\theta - \phi < 0$ for all $\theta < \theta^*$. Thus the integral on the right-hand side of (14) must be negative, and $k'(I^*) > k'(\hat{I})$. When deductions are only generated by depreciation, asymmetric taxation leads to underinvestment. The tax benefits which are lost exceed the contribution to taxable cash flow in the sheltered states.

To summarize, then, depreciation and interest deductions have exactly opposite effects, in determining the result of the tax asymmetry on the firm's scale. When all deductions are debt related, the firm overinvests under asymmetric taxation, and when they are all due to depreciation, the firm underinvests. The ambiguity which arises when both types of deductions are present is thus not particularly surprising.

V Asymmetric taxation and stockholder–bondholder conflicts

Black and Scholes (1973) originally noted that equity in a firm with risky debt is a call option on the value of the firm as a whole. When the debt is already outstanding, this may lead shareholders to make investment decisions which do not maximize the value of the entire firm. Myers (1977) has shown that in such a situation shareholders have an incentive to underinvest in projects with positive Net Present Value.

Our model can provide a simple formalization of the Myers (1977) result. Suppose there is an outstanding debt claim on the firm, with face payment B and interest rate r. The firm must finance an opportunity to invest in a new project solely with new outside equity.[6] Thus we can view the shareholders as solving P1, except that B and r are viewed as parameters so that equation (7) is deleted from the constraint set. By the same arguments that generated P2 from P1, the investment allocation which solves this problem will maximize the present value of the total equity less the amount invested, or

P3:

$$\max_I \int_0^\infty p(\theta) \max[k(I)\theta - B(1+r) - \tau \max\{k(I)\theta - \phi I - rB, 0\}, 0] d\theta - I \quad (16)$$

There are two $\max\{\cdot,\cdot\}$ functions in this objective function. The interior one, however, will always be positive if the firm defaults at a value of θ higher than that at which it stops paying taxes (i.e., when the solvent firm always pays taxes). This will occur as long as $B(1+r) > \phi I + rB$, or as long as the face value of the debt exceeds depreciation deductions. Let us consider this case first, and let I^{**} be the optimum for P3. The first-order condition for this case is:

$$k'(I^{**}) \int_{\hat\theta}^\infty p(\theta)\theta d\theta(1-\tau) = 1 - \tau\phi \int_{\hat\theta}^\infty p(\theta)d\theta \quad (17)$$

where $\hat\theta$ is the point at which default occurs. It solves:

$$k(I^{**})\hat\theta = rB + \frac{B - \tau\phi I^{**}}{1-\tau} \quad (18)$$

Two consequences are apparent from equation (17). First, relative to the case where the firm is symmetrically taxed and there is full information, the firm invests less. This contrasts markedly with the tax asymmetry, which in general had an ambiguous effect on the firm's scale. To write (17) in a form comparable to (14), we combine it with (11), which after rearranging yields:

$$[k'(I^{**}) - k'(\hat I)] \int_0^\infty p(\theta)\theta d\theta(1-\tau) = \tau \int_0^{\hat\theta} p(\theta)\left[k'(I^{**})\theta \frac{(1-\tau)}{\tau} + \phi \right] d\theta \quad (19)$$

In contrast to (14), the integrand on the right-hand side of (19) is positive for all θ. Over the default states the equity holders fail, because of the debt claim against them, to enjoy the benefits of either the cash flow or deductions generated by the marginal investment. Thus, $k'(I^{**}) > k'(\hat I)$ and there is underinvestment. This is, in the context of our model, the Myers (1977) result.

The second point to be made about the first-order condition (17) is that the tax asymmetry is not manifest in it. The asymmetry affects only transactions between the government and the bondholders who inherit the firm in default. Yet it is important to realize that this does not imply that the tax asymmetry is not of economic significance. Indeed it may serve to intensify conflicts of interest between shareholders and bondholders. A consideration of Case 1 from the previous section makes this clear. When the firm's investment is non-depreciable (i.e., $\phi = 0$), the tax option distorts the firm's investment in exactly the opposite direction from the distortion due to the equity option. With symmetric taxation the best policy for the firm as a whole is $\hat{I}$ which is larger than I^{**}, the best policy for the equity holders. With asymmetric taxation, and $\phi = 0$, the best policy for the firm as a whole is even larger, but the best policy for the equity holders is unchanged. Thus, $I^{**} < \hat{I} < I^*$, and the asymmetric taxation makes the conflict of interest worse.

This result is a direct analogue for the 'Myers problem' to one in Green and Talmor (1985) concerning the effect of asymmetric taxes on the 'risk-incentive' problem discussed in Jensen and Meckling (1976). There we showed that while the equity option leads shareholders to overinvest in risky projects relative to safer ones, the tax option has the opposite effect. It encourages firms to insure their deductions by overinvesting in safer assets. Since the benefits of this insurance, however, flow through entirely to existing debt holders, equity claimants in control of the firm have no incentive to lower the value of the firm's tax liability in this way. Thus, if the outstanding debt obligations are large enough that the firm defaults at a level of earnings higher than that which exhausts its deductions, the agency problem is aggravated by the tax asymmetry.

Even with a positive depreciation rate (up to $\phi I < B$), the equity option induces an incentive to underinvest, and $I^* > I^{**}$. These two quantities, however, can no longer be ordered relative to the symmetric tax, full information level. Thus, the distortion may be more or less severe under asymmetric taxation but in any case is still present. To see this subtract (17) from (12) to obtain:

$$[k'(I^*) - k'(I^{**})] \int_0^\infty p(\theta)\theta d\theta (1-\tau) \tag{20}$$

$$= -\tau \left[k'(I^*) \int_0^{\theta^*} p(\theta)\theta d\theta + k'(I^{**}) \int_0^{\theta} \frac{(1-\tau)}{\tau} p(\theta)\theta d\theta + \phi \int_{\theta^*}^{\theta} p(\theta)d\theta \right]$$

The right-hand side of this expression is clearly negative, so $k'(I^{**}) > k'(I^*)$, and the shareholders overinvest when maximizing the value of their own claim relative to the level of activity they would choose in the absence of any moral hazard.

When the firm is less highly levered, so that $B < \phi I$, the tax option has a higher 'exercise price' than the equity option. The shareholders have redundant deductions at levels of earnings higher than the point at which they default, and $\theta^* > \hat{\theta}$. In this situation, the level of investment which maximizes the value of the equity claim is characterized by the first-order condition:

$$k'(I^{**})\left[\int_{\hat{\theta}}^{\infty} p(\theta)\theta d\theta - \tau \int_{\theta^*}^{\infty} p(\theta)\theta d\theta\right] = 1 - \tau\phi \int_{\theta^*}^{\infty} p(\theta)d\theta \qquad (21)$$

At first glance a comparison of (21) with (12) would suggest $I^{**} < I^*$, because the only difference appears to be in the first term on the left-hand side. This is smaller in (21) because the integral is only taken over the states with no default. This conclusion is unwarranted, however, because θ^*, which is defined in (13), depends non-monotonically on the optimal investment. Thus, when the equity claim earns tax forgiveness in some states of the world, the equity and tax options interact in complex, and potentially offsetting ways. The Myers result may not hold in this case. In fact, it is quite possible that there are some capital structures in that range which result in more investment by shareholders then when the firm is unlevered.

Table 4.1 summarizes the interaction between the equity and tax options, and the relationship between their effects on the firm's scale of investment (the results described above) and on the optimal mix of investment projects undertaken (Green and Talmor (1985)).

VI Conclusion

This paper analyzes the distortionary effects on the scale of corporate investments caused by the asymmetric taxation of losses and gains. More specifically, we have attempted to trace this ambiguity to conflicting incentives engendered by deductions from different sources. If deductions are due to interest expense alone (or other fixed deductions), the firm overinvests relative to its optimal policy under symmetric taxation. If they are due solely to deductions that are proportional to the investment, such as depreciation, there is less investment at the optimum.

We also considered the possibility that with debt already in place, shareholders may choose policies which maximize the value of their own claim but do not maximize the value of the firm as a whole. This complicates the problem, but in instructive ways. For firms which are highly levered, the incentives due to the asymmetries in the equity payoffs will dominate those due to the non-linear taxation. In this situation the tax asymmetry will aggravate conflicts of interest between bondholders and shareholders, along with the attendant agency costs.

Table 4.1. *Summary of incentive effects*

	Asymmetric taxation	Stockholder–bondholder conflicts	Effect of tax asymmetry on stockholder–bondholder conflict	
			$B > \phi I$	$B < \phi I$
Mix of projects	Less risky projects	More risky projects (*Jensen and Meckling*)	Aggravates	Ambiguous
Scale of investment	Generally ambiguous $\phi = 0$: overinvestment $rB = 0$: underinvestment	Underinvestment (*Myers*)	Aggravates	Ambiguous

NOTES

* The authors wish to thank A. Auerbach, R. Dammon, A. Pitts, and J. Franks for very useful comments on this research. Green thanks the Center for Public Policy Research at Carnegie-Mellon for support while this work was conducted.
1 See Cooper and Franks (1983) for an extended discussion of barriers to a full recovery of unused losses.
2 See Domar and Musgrave (1944), Stiglitz (1969), Mossin (1968), Atkinson and Stiglitz (1980, Chapter 4), Cooper and Franks (1983), Green and Talmor (1985), and Majd and Myers (1984). The interactions between investment and financing under asymmetric taxation are analyzed in Dammon and Senbet (1985).
3 See, in particular, Galai (1983) and Pitts and Franks (1984).
4 Many of the results in the paper, which depend only on the option-like nature of the tax liability, are robust to this assumption. This is clear from Green and Talmor (1985) and Auerbach (1984).
5 See, for example, the development in Fama and Miller (1972).
6 Like Myers (1977), our analysis begs the question of why the firm does not first retire the debt and then invest.

REFERENCES

Atkinson, A. B. and J. E. Stiglitz (1980). *Lectures on Public Economics*. McGraw-Hill, New York.
Auerbach, A. J. (1984). 'The Dynamic Effects of Tax Law Asymmetries.' Mimeo, University of Pennsylvania.
Baron, D. P. (1975). 'Firm Valuation, Corporate Taxes, and Default Risk.' *Journal of Finance*, 30, 1251–1264.
Black, F. and M. Scholes (1973). 'The Pricing of Options and Corporate Liabilities.' *Journal of Political Economy*, 81, 637–659.
Cooper, I. and J. R. Franks (1983). 'The Interaction of Financing and Investment Decisions When the Firm has Unused Tax Credits.' *Journal of Finance*, 38, 571–583.
Dammon, R. M. and L. W. Senbet (1984). 'Tax Effects of Production and Finance.' Unpublished working paper.
Domar, E. D. and R. A. Musgrave (1944). 'Proportional Income Taxation and Risk-Taking.' *Quarterly Journal of Economics*, 58, 388–422.
Fama, E. F. and M. H. Miller (1972). *The Theory of Finance*. Holt, Rinehart and Winston, New York.
Galai, D. (1983). 'Corporate Income Taxes and the Valuation of Claims on the Corporation.' Unpublished working paper.
Green, R. and E. Talmor (1985). 'The Structure and Incentive Effects of Corporate Tax Liabilities.' *Journal of Finance*, 40, 1095–1114.
Jensen, M. and W. Meckling (1976). 'Theory of the Firm: Managerial Behavior, Agency Costs and Ownership Structure.' *Journal of Financial Economics*, 3, 305–360.
Majd, S. and S. C. Myers (1984). 'Valuing the Government's Tax Claim on Risky Assets.' Unpublished working paper.

Mossin, J. (1968). 'Taxation and Risk-Taking: An Expected Utility Approach.' *Economica*, **35**, 74–82.

Myers, S. M. (1977). 'Determinants of Corporate Borrowing.' *Journal of Financial Economics*, **5**, 147–175.

Pitts, C. G. C. and J. R. Franks (1984). 'Corporate Tax as a Contingent Claim and the Implications for Financing and Investment Decisions.' Unpublished working paper.

Ross, S. (1978). 'The Valuation of Risky Streams.' *Journal of Business*, **51**, 453–475.

Stiglitz, J. E. (1969). 'The Effects of Income, Wealth, and Capital Gains Taxation on Risk-Taking.' *Quarterly Journal of Economics*, **83**, 263–283.

Talmor, E., R. A. Haugen and A. Barnea (1985). 'The Value of the Tax Subsidy on Risky Debt.' *Journal of Business*, **58**, 191–202.

BANKING

5 Credit rationing and collateral

JOSEPH STIGLITZ and ANDREW WEISS*

I Introduction

For generations, economists have resorted to blaming 'imperfections' in the capital market for a whole host of phenomena, and institutional economists have criticized the relevance of much of traditional neo-classical analysis because of its reliance on the assumption of perfect capital markets. We agree with that criticism. We would argue, however, that economic theory should 'explain' institutional structures, at least those that take on the prominence that 'capital market imperfections' have. These are matters of more than just academic interest: if the nature of the imperfections are, in some sense, endogenous, then government policies may well affect them; they cannot simply be taken as given.

This paper is part of a research program aimed at explaining certain key elements of the capital market.[1] Many of the central aspects of this market can be understood once the asymmetries of information, and the costs of acquiring information are taken into account.[2] Earlier studies have shown how these informational imperfections may make it very costly for firms to raise funds on the equity market (Greenwald, Stiglitz and Weiss (1984)), and why they may give rise to credit rationing (Stiglitz and Weiss (1981) and (1983)). In particular, in our earlier study, we argued that banks might not raise the rate of interest they charged on loans, even in the presence of an excess demand for credit, because to do so might lower the return they receive. This may happen either because of the incentive effects – at higher interest rates, borrowers undertake riskier projects – or because of adverse selection effects – at higher interest rates, safer borrowers no longer apply for loans, so that the proportion of risky borrowers in the applicant pool increases.

In our 1981 study, we showed that increasing collateral had positive incentive effects, but could, under a variety of plausible conditions, have adverse selection effects: borrowers who were willing to put up more collateral undertook, on average, riskier projects. We did not, however, allow banks to choose collateral requirements and interest rates simultaneously; doing so allows for the possibility of banks using the loan contract (specified by an interest rate-collateral combination) as a self-selection device.

In this paper we allow banks to simultaneously choose interest rates and collateral requirements. We show that when there are heterogeneous borrowers, and several techniques, or projects, are available to each borrower, this increase in the dimensionality of contracts available to banks does not in general eliminate credit rationing. (Even if borrowers were homogeneous allowing banks to simultaneously choose interest rates and collateral requirements does not eliminate rationing – each bank would require borrowers to use all their assets as collateral but the bank's optimal interest rate subject to this constraint may still entail rationing. Similarly if there is a continuum of heterogeneous borrowers but only one possible technique banks will demand collateral equal to the wealth of the wealthiest applicants, but within that class of applicants there may be sufficient residual heterogeneity to sustain a credit rationing equilibrium.)

Although the bank has an additional instrument, it still cannot obtain perfect control. As long as that is the case, rationing may occur. Changing any of the terms of the contract (separately or together) in such a way as to decrease the demand for loans – increasing the interest rate or the collateral requirements – may at the same time decrease the expected return on the loan, either because the mix of applicants changes adversely or because the borrowers undertake riskier actions. The insights of our earlier analysis remain valid in this more general setting.

We show in particular that there exist complete pooling equilibria (in which only one type of bank contract is offered) and separating equilibria (in which there exists at least two contracts: the mix of borrowers accepting each differs). Each of these equilibria may be characterized by credit rationing. In our earlier study, if there were several identifiable types of individuals, rationing only occurred among one type (that is, only for one group is it the case that some obtained credit while other, apparently identical applicants, are denied credit). In this model all groups may be rationed.

It is important, at this juncture, to reiterate five points we made in our earlier studies.

First, we do not claim that there always will be credit rationing, only that it will arise under some, not implausible, circumstances.

Second, there may exist a Walrasian equilibrium, an interest rate (or an interest rate-collateral combination) at which demand equals supply. But this is not a competitive equilibrium, in the sense in which that term ought to be used.[3] It may be in the interest of any bank to lower its interest rate.

Third, though we focus our analysis on rationing within competitive markets, exactly the same arguments can be used to show that a monopoly bank would engage in credit rationing.

Fourth, we do not claim that our model provides the only explanation of credit rationing. Government imposed interest rate ceilings on loans may, for instance, give rise to credit rationing.[4]

Fifth, (constrained) Pareto efficient allocations may be characterized by credit rationing. Thus, the presence of rationing is not, in itself, evidence of market inefficiency (given the costliness of information). It turns out, however, that the market is not constrained Pareto efficient: both the interest rates charged and the pattern of allocation of capital are different from what they would be if the government were directly controlling the credit market to keep contracts on the Pareto frontier.

II The model

The economy consists of a large number of banks, borrowers, and depositors. Each borrower chooses one, and only one technique, but requires bank financing for its projects. Banks offer loan contracts, characterized by a collateral requirement, C, and an interest rate, r. Borrowers can apply to as many banks as they wish (there are no application costs). If they get accepted by several banks, they choose the loan contract which maximizes their expected utility.

In the simplest version of the model we present, each bank is allowed to offer only one contract form. Each bank has a great deal of statistical information about the market: it knows the distribution of borrowers. In the version we focus on here, all borrowers have the same utility function and investment ability; they differ only in their wealth. Banks know not only the distribution of wealth, but also how wealth affects behavior. On the other hand, they cannot tell who is of which type, nor can they directly control behavior (or infer what investment projects the individual undertook from the outcomes). Each bank also knows the contract offers of the other banks (though not the identity of the individuals to whom it has made offers). On the basis of this information, or on the basis of experience, it makes an inference concerning the consequences of offering alternative contracts, assuming the behavior of the other banks remains unchanged.[5] It chooses the contract which maximizes its expected return. Given its supply of funds, it then randomly allocates its funds among the applicants, taking into account the fact that not all of those whose applications it accepts will accept it.[6]

Depositors allocate their funds among the banks yielding the highest return. Since in equilibrium the return to all contracts will be the same, competition will ensure that the rate of return offered depositors by all banks will be the same, and equal to the expected return on any loan. Thus, in this simple version of the model, we can take the supply of funds available to each bank as fixed, and equal to its pro rata share of the aggregate funds of depositors.[7]

Thus equilibrium is described by a configuration of loan contracts, each characterized by $\{C, r\}$ such that all loan contracts offered yield the same expected return; and such that there does not exist another contract which any firm could offer which would yield a greater expected return. Our objective is to analyze the alternative forms which equilibrium can take, and in particular, to ascertain the circumstances under which credit rationing may occur.

We now present the details of the model.

Borrowers

For simplicity, we assume that there are two types of borrowers, who differ only in their wealth; they have the same (risk averse) utility function, and the same set of available techniques. (As will be made clear below, if borrowers were assumed to have different sets of techniques available we would be able to obtain the central results of our paper, concerning the existence of credit rationing in the presence of collateral, more easily.) All techniques cost the same ($1) and have two outcomes. If they are successful they yield a return R, if unsuccessful they yield the return zero. The probability of success is $p(R)$, and we assume[8]

$$p'(R) < 0 \qquad p''(R) < 0 \qquad (1)$$

Projects with higher returns have a lower probability of success, and thus can be thought of as riskier. See Figure 5.1a.

The expected return to the project is just $p(R)R$. This may increase or decrease with R. For simplicity, we assume that $p(R)R$ has the inverted U-shape of Figure 5.1b, with the R which maximizes expected return denoted by R^0. R^0 is the solution to

$$p'(R)R + p = 0 \qquad (2)$$

Borrowers must make two decisions. The first concerns the financing of the project. They must decide which loans to apply for, and if they apply for more than one loan and more than one of their applications are accepted they must decide which contract to accept.

Secondly, having obtained a loan, they must decide which technique to choose.

We solve the second problem first. The expected utility from choosing

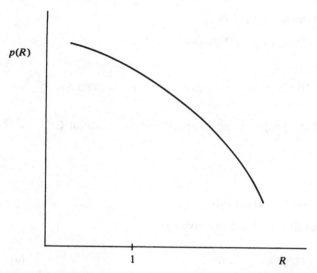

Figure 5.1a Projects with a higher return if successful have a lower probability of success

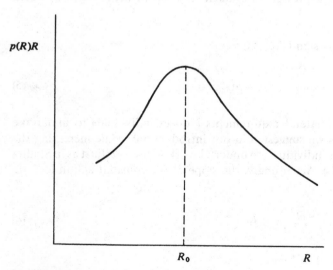

Figure 5.1b R_0 maximizes expected return

technique 'R' with contract $\{C, r\}$ is

$$EU = U(Y_1(R; r))p(R) + U(Y_0(C))(1 - p(R)) \tag{3}$$

where

$Y_1(R; r) =$ income if the R project is successful, given contract $\{C, r\}$[9]
$ = A + R - (1 + r)$

$Y_0(C) =$ income if the project is unsuccessful, given collateral C[10]

$ = A - C$

where

$A =$ individual's total wealth

The first order condition of the borrower is

$$\frac{\partial U}{\partial R} = (U_1 - U_0)p' + pU_1' = 0 \tag{4}$$

where

$U_1 = U(Y_1)$, utility if project is successful

$U_0 = U(Y_0)$, utility if project is unsuccessful

We can solve for the project undertaken at each contract $R = R(r, C)$. From (4),

$$\text{sign}\, \frac{dR}{dC} = \text{sign}\, U_0' p' < 0$$

$$\text{sign}\, \frac{dR}{dr} = \text{sign}\, -p' U_1' - pU_1'' > 0 \tag{5}$$

Increasing the collateral requirements induces individuals to undertake safer projects (as we suggested in our introduction), while increasing the interest rate leads individuals to undertake riskier projects (just as in Stiglitz and Weiss (1981)). Accordingly, the slope of the constant action loci are positive and given by

$$\left. \frac{dr}{dC} \right|_{\bar{R}} = \frac{U_0' p'}{p' U_1' + pU_1''} > 0 \tag{6}$$

These are depicted in Figure 5.2.

Note that if individuals were risk neutral, the first order condition could

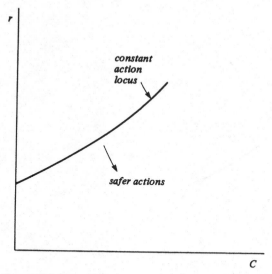

Figure 5.2 Constant action loci are upward sloping. Higher collateral is associated with safer action

be rewritten as

$$p'R + p = p'(1 + r - C) < 0 \tag{7}$$

implying that (comparing (7) and (2)) the individual chooses a level of risk taking beyond that which maximizes the expected return:

$$R(r, C) > R^0 \tag{8}$$

Using standard techniques (Diamond and Stiglitz (1974)) it can be shown that an increase in risk aversion reduces risk-taking (R). In particular, if individuals are risk averse

$$(U_1 - U_0)/U_1' < R - (1 + r) + C$$

Thus, if individuals are sufficiently risk averse,

$$R(r, C) < R^0$$

We also depict (in Figure 5.3) the indifference curves. Since increasing the interest rate or the collateral requirement lowers the individual's utility, the indifference curve is negatively sloped. Using the envelope theorem, we obtain

$$\left.\frac{dr}{dC}\right|_U = -\frac{(1-p)U_0'}{pU_1'} < 0 \tag{9}$$

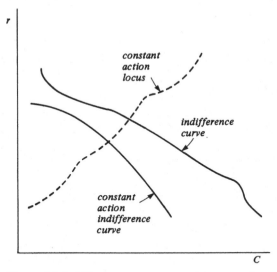

Figure 5.3 Indifference curves are not in general convex

The indifference curves are, of course, only defined for feasible values of collateral. Not all of the wealth of the individual is collateralizable. Future wages, pension funds, durable consumption goods, and trust funds are not in general collaterizable. We assume that the maximum value of collateral to the ith individual is C^i. Thus the set of feasible contracts are those for which[11]

$$C \leqslant C^i$$

The set of preferred contracts of borrowers is not in general convex. This non-convexity is a reflection of the non-convexity which arises in general with incentive-moral-hazard problems. If the choice of technique were fixed, the indifference curve would be quasi-concave (because of the standard arguments concerning diminishing marginal utility) and the preference sets convex. But as Figure 5.3 makes clear, as the individual moves along his indifference curve towards higher values of C, he undertakes less risky projects (he loses more in the event of failure). How much of a reduction in r he has to be given to compensate him for any given increase in C depends in part on the likelihood that he will have to forfeit his collateral which decreases as C increases: this makes his indifference curve flatter.

This can be seen more formally by noting in eq. (9) that as C increases and r decreases, U_0'/U_1' increases while $(1-p)/p$ decreases. The net effect on the slope of the indifference curve is ambiguous.

Comparison among borrowers

For simplicity, we shall, for most of the analysis, assume that there are only two groups, the rich and the poor, denoted by subscripts p and r. A_p denotes the total wealth of the poor, C_p is the collaterizable wealth of the poor, I_p is the indifference curve of the poor. We assume that

$$A_r > A_p \qquad C_r > C_p$$

the rich have both more total wealth and more collateralizable wealth.

It is ambiguous whether the indifference curve of a wealthy individual through a point in $\{r, C\}$ space is steeper or flatter than that of a poor individual. If there is decreasing absolute risk aversion, at a fixed p the poor's indifference curve is steeper: With decreasing absolute risk aversion

$$\frac{d \ln(U_0'/U_1')}{dA} = \frac{U_0''}{U_0'} - \frac{U_1''}{U_1'} < 0; \quad \text{thus} \quad \frac{d(-U_0'/U_1')}{dA} > 0$$

But poor individuals undertake safer projects (see Stiglitz and Weiss (1981)). In Appendix A we show that the relative magnitude of the two effects depends on the specific parameter values of the problem.

Note also that the indifference curves of rich and poor borrowers may cross more than once, and may touch without crossing (Figure 5.4).

We summarize our findings about borrowers' behavior by the following list:

Property 1. For any borrower, an increase in collateral induces safer actions

Property 2. For any borrower, an increase in the interest rate charged increases risk taking

Property 3. Risk neutral borrowers undertake actions which are riskier than R^0 (the project that maximizes expected return)

Property 4. An increase in risk aversion leads to a lower value of R

Property 5. Sufficiently risk averse borrowers undertake actions that are safer than R^0

Property 6. Preference sets are in general not convex. (Along any indifference curve, higher levels of collateral correspond to safer actions.)

Property 7. At any contract, with decreasing absolute risk aversion wealthier borrowers undertake riskier projects, but may have steeper or flatter indifference curves than poor borrowers

Bank profits

The expected gross return per dollar loaned of a bank (given a particular

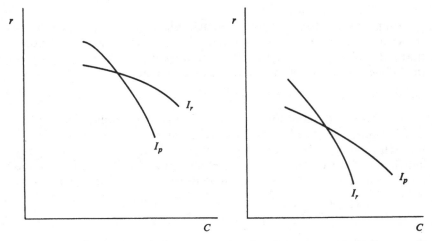

Figure 5.4 If the rich and the poor undertake the same projects the poor's indifference curves would be steeper; but the rich undertakes riskier projects so the rich's indifference curves would be steeper

type of borrower) is given by

$$v(r, C) = p(R(r, C))(1+r) + (1 - p(R(r, C))C$$
$$\underbrace{}_{\substack{\text{return if project} \\ \text{succeeds}}} \quad \underbrace{}_{\substack{\text{return if} \\ \text{project fails}}}$$

yielding iso-profit loci with slope

$$\left.\frac{dr}{dC}\right|_{\bar{v}} = -\frac{p'[1+r-C]\dfrac{dR}{dC}+1-p}{p'[1+r-C]\dfrac{dR}{dr}+p} \tag{10}$$

If p were fixed, the iso-profit focus would be a straight line with slope $-(1-p)/p$. But, with p variable, even the sign of the slope of the bank's iso-profit line is indeterminate.

For any particular borrower, increasing collateral increases the bank's expected return, both because it increases its return when the borrower defaults (the second term of the numerator) and because it reduces the likelihood of default (the first term of the numerator). On the other hand, increasing the interest rate increases the return to the bank if the borrower does not default (the second term of the denominator) but increases the likelihood of a default (the first term of the denominator).

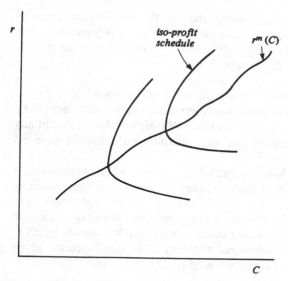

Figure 5.5 $r^m(C)$ gives the interest rate which maximizes the basic return at any level of collateral

We assume that there exists a unique interest rate which, for any given C, maximizes the bank's return; it is the solution to

$$p'(1+r-C)(dR/dr)+p=0 \qquad (11)$$

and is denoted by $r^m(C)$. For $r > r^m(C)$, the bank's return is lowered because the increasing risk-taking of borrowers offsets the direct effect on bank profits from a higher interest rate. We depict $r^m(C)$ in Figure 5.5, as well as the bank's iso-profit locus. Note that if we assume that

$$dv(r, C)/dr \gtreqless 0 \text{ as } r \lesseqgtr r^m(C) \qquad (12)$$

then the iso-profit locus is negatively sloped below $r^m(C)$ and positively sloped above it. (Obviously, by definition, at r^m, $\dfrac{dv}{dr} = 0$, $\dfrac{dv}{dr} \gtreqless 0$ as $r \lesseqgtr r^m$. But here (12) is assumed to hold globally.)

Comparison of slopes of iso-profit locus and indifference curve
Since individuals are risk averse, it immediately follows that, if there were no choice of technique, in order to remain on the same indifference curve individuals would require a reduction in the interest rate charged to compensate for an increase in collateral which represented more than the actuarially fair value of the loss in collateral. With fixed R, the slope of the

iso-profit locus is $-(1-p)/p$, while that of the indifference curve is $-U_0'/U_1' \times (1-p)/p < -(1-p)/p$. On the other hand, with variable R, this need not be the case; indeed, near $r^m(C)$, the slope of the iso-profit locus is always greater than that of the indifference curve.

Comparison of iso-profit loci for different borrowers

It should be clear that since richer borrowers, at any given contract $\{C, r\}$, undertake riskier projects, profits are lower. We also postulate that at any level of collateral the interest rate that maximizes the bank's expected return is lower for the rich.[12]

We let $v_x(\ )$ denote the bank's expected gross return when the proportion x of its borrowers are poor. $v_z(\ )$ denotes the bank's expected return when its borrowers are a random sample (equally weighted) of the population, i.e., z is the proportion of poor borrowers in the population. We again depict the iso-profit loci, given the particular mix of applicants. We denote by $r_z^m(C)$ the interest rate which maximizes the banks' expected return, given collateral C, and given a proportion x of poor borrowers.

Characterization of equilibria

In the context of our model we can illustrate several possible characterizations of equilibria:

(a) There exist *pooling* equilibria: different types of borrowers choose the same contract;
(b) There exist *complete separating* equilibria: only one type takes each contract;
(c) There exist *partially separating equilibria* with the quality mix differing across loan contracts;
(d) There exist equilibria in which there is no rationing;
(e) There may be rationing for all contracts;
(f) There may be rationing for some, but not all, contracts.

Our objective is not to undertake here an exhaustive taxonomy of the circumstances for (a)–(f), but rather to present some of the more interesting features of these equilibria.

We shall focus our attention on equilibria in which at least some rationing occurs. Let N^* be the total number of potential borrowers (in this simple version, this is independent of the interest rate charged, so long as the loan contracts are 'acceptable' to both groups of borrowers). Let $L(i)$ be the supply of funds (real resources) as a function of the return offered to depositors. Thus, we focus on situations for which, in equilibrium,

$$N^* > L(i)$$

We began this study, it will be recalled, with the observation that an increase in collateral has positive incentive effects, but potentially negative adverse selection effects. The adverse selection effects arise in this simple model in the presence of rationing only when an increase in collateral precludes one group (the poor) from borrowing. Thus, if there is rationing, at least one of the contracts offered must be at C_p or C_r.

II.1 Pooling equilibrium with rationing

Typically, in models of asymmetric information where self-selection mechanisms are available and the slopes of the agents' indifferences curves differ, pooling equilibria do not exist (see Rothschild and Stiglitz (1976)). Pooling equilibria exist in our model for either of two reasons. First, the limited collateral of poor borrowers makes their set of feasible contracts closed and bounded. Hence, contracts requiring C_p of collateral cannot necessarily be broken. Second, the indifference curves of rich and poor borrowers do not necessarily satisfy the single crossing property.[13]

If there exists a pooling equilibrium with rationing, it must lie along the locus $r_z^m(C)$. Otherwise, the lender could simply increase the interest rate charged, obtaining a random sample of the population, and accordingly increase its profits. By the same token, it can increase its collateral requirements, up to C_p, adjusting r simultaneously, and again increase its profits. We denote the contract $\{r_z^m(C_p), C_p\}$ by F^*.

The question is, can this pooling equilibrium be broken, under the assumption that each bank believes that the other banks will continue to make the same set of loans they are currently making, regardless of the actions that it undertakes? Recall that we asserted earlier that the rich individual's indifference curve through any contract may be more or less steep than the poor's. The two cases are depicted in the two parts of Figure 5.4. In either case, the equilibrium cannot be broken (locally) an an *increase* in collateral; for increasing C beyond C_p results in only rich individuals accepting the contract, and the bank's profits from such loans is lower. If the poor's indifference curve is flatter than that of the rich (which will be the case if there is a considerable difference in the projects undertaken), then any contract with less collateral than C_p that is taken up by the poor will be taken up by the rich: there is no (nearby) contract which can break the contract F^*.

Define

$$\tilde{r}_p(C; EU_p\{F^*\})$$

as the interest rate yielding the same expected utility as F^* to the poor when the collateral requirement is C; and define $\tilde{r}_r(C; EU_r\{F^*\})$ similarly for the rich. We require that for all C for which

$$v_p(\tilde{r}_p, C) \geqslant v_p\{F^*\} \tag{13a}$$

$$\tilde{r}_r(C; EU_r\{F^*\}) \geqslant \tilde{r}_p(C; EU_p\{F^*\}) \tag{13b}$$

where $EU_r\{K\}$ is the rich individual's expected utility at contract $\{K\}$ and we have used the obvious notation: $v_p\{F^*\} = v_p(r_z^m(C_p), C_p)$; more generally $v_p\{K\}$ is the bank's expected profit from contract K with a fraction x of applicants being poor. In these circumstances, the contract F^* cannot be broken by a contract with less than C_p. If the contract F^* is to be broken, it must be broken by a contract that only attracts the rich. By the same argument as given above, the contract which maximizes the bank's return, if it lends only to the rich, is $\{r_r^m(C_r), C_r\}$ and is denoted by G.[14] see Figure 5.6. We denote by G' the contract with $C = C_r$ which makes the (rich) individual indifferent between it and F^*, that is

$$EU_r\{F^*\} = EU_r\{G'\}$$

(Figure 5.7). There are two possibilities. If $EU_r\{G\} > EU_r\{G'\}$, then the bank compares the return at G and F^*. If $EU_r\{G\} < EU_r\{G'\}$, the bank compares the return at G' and F^*. It immediately follows that:

Proposition 1. There may exist a pooling equilibrium with rationing, with collateral C_p and interest rate $r_z^m(C_p)$, provided

(i)   the indifference curves (defined for values of $C \leqslant C_p$) of the poor are

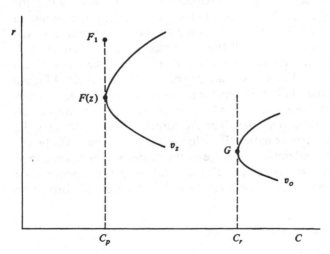

Figure 5.6. $F(z)$ maximizes bank's return at C_p with $x = z$; G maximizes bank's return at C_r

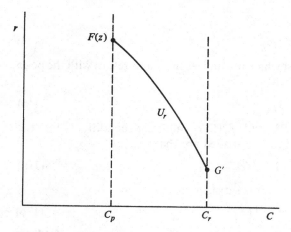

Figure 5.7 G' with contract at $C = C_r$ which makes the rich indifferent to it at $F(z)$; G' may be above or below G

flatter than those of the rich (or more precisely inequalities (13a) and (13b) are satisfied)

(ii) $L(i) < N^*$, where $i = v_z\{F^*\}$

(iiia) $v_z\{F^*\} > v_r(G)$

 or

(iiib) $EU_r\{G\} < EU_r\{G'\}$ and $v_z\{F^*\} > v_r\{G'\}$.

It is easy to confirm that these conditions can in fact be easily satisfied.

II.2 *Rationing with separating equilibrium*

We shall now show that even if contracts sort loan applicants, so that the distribution of borrowers varies across contracts, it may be the case that at every contract borrowers are rationed. The rationing equilibrium we shall describe has loans being made at collateral requirements C_p and C_r. Since only the rich apply at C_r, if there is rationing at C_r, then $r(C_r) = r_r^m(C_r)$, so the equilibrium contract is the contract we denoted earlier by $\{G\}$. Assume the rich prefer the contract $\{G\}$ to the contract offered at C_p. Then any rich individual offered both will choose $\{G\}$. Hence, the proportion of poor borrowers accepting contracts at C_p is $\hat{x} > z$. Let $F(\hat{x})$ be the contract which, at C_p, maximizes v given $x = \hat{x}$.[15] If $\{F(\hat{x}), G\}$ constitutes a (partially) separating equilibrium

$$v_{\hat{x}}\{F(\hat{x})\} = v_0\{G\} \tag{14}$$

For there to be a separating equilibrium, then, we require that there exists an $\hat{x}$ satisfying (14) for which

$$EU_r\{F(\hat{x})\} < EU_r\{G\} \tag{15}$$

Since the rate of interest which maximizes the loan's return with the poor is higher than with the rich,

$$r_{\hat{x}}^m(C_p) > r_z^m(C_p) \tag{16}$$

or $F(\hat{x})$ lies between F^* and $r_1^m(C_p)$. *Sufficient* conditions for the inequalities (14) and (15) to be satisfied are that

$$EU_r(r_z^m(C_p), C_p) < EU_r\{G\} \tag{17a}$$

((16) and (17a) imply that (15) is satisfied); and

$$v_1\{F(1)\} > v_0\{G\} > z_z\{F^*\} \tag{17b}$$

It is immediate that given the appropriate continuity assumptions, if (17b) is satisfied, there exists an $\hat{x}$ for which (14) is satisfied.

Can this equilibrium be broken? The answer to this depends on whether there exists a contract which separates out the poor and the rich with $C < C_p$. If the indifference curve through $F(\hat{x})$ of rich borrowers lies everywhere above that of poor borrowers, then the equilibrium cannot be broken. We have thus established

Proposition 2. If $L(i) < N^*$ where $i = v_r\{G\}$ and inequalities (13) are satisfied, then there exists a (partially) separating equilibrium with credit rationing at both contracts.[16]

II.3 Stability of sorting equilibria

Although we do not undertake a formal analysis of stability here, we note that if, for some reason, fewer banks made loans at the high collateral contract in a sorting equilibrium, there would be more rich borrowers applying to the low collateral contract, lowering the mean return at that contract. This would make the high collateral contract more attractive (to the bank) than the low collateral contract. Consequently banks would switch back to offering high collateral contracts, restoring the equilibrium. Conversely, if, for some reason, fewer banks made loans at the low collateral contract, the excess funds would be offered to high collateral borrowers, which would, in turn, increase the return at the low collateral contract. Consequently the quantity of low collateral loans would increase, reversing the initial perturbation.

There is clearly an externality between high collateral and low collateral contracts, of a kind that is not unusual in the context of adverse selection problems. (See Greenwald and Stiglitz (1985b).) If a bank could precommit itself to making a certain proportion of high collateral loans (without affecting the interest rate it pays depositors) it would. By increasing the number of high collateral loans, it increases the return it obtains on the low collateral loans, without reducing the return it obtains on the high collateral loans.

III Alternative equilibrium concepts

As Rothschild and Stiglitz (1976) made clear in their original study, the nature of the equilibrium depends critically on specific assumptions concerning the set of available actions (strategies) of the informed (borrowers) and the uninformed (banks). We have explored several modifications on our basic model. While some of these modifications leave the results essentially unaffected, some of them have fundamental consequences. After describing these alternatives and exploring their consequences, we summarize our views concerning the appropriateness of the alternatives for the market situation under examination.

III.1 Two contracts

The simplest modification allows each bank to offer more than one contract. We shall show that strategies that generated a separating equilibrium in the previous model also generate a separating equilibrium when we allow each bank to offer several different contracts.

Assume the conditions for a sorting equilibrium are satisfied (Proposition 2), and suppose a bank sought to break this equilibrium by offering a set of contracts which would, in total, increase its expected returns.

The borrower, in deciding on his application strategy, must take into account two facts: (i) the loan that he applies for conveys information to the bank; and (ii) the bank will only fund those loan applications which yield the highest return, given the information that the bank has (including the information revealed by the application).

To see how these inferences would be drawn, consider two contracts A and B being offered by a bank. If one of the contracts, say A, is not feasible for the poor borrowers or if it is dominated for the poor by not getting credit at all, then banks would infer that if A were chosen it was chosen by a rich borrower and that borrower would not get credit at contract B. In the more interesting case A and B are feasible for both borrowers and dominate not getting credit.

Let us assume we are in the separating equilibrium with rationing. Each bank is offering either contract G or contract $F(\hat{x})$. Consider a bank considering offering a contract pair $\{J, K\}$. This contract pair will only be offered if it generates a return greater than $v\{F(\hat{x})\} = v\{G\}$: the return achieved by the banks offering a single contract. Suppose one (or both) of the deviating bank's contracts, say J, lies above C_p. Because contract G generates the maximum return on loans to rich borrowers, J must generate a return to the bank less than or equal to $v\{F(\hat{x})\}$. If the pair generates a return strictly greater than $v\{F(\hat{x})\}$, contract K must be generating a higher return than does contract J. We assume that banks cannot commit themselves to funding the contracts they offer in any predetermined ratio. Given that assumption, the deviating bank will not fund contract J.

The reason contract J is not funded in the case where the deviating bank would be rationing credit is clear; in that case it will only fund its most profitable contract. If the deviating bank was not rationing credit this must be due to the bank having increased the supply of loanable funds by offering an interest rate greater than $v\{F(\hat{x})\}$. However, in that case contract J would generate losses for the bank and would not be funded. In either case borrowers realize that contract J will not be funded. They also realize that by applying for contract J they will be labeled as a rich borrower and consequently would be denied credit at contract K. Therefore, no borrowers apply for contract J. Consequently offering the pair $\{J, K\}$ reduces to only offering a singleton contract K. As we have shown, the separating equilibrium we constructed cannot be broken by a bank offering only one contract.

Let us now consider the case where both contracts demand less than C_p of collateral. Recall our assumptions that the indifference curves of the rich and poor borrowers only cross once and that the indifference curves of poor borrowers through $F(\hat{x})$ are flatter than those of rich borrowers. From those assumptions it follows that one of the contracts offered by the deviating bank must attract a proportion of poor borrowers less than or equal to $\hat{x}$. That contract(s) generates a return no greater than $v\{F(\hat{x})\}$. Consequently, from our previous argument, that contract will not be funded. The contract pair is again equivalent to only offering a singleton contract.

It should be obvious the argument we have presented can easily be extended to encompass the case where banks can offer more than two contracts.

While we have established that allowing each bank to offer several contracts does not affect the viability of the single contract equilibria described in the previous section, we have not precluded the existence of other equilibria. This possibility is the subject of on-going research by the authors. We conjecture that there are interesting rationing equilibria in which each bank offers several contracts.

III.2 Pooling equilibrium: another perspective

In our earlier analysis, we simply borrowed the basic conceptual framework employed by Rothschild and Stiglitz (1976) to argue that when the rich individual's indifference curve was flatter than the poor's the pooling equilibrium could be broken. Our model, however, differs in an important way from that of Rothschild and Stiglitz. In their model, the uninformed insurance company makes the first move, offering to potential buyers of insurance an array of insurance contracts. Buyers then accept or reject these offers.

Here, there are four moves: first the bank makes an offer of a loan contract; then borrowers apply; then the bank accepts some of these applications; and then borrowers accept one of the acceptances. (For simplicity we assume each bank has a fixed supply of loanable funds on which they have committed themselves to pay the equilibrium interest rate i. If their return is less than i, depositors are paid out of the bank's equity.)

Banks may thus be in a position to observe the offers of other firms (not necessarily who is offered what loans, but the kinds of contracts that are being made available). The bank can thus make an inference about who will accept their loan. On the basis of this inference, they can decide which, if any, of their loan applications to accept, and, if they have offered several loan contracts, their allocation of loanable funds among the contracts they offered. Potential borrowers, knowing this, will adjust their loan application strategy accordingly.

We have already provided one example of how this kind of information can be employed. We argued that the equilibrium in which each bank offers only one contract remained an equilibrium even if a bank decided to make available two loan contracts: potential borrowers would only apply for one of the two loan contracts.

We now wish to argue that there is a perfect equilibrium with pooling, even when, in the Rothschild–Stiglitz analysis, there would not be. Consider the pooling equilibrium of Section II.1, but assume that the indifference curve of the rich is flatter than that of the poor. In the standard analysis, if a bank offered a contract between the two indifference curves, only the safe, poor borrowers would purchase it; and this would break the pooling equilibrium.

But now consider the banks offering the pooling contract that we denoted earlier by F^*. They know that if they lose the safe borrowers this contract will not earn the required rate of return i. Denote the new contract lying between the indifference curves of the poor and rich by H. Banks know that only the safe borrowers will prefer H to F^* and that the bank offering the new contract will find it profitable to lend at those terms when F^* is offered. If we postulate that each bank has some alternative asset (a safe investment) yielding a return ε less than i, all banks that offered contract F^* will find it optimal to allocate their funds to this alternative asset. No loans will be extended at F^*. The applicant pool at the new contract, denoted by H, that, if offered the contract, will accept it, consists of the entire population. This contract will earn strictly less than i, since, at H, collateral is lower, and F^* maximizes the return for the population as a whole at C_p. The bank offering H will realize that it would have done better had it stuck to the original contract of offering just F^*. Thus F^* is an equilibrium.

The extra moves allow, in effect, the bank to react to the contracts offered by other banks. Whether one views this as providing the appropriate equilibrium for the market depends on at least three questions:

(1) Though the equilibrium is a (sub-game perfect) Nash equilibrium it has the property that an action by a small firm can alter the behavior of each of the other firms in the economy,[17] which seems inconsistent with standard competitive behavior. In a sense, it gives enormous market power to any one firm. (It may, of course, be the case that with imperfect information there is always inherently some degree of market power.) The central question then is whether the particular way of modeling market power implicit in these models captures well the nature of imperfect competition arising in these markets.[18]

(2) The availability of an alternative investment opportunity is critical. If such an opportunity were not available,[19] the best the firm might be able to do would be to lend to the remaining loan applicants, knowing that in doing so it would encounter losses. Of course, this could (or should) have been anticipated, so that in fact no bank would have offered the contract $\{F^*\}$ originally. This is simply another way of stating that, in these circumstances, $\{F^*\}$ would not be an equilibrium.

(3) The role of commitment. The kinds of commitments which are feasible (plausible) has an enormous effect on the nature of the equilibrium.

Consider, for instance, the pooling equilibrium. Pooling equilibria are almost always inefficient. One group is subsidizing the other group. The action of the subsidized group is altered in order to obtain the subsidy. If the high risk group would only admit to its higher risk, the low risk group would be able to give them the same level of utility, but at less cost.

Thus, at the pooling equilibrium $\{F^*\}$, the wealthy are being subsidized (that is, the expected return on loans to the wealthy is lower than i). Consider what happens if we increase the collateral requirements for the wealthy, from C_p to C_r, adjusting the rate of interest in such a way as to keep the wealthy individual on the same indifference curve. The bank's return from this borrower increases.

Let us now assume that the sequence of actions we have modeled is modified in the following simple way.[20] We first allow the bank to announce a single contract, or a set of contracts, among which the borrower is allowed to select later; the borrower does not have to reveal which of the contracts it will choose until after the bank has accepted its loan application. Borrowers then apply to banks. Banks then accept applications. After the bank has committed itself to allowing borrowers to have a choice, borrowers tell the bank which of the possible contracts they wish to accept.

In that case, if a bank offered the pair $\{F^*, G'\}$, where G' is the contract with $C = C_r$ which is just preferred by the rich to $\{F^*\}$, all rich individuals who were accepted would accept G'. Clearly, this contract pair would break the pooling equilibrium.

The question is, can the bank commit itself to lending to the rich, once they have announced who they are (by their preference for contract G' over F^*)? Obviously, if they cannot, the rich would know that once they announce that they preferred G' to F^*, the bank would not lend to them; hence, allowing for the possibility of making choices after the bank's acceptances would leave the equilibrium unaffected.[21]

III.3 Competition for depositors

One problem that frequently arises in applications of game theoretical notions of equilibrium to markets of this sort is how to model the response of depositors to a new interest rate (on deposits)-loan contract combination where the new interest rate is higher than that offered by other banks but the loan contract is less attractive than the contract offered to borrowers by other banks. This is not a problem in the *rationing* equilibria discussed below. In those equilibria banks are paying depositors an interest rate reflecting the maximum possible return per dollar loaned.

In a non-rationing regime one might argue that the high interest rate offered depositors would attract all the depositors. Since no other bank would have any loanable funds, the bank would attract all borrowers that preferred its contract to not getting credit. This new interest rate – loan contract combination may then generate an excess supply of loanable funds. Yet in general the higher gross return the bank makes on each loan would outweigh the epsilon increase in the interest rate paid depositors less the loss to the bank from having some deposits that are not loaned out.[22]

On the other hand, one might argue that depositors would not find the interest rate being offered by the bank credible. The bank can only pay that interest rate if it attracts borrowers. Since the contract it is offering borrowers is less attractive than the contracts being offered by other banks it only attracts borrowers if it attracts depositors.

If depositors believe the new contract will attract all depositors they will also believe it will attract borrowers, consequently they would deposit their funds with the new contract and their beliefs would be fulfilled. On the other hand, if depositors believe the other banks would not lose their depositors they would infer that the new contract would not attract borrowers and the proposed return would not be paid; consequently depositors would not deposit funds with the banks offering the new contract, and these (opposite) beliefs would be fulfilled.

Following the notion of credibility defined in Stiglitz and Weiss (1983) we require that for a new contract to break an equilibrium it must offer an interest rate to depositors and a loan contract to borrowers that makes neither depositors nor borrowers worse off, and makes either depositors or borrowers strictly better off. This restriction can be motivated by beliefs on the part of either depositors or borrowers that (when this condition is not satisfied) the bank will be unable to pay the interest rate or finance the loan contract it announces.

III.4 Additional instruments

One of the original motivations for this study was to explore the consequences of providing the bank with additional instruments (besides the interest rate) with which to select among applicants and with which to affect the behavior of borrowers. We have shown that allowing for collateral strengthens the basic qualitative results of our earlier analysis: there still may be credit rationing, though now all may experience rationing simultaneously, while in our 1981 paper only one group would be rationed in any equilibrium.

A natural question that arises is, "Will providing the bank still more instruments affect our results?" It is our contention that so long as an informational problem remains, credit rationing may occur.

We consider here only one additional instrument: requiring borrowers to provide more equity. In our model, this instrument is completely redundant, so long as providing more equity reduces the amount of collateral that a borrower can provide.

To see this, we compare two loan contracts a and b. 'a' demands C units collateral and e units of equity; 'b' demands $C + \Delta$ units of collateral and $e - \Delta$ units of equity. We shall show that the return of the bank is the same from both contracts.

The payoff to a borrower from a is 0 if the project fails and $R - (1-e)(1+r_a) + C(1+i)$ if the project is successful, where R is the technique induced by contract a, r_a is the interest rate charged in contract a and collateral earns the risk-free return i.[23] If contract b were also to induce the borrower to choose R, the interest rate r_b charged in contract b must be such that the return to the borrower, if the project is successful, is the same as for contract a (note the return to the borrower for a failure is the same in either case). That is

$$R-(1-e)(1+r_a)+C(1+i) = R-(1-e+\Delta)(1+r_b)+(C+\Delta)(1+i) \qquad (20)$$

$$(1+r_b) = \frac{\Delta(1+i)+(1-e)(1+r_a)}{1-e+\Delta} \qquad (21)$$

The bank's return from contract a is equal to its return from b iff

$$p(R)(1-e)(1+r_a)+[1-p(R)]C(1+i)-(1-e)(1+i)$$
$$\overset{?}{=} p(R)(1-e+\Delta)(1+r_b)+[1-p(R)](C+\Delta)(1+i)-(1-e+\Delta)(1+i)$$

Substituting for $1+r_b$ from (21)

$$p(R)(1-e)(1+r_a)+[1-p(R)]C(1+i)-(1-e)(1+i)$$
$$\overset{?}{=} p(R)[\Delta(1+i)+(1-e)(1+r_a)]+[1-p(R)](C+\Delta)(1+i)$$
$$-[1-e+\Delta](1+i)$$
$$0 \overset{?}{=} p(R)\Delta(1+i)+[1-p(R)]\Delta(1+i)-\Delta(1+i)$$
$$0 = 0$$

Thus we can see that for any technique induced by one loan contract, any other loan contract requiring the same commitment of loanable funds, and that also induces that technique, generates the same profit to the bank. From the bank's point of view the allocation of liquid funds demanded from the borrower between equity and collateral is immaterial.

Thus, though we have assumed banks only impose collateral requirements, the results are identical to what they would be if they could have imposed, in addition, equity requirements.

IV Further remarks

We have assumed throughout that when a bank makes a loan, it only knows that the borrower has at least the collateral required for that loan. If the bank could compel borrowers to reveal how much wealth they had, then, of course, the bank could identify precisely who is rich and who is poor. We do not allow the bank to do this. Since borrowers have an incentive to signal that they are poor, and hence will undertake safe projects, we are only assuming that borrowers can conceal some of their assets from banks, not that they can persuade banks to overvalue their assets. Presumably the first type of deception is harder for banks to detect than the second.

Second, in most of the analysis we have assumed that individuals, regardless of their wealth, have the same investment opportunity set. Had we assumed that they differed in their opportunity sets, it would have been trivial to construct examples of credit rationing with (or without) self-selection. What is surprising in the analysis we have presented is that heterogeneity among borrowers stemming solely from unobserved differences in wealth is sufficient to generate credit rationing even when there are sufficient instruments available to sort borrowers.

Of course, if all borrowers were identical there could still be rationing at a contract demanding full collateral for those borrowers. In that case there is only one source of market imperfection – the incentive effect of contracts – and two instruments, collateral and the interest rate. However, the extra instrument still does not eliminate rationing. In the other extreme case in which each individual has only one available technique – so there are no incentive effects of contracts – heterogeneity among borrowers with a given level of liquid funds may also create rationing equilibria. This is the case if the distribution of borrowers is such that the bank optimal contract lies at an interior point in $\{r, C\}$ space.

V Conclusion

The basic principle that we enunciated in our earlier paper, that the terms of a contract affect both the mix of applicants and the actions which they take, and that as a result banks might wish to offer contracts which generate a higher level of expected utility to the borrower than he could obtain elsewhere, is a general one: its validity holds whether or not there are self-selection mechanisms available. What is required is that, given whatever mechanisms are available for extracting information concerning the mix of applicants and the actions they take, there is a residue of imperfect information. Although one can construct examples in which there is no such residue (see Bester (1985), Besanko and Thakor (1984b) or Milde and Riley (1984)), we would argue that, in real markets, there is. Accordingly, there is the possibility of credit rationing.

Finally, to reiterate two points we made in our earlier papers:

(1) There may be in these models a contract at which demand for loans equals the supply; but no bank is compelled to offer the market clearing contract. If lowering the interest rate or the collateral requirements or both increases its profits, it will do so.

(2) We are not contending that market equilibria are always

characterized by credit rationing, only that there are demand and supply relationships for which there is credit rationing.

This paper has established not only that there can be credit rationing, but that there can be rationing at several different loan contracts. Our rationing equilibria have interesting macro-economic implications: monetary policy may work more through its consequences for the availability of credit than through its effects on interest rates. Indeed, in our equilibrium with two different credit contracts, a tightening of credit will leave unaffected the interest rates charged on each contract; all the restriction in credit availability will be felt in a reduction in the number of low collateral contracts (that is, the impact will not be uniform across credit types); and the weighted average interest rate (with the weights being the relative quantities of the different contracts supplied) actually falls.

APPENDICES

A Effect of increases in wealth on slope of indifferences curve

From (5)

$$\text{sign}\frac{d\left(\dfrac{dr}{dC}\Big|_{\bar{v}}\right)}{dA} = -\text{sign}\left\{pU_1'\left[-p'(R)U_0'\frac{dR}{dA}+(1-p)U_0''\right]\right.$$

$$-(1-p)U_0'\left[p'U_1'\frac{dR}{dA}+pU_1''\left(1+\frac{dR}{dA}\right)\right]\right\}$$

$$= -\text{sign}\left\{p(1-p)\left[U_1'U_0''-U_0'U_1''\left(1+\frac{dR}{dA}\right)\right]-p'U_0'U_1'\frac{dR}{dA}\right\}$$

$$= -\text{sign}\left\{p(1-p)[U_1'U_0''-U_0'U_1''][p(1-p)U_1''+p'U_1']U_0'\frac{dR}{dA}\right\}$$

From decreasing absolute risk aversion

$$\left|\frac{U_1''}{U_1'}\right|=\left|\frac{U_0''}{U_0'}\right|$$

therefore

$$p(1-p)[U_1'U_0''-U_0'U_1'']<0 \tag{A.1}$$

From (5)

$$\text{sign}\frac{dR}{dA}=\text{sign}\left\{(U_1'-U_0')p'+pU_1''\right\}=-\text{sign }p_1'\left\{\frac{U_1'-U_0'}{U_1-U_0}-\frac{U_2''}{U_1'}\right\}\gtrless 0$$

as there is decreasing or increasing absolute risk aversion. This is derived simply by viewing U' as a function of U. Therefore, decreasing absolute risk aversion implies

$$-[p(1-p)U''_1 + p'U'_1]U'_0 \frac{dR}{dA} > 0 \tag{A.2}$$

The first and second order conditions for profit maximization do not preclude the absolute value of (A.2) being greater than the absolute value of (A.1). Consequently, the indifference curves of rich borrowers through a contract can be steeper (or flatter) than the indifference curves of poor borrowers.

B Rationing at one contract

In the text, we analyzed rationing at the pooling and partially separating equilibria. The third form of rationing equilibrium consists of rationing at only one of two contracts.[24] There can be rationing either at only the high collateral contract or only the low collateral contract.

Rationing at only the high collateral contract
The fact that there is rationing at only the high collateral contract means that everyone in fact obtains a loan. Thus the equilibrium rate of interest is the solution to

$$L(\hat{\imath}) = N \tag{B.1}$$

which we denote by $\hat{\imath}$.

The contract rate (to borrowers) yielding this expected return (with $C = C_r$) we denote by $\hat{G}$. It is the solution to

$$v[\hat{G}] = v_r[\hat{r}, C_r] = \hat{\imath} \tag{B.2}$$

Since there is rationing, it must be the case that the bank cannot increase its interest rate without adversely affecting itself. Since $\hat{\imath} \leqslant i^*$, except for the singular case where $\hat{\imath} = i^*$, this must imply that if the bank increases the interest rate charged, it loses all its customers. Thus the low collateral contract must solve

$$U_r\{\hat{G}\} = U_r\{F(x)\} \tag{B.3}$$

Finally, the number of loans issued at the high collateral contract must be such as to make the low collateral loans yield a return of $\hat{\imath}$, i.e., $\hat{x}$ solves

$$v[F(\hat{x})] = \hat{\imath} \tag{B.4}$$

There exists an x solving (B.4) provided only that

$$v_1\{F(1)\} > \hat{\imath} > v_2\{F(2)\} \tag{B.5}$$

Moreover, for rationing at G it is necessary that

$$v_2\{F(z)\} < \hat{\imath} \tag{B.6}$$

(Otherwise, the pooling contract would break this $\{G\}$ contract.)

Rationing at only the low collateral contract

Proposition 3a. Consider a contract G', requiring collateral C_r and interest rate $r \leqslant r_0^m$, such that $v_0(G') = v_z(F(z))$, and $U_r(G') < U_r(F(z))$. Then there is rationing at contract $F(z)$ but not at G', if there exists a value of β between 0 and 1 satisfying

$$L(v_0(G')) = R + \beta P \tag{B.7}$$

Both rich and poor borrowers apply for loans at contract $F(z)$. The rich borrowers that fail to obtain a loan at $F(z)$ take a loan at G'. The number of loans granted at $F(z)$ is such that when all rejected rich borrowers get credit at G' the number of loans granted is equal to the supply of loanable funds at $i = v_0(G') = v_z(F(z))$. That is, if β represents the proportion of applicants getting loans at contract $F(z)$, then $L(v_0(G')) = R + \beta P$. Banks would not raise the interest rate of the low collateral loan despite credit being rationed since the adverse incentive effects of a higher interest rate would lower their return. Given the interest rate paid depositors banks would lose money if they were to lower the interest rate at G, while a higher interest rate would cause each bank to lose its borrowers.

Proposition 3b. Consider a contract G'', requiring collateral C_r and interest rate $r \leqslant r_0^m$, such that $v_0(G'') = v_1(F(1))$, and $U_r(G'') > U_r(F(1))$. Then there is rationing at contract F but not at G'', if there exists a value of β satisfying (B.7), when G' is replaced by G''.

All the rich borrowers get credit at contract G'', their preferred contract. Some, but not all, of the poor borrowers get credit at contract F. Banks pay depositors an interest rate $i = v_0(G'') = v_1(F(1))$. Again if we let β represent the proportion of applicants at $F(1)$ that get credit, this is a rationing equilibrium where β is chosen such that $L(v_0(G'')) = \beta P + R$. For the same reasons as described above, no bank would have an incentive to change either contract $F(1)$ or G''.

Proposition 3c. Consider a contract G^*, requiring collateral C_r and interest rate $r \leqslant r_r^m$, such that $v_0(G^*) = v_x(F(x))$, where x lies between z and 1, and $U_r(G^*) = U_r(F(x))$. Then there is rationing at contract F but not at G^*, if there exists a value of β satisfying (B.7), when G' is replaced by G^*.

The proportion of rich borrowers accepting contract $F(x)$ generates the ratio x, which is required to equate the banks returns from contract $F(x)$ and G^*. A banking raising the interest rate at collateral C_p would face a distribution z of poor borrowers, and would lose money. Similarly any deviation in the interest rate offered at the high collateral contract would either cause the bank to lose money, or would dissuade borrowers from applying to that bank.

Note that, despite the equalities, the situation described in Proposition 3c is not degenerate. Consider the values of G' and G'' defined in Propositions 3a and 3b and $U(G') > U(G'')$. By continuity there exists a proportion x of poor borrowers at the low collateral contract, $z < x < 1$, and a value of $G^{\#}$, lying between G' *and* G'' such that $v_0(G^{\#}) = v_x(F(x))$ and $U_r(G^{\#}) = U_r(F(x))$ simultaneously.

NOTES

* The views expressed are not necessarily those of Bell Communications Research. Financial support from the National Science Foundation and the Hoover Institution, Stanford, is gratefully acknowledged. Earlier versions of this paper were presented at seminars at Yale University and the Institute for Mathematical Studies in the Social Sciences, Stanford University. We are grateful for the helpful comments of the participants in those seminars. We are also indebted to Gerhard Clemenz, Oliver Hart, Martin Hellwig and John Riley for helpful comments.

1 That research program itself is part of a larger research program aimed at ascertaining the extent to which a variety of features of the economy can be explained by informational imperfections. We have been particularly concerned with seeing how informational imperfections explain wage and price rigidities, and how these in turn can explain certain key macro-economic phenomena. See, for instance, Stiglitz (1976), (1984a), (1984b) and (1985), Weiss (1980), Nalebuff and Stiglitz (1982), Shapiro and Stiglitz (1984), Greenwald and Stiglitz (1985a) and (1985b), Greenwald, Weiss and Stiglitz (1984).

2 See also Stiglitz (1982) and (1985b).

3 Conventional competitive analysis has imposed price-taking behavior as an *assumption*, just as it has imposed the market clearing condition as part of the *definition* of equilibrium. The essential feature of *competitive* markets, we would argue, is the smallness of the participants in the market (relative to the size of the market). Whether, in such situations, the participants in the market take prices as given, and whether equilibrium is characterized by demand equaling supply, are properties to be derived from the more primitive assumptions of the model.

4 Though interest rate ceilings imposed on deposit accounts do not. Thus, the fact that savings and loan associations had federally imposed ceilings on the interest rates they could pay to depositors may have limited the supply of funds available to the mortgage market in the post World War II period. But mortgage rates were not at the maximum rates imposed by usury laws. Hence, the widely observed phenomena of rationing of mortgages cannot be explained by governmentally imposed interest rate ceilings.

It should be emphasized that, with imperfect information, there need not be the negative welfare aspects associated with governmentally imposed rationing under perfect information.

5 We shall be more precise later concerning what exactly this entails.

6 Banks are assumed to be large enough that they can ignore the stochastic variations in the percentage of the applicants that it accepts that accept it.

7 That is why we assumed earlier that each bank chooses the contract which maximizes its expected return. When it does this, this will be precisely zero, so the bank is indifferent concerning its scale of operations. As is usually the case in such models, although the scale of each bank is of no consequence, the aggregate distribution of loan contracts by types is determinate.

8 The condition that $p'' < 0$ is imposed to ensure that the second order condition is satisfied. Most of our results would go through even if $p'' > 0$, though we would have to be careful to ensure that the project undertaken maximizes expected utility, rather than minimizes it.

9 Since when the project is successful, the bank returns the collateral, the value of C is of no concern in that state, though r and R clearly are. To simplify the exposition we are evaluating A and C at their values at the end of the investment period including any interest they may have generated.

10 If the project is unsuccessful, the individual forfeits his collateral; hence his income depends on the amount of collateral he has had to put up, but it does not depend either on R or r.

11 In addition, the individual must obtain at least as great a level of expected utility as he would if he did not undertake the project, i.e.

$$EU > U(A)$$

We assume throughout our analysis that this latter constraint is not binding.

12 This can be shown to be true for the two activity case. We do not derive here conditions ensuring that it will always be true.

13 The single crossing property requires that one type of borrower has unambiguously steeper indifference curves than the other.

14 We denote the interest rate which maximizes the return to the bank lending to an individual of type i with collateral C by $r_i^m(C)$,

$$r_p^m(C) = r_1^m(C) \quad \text{and} \quad r_r^m(C) = r_0^m(C)$$

15 Thus $F^* = F(z)$.

16 In Appendix B we consider separating equilibria with rationing at only one contract.

17 This is basically the same criticism raised earlier by Rothschild and Stiglitz against the reaction equilibrium concepts: their analysis purported to describe competitive markets with imperfect information. A basic property of competitive markets should be that each firm believes its actions have no effect on the actions of the other firms.

Two other criticisms have been levied against these reaction equilibria. (a) Most imposed somewhat arbitrary restrictions on the set of admissible strategies. For example Wilson (1977) suggested that firms could react by dropping contracts, but could not add additional contracts. (b) They used a static model to analyze what was essentially a dynamic situation. The model we have just discussed shows that the second of these criticisms was in fact not substantive. Our model is explicitly dynamic.

The fact that one can 'convert' a 'reaction' equilibrium into a Nash equilibrium of an alternating move game is not, of course, surprising. The central economic issues, about whether the restrictions concerning the sequencing of moves and the set of available actions and strategies are reasonable remain, as do the associated issues of whether the resulting model provides a good description of a competitive market.

18 We believe that one cannot answer these questions in the abstract. Different models are appropriate to different situations. In particular, the possibility of a response of a lender of not extending any loans is, we think, especially germane in the context of rationing models where the lender is rejecting some applicants anyway.

19 One can think of the bank as having only limited managerial resources: it either enters the loan market (in which case the best it can do is to make loans); or it can enter the investment market. Limitations on available opportunities have much the same effect as commitments, discussed below.

20 A similar example was first suggested to us by Gerhard Clemenz.

21 Similar issues of commitment arise in the Rothschild–Stiglitz analysis of the insurance market. If firms could commit themselves to offering two insurance policies in fixed ratios, then in those situations where, without the commitment, no equilibrium exists, there now exists an equilibrium, with the high risk individuals obtaining complete insurance, subsidized by the low risk individuals. Any firm that attempted to steal the good (low risk) customers, would observe that a corresponding number of bad (high risk) customers were simultaneously placed on the market, since as the existing insurance firms lose their good risks, they simultaneously cancel the policies of the bad risks. Hence any firm attempting to steal only the good risks would find itself facing an applicant pool reflecting the distribution of risks in the population, and it would make a loss.

22 This problem is not peculiar to credit markets or markets with asymmetric information: in any product-factor market a firm could become a monopolist in the product market by offering a factor price above the market price of the factor. In general these monopoly rents could outweigh the costs associated with the higher factor price.

23 Note the slight modification from the earlier model where the value of collateral was measured as of the end of the period.

24 A fourth form about which we will say little, is that where there is a single contract offered, $\{G\}$ at which there is rationing. This will be an equilibrium if

(i) $L(i^*) \leqslant R$, and

(ii) $v_0(G) \geqslant v_1(F(1))$.

These conditions are, of course, stronger than is required for rationing at G.

REFERENCES

Besanko, D. and A. Thakor (1984a). 'Competitive Equilibrium in the Credit Market Under Asymmetric Information.' Northwestern University Discussion Paper.
Besanko, D. and A. Thakor (1984b). 'Collateral and Rationing: Sorting Equilibria in Monopolistic and Competitive Markets.' Northwestern University Discussion Paper.
Bester, H. (1985). 'Screening Versus Rationing in Credit Markets with Imperfect Information.' *American Economic Review*, **75**, 850–855.
Bhattacharya, S. (1980). 'Nondissipative Signaling Structures and Dividend Policy.' *Quarterly Journal of Economics*, **95**, 1–25.
Blinder, A. (1984). 'Notes on the Comparative Statics of a Stiglitz–Weiss Bank.' Mimeo.
Blinder, A. and J. E. Stiglitz (1983). 'Money, Credit Constraints and Economic Activity.' *American Economic Review*, **73**, 297–302.
Diamond, P. and J. E. Stiglitz (1977). 'Increases in Risk and in Risk Aversion.' *Journal of Economic Theory*, **14**, 337–360.
Gale, D. and M. Hellwig (1985). 'Incentive-Compatible Debt Contracts: The One Period Problem.' *Review of Economic Studies*, **52**, 647–664.
Gausch, J. L. and A. Weiss (1980). 'Wages as Sorting Mechanisms in Competitive Markets with Asymmetric Information.' *Review of Economic Studies*, **47**, 149–165.
Gausch, J. L. and A. Weiss (1982). 'An Equilibrium Analysis of Wage-Productivity Gaps.' *Review of Economic Studies*, **49**, 485–497.
Greenwald, B. and J. E. Stiglitz (1985a). 'Money, Imperfect Information, and Economic Fluctuations.' Lecture presented at CEME Conference in Nice, June.
Greenwald, B. and J. E. Stiglitz (1985b). 'Externalities in Economies with Imperfect Information and Incomplete Markets.' *Quarterly Journal of Economics*, forthcoming.
Greenwald, B., A. Weiss and J. E. Stiglitz (1984). 'Informational Imperfections in the Capital Markets and Macro-economic Fluctuations.' *American Economic Review*, **74**, 194–200.
Keynes, J. M. (1936). *The General Theory of Employment, Interest and Money*. Macmillan, London.
Milde, H. and J. Riley (1984). 'Signalling in Credit Markets.' UCLA Discussion Paper.
Nalebuff, B. and J. E. Stiglitz (1983). 'Equilibrium Unemployment as a Worker Selection Device.' Mimeo, Princeton University.
Neary, P. and J. E. Stiglitz (1982). 'Expectations, Asset Accumulation and the Real-Balance Effect.' Paper presented at Dublin meetings of the Economic Society, September.
Riley, J. (1975). 'Competitive Signalling.' *Journal of Economic Theory*, **10**, 174–186.
Riley, J. (1979). 'Informational Equilibria.' *Econometrica*, **47**, 331–360.
Riley, J. (1984). 'Competitive Signalling Reconsidered.' UCLA Working Paper No. 294.
Rothschild, M. and J. E. Stiglitz (1976). 'Equilibrium in Competitive Insurance Markets.' *Quarterly Journal of Economics*, **80**, 629–649.
Shapiro, C. and J. E. Stiglitz (1984). 'Equilibrium Unemployment as a Worker Discipline Device.' *American Economic Review*, **74**, 350–356.

Stiglitz, J. E. (1972). 'Some Aspects of the Pure Theory of Corporate Finance: Bankruptcies and Take-overs.' *Bell Journal of Economics and Management Science*, **3**, 458–482.

Stiglitz, J. E. (1976). 'Prices and Queues as Screening Devices in Competitive Markets.' IMSSS Technical Report No. 212, Stanford University.

Stiglitz, J. E. (1982). 'Ownership, Control and Efficient Markets: Some Paradoxes in the Theory of Capital Markets.' In K. Boyer and W. Shepherd (eds), *Economic Regulation: Essays in Honor of James R. Nelson*. Michigan State University Press, Michigan.

Stiglitz, J. E. (1984a). 'Price Rigidities and Market Structure.' *American Economic Review*, **74**, 350–356.

Stiglitz, J. E. (1984b). 'Theories of Wage Rigidity.' NBER Working Paper No. 1332.

Stiglitz, J. E. (1984c). 'Competitivity and the Number of Firms in a Market: Are Duopolies More Competitive Than Atomistic Markets?' Mimeo, Princeton University.

Stiglitz, J. E. (1985a). 'Information and Economic Analysis: A Perspective.' *Economic Journal Supplement*, **95**, 21–42.

Stiglitz, J. E. (1985b). 'Credit Markets and the Control of Capital.' *Journal of Money, Credit and Banking*, **17**, 133–152.

Stiglitz, J. E. (1985c). 'Equilibrium Wage Distributions.' *Economic Journal*, **95**, 595–618.

Stiglitz, J. E. and A. Weiss (1983). 'Incentive Effects of Terminations: Applications to the Credit and Labor Markets.' *American Economic Review*, **73**, 912–927.

Stiglitz, J. E. and A. Weiss (1985). 'Sorting out the Difference Between Screening and Signaling Models.' Columbia University Discussion Paper No. 225.

Weiss, A. (1980). 'Job Queues and Layoffs in Labor Markets with Flexible Wages.' *Journal of Political Economy*, **88**, 526–538.

Weiss, A. and J. E. Stiglitz (1981). 'Credit Rationing in Markets with Imperfect Information.' *American Economic Review*, **71**, 393–410.

Weiss, A. and J. E. Stiglitz (1984). 'Credit Rationing and Collateral.' Mimeo, Bellcore.

Wette, H. (1983). 'Collateral in Credit Rationing in Markets with Imperfect Information.' *American Economic Review*, **73**, 442–445.

Wilson, C. (1977). 'A Model of Insurance Markets with Incomplete Information.' *Journal of Economic Theory*, **16**, 167–207.

COMMENT OLIVER D. HART*

Over the last few years, Joe Stiglitz and Andy Weiss have written a number of papers on credit rationing (e.g., Stiglitz and Weiss (1981)), and I thought that it might be useful if I address this work generally rather than focussing specifically on the current paper.

Economists have long struggled to understand the phenomenon of rationing in certain markets, particularly labor and credit markets. While not everybody agrees about the relevance of this phenomenon, for many economists, e.g. Keynesians, such rationing is one of the most striking and important instances of market failure in modern capitalist economies. But, assuming the phenomenon exists, how do we explain it? The problem is, of course, that if a good is in excess demand, we would expect either unsatisfied buyers or opportunistic sellers to bid up its price; and equally if it is in excess supply, we would expect price to fall. That is, in an economy which satisfies the standard neoclassical assumptions, it is not clear that rationing can be an equilibrium phenomenon, i.e. how it can persist.

Much of the economists' intuition about this issue is based on the case where agents have perfect information, or at least common information. In the last few years, a great deal of research has considered the consequence of relaxing this assumption. The Stiglitz–Weiss (henceforth SW) papers are a leading example of this type of work. Their goal is to try to explain rationing as an equilibrium phenomenon by introducing various asymmetries of information between economic agents. The focus is on the credit market, although, in related work, Weiss (1980) has extended some of these ideas to explain involuntary unemployment in the labor market.

My comments will be in two parts. First, I will set up a variant of a model SW have used. Secondly, I will give a critical discussion of this model. I will end with some concluding remarks.

It is worth noting first that, while SW are concerned to understand rationing under perfect competition, the same intellectual puzzle arises in expaining the phenomenon under imperfect competition. In particular,

	Return in £	Probability
Project 1:	0	1/3
	15	1/3
	30	1/3
Project 2:	0	4/5
	40	1/5

why should a monopolistic seller ever ration his customers? The point is that if there is excess demand, the monopolist can increase profit by raising price and choking off demand that way. Since the monopolistic case presents the same basic problems and turns out to be much easier to analyze, I shall concentrate on it in what follows. That is, I will consider the case of a single monopolistic bank which wishes to make loans to a number of perfectly competitive customers.

SW in fact present two theories of credit rationing under asymmetric information, one based on moral hazard and the other on adverse selection (a similar moral hazard theory was developed independently by Keeton (1979)). I shall focus mainly on the moral hazard theory, which can be illustrated using the following very simple example. Suppose that a monopolistic bank has funds £F to lend out, and that it faces many identical potential borrowers, whom we shall call firms. Assume that the £F is just enough to cover the investment of *one* of these firms and so the question is which firm gets the funds and on what terms. Suppose further that firms have no funds of their own and no collateral.

Assume that each firm can undertake two sorts of projects, with (uncertain) returns as indicated in the table. Suppose also that each project involves a disutility of effort by the firm's manager, which is equivalent to a monetary cost of £1. Finally, assume that firms are risk neutral with respect to net return, but that net return can never become negative (recall that the firm has no initial wealth).

We consider two regimes, the first-best where the parties have the same information, and the second-best where there are some asymmetries of information.

First-best

In the first-best, the firm's return R, and the choice of project, are both publically observable. Hence in this case the contract between the bank and the firm to which it lends can be a contingent one, in the sense that it can specify the project to be undertaken and make the debt repayment a function of the project's ex post return. Since the bank is a monopolist facing a large number of potential customers, we suppose that it has all the bargaining power, i.e. it sets the terms of the contract. Now the bank must leave the firm at least £1 of profit to compensate the manager for his effort. Hence an optimal contract will state that the firm must hand over to the bank the full return from its investment except for £1. This makes the firm indifferent about the project undertaken, but the bank will want project 1 since it has a higher expected return. Hence the contract will also specify that project 1 should be undertaken (actually this is not strictly necessary since, given that the firm is indifferent about the project, it will presumably be prepared to do what the bank wants anyway (see also note 2 below)).

Observe that there is no credit rationing here. The firms which do not receive credit are no worse off than the firm that does. This is because the bank chooses the terms of the contract to make the firm just indifferent between borrowing and not, i.e. the bank squeezes all the surplus out of the transaction.

Second-best

We now consider the case where: (a) only the firm observes the ex post return, R: and (b) the bank cannot observe the choice of project.[1] Hence contingent contracts can no longer be written. In fact, the only feasible contract now is one that specifies a noncontingent amount D that the firm must repay to the bank. Of course, this payment is only going to be feasible for the firm in states where the ex post return $R \geqslant D$. If $R < D$, we follow the SW assumption that the firm goes *bankrupt* and pays the bank what it can, i.e. R.

At what level should the bank set D? The problem is that, as D changes, so may the firm's choice of project and this imposes a kind of externality on the bank. In particular, given that the firm receives $R - D$ if $R \geqslant D$ and 0 if $R < D$, we see that, if $D < 15$, the firm will choose project 1 since

$$(1/3)(0) + (1/3)(15 - D) + (1/3)(30 - D) > (4/5)(0) + (1/5)(40 - D) \quad (1)$$

On the other hand, if $35 \geqslant D > 15$, it is easy to see that the firm will choose project 2 (note that if $D > 35$, the firm's profit falls short of the manager's effort cost and so the firm won't borrow at all). Finally, if $D = 15$, the firm is just indifferent between the two projects.

The problem facing the bank is then the following. If it wants the firm to choose project 1, it must set $D \leqslant 15$. Since in this case, the bank's profit,

$$(1/3)(0) + (1/3)D + (1/3)D \quad (2)$$

is increasing in D, the bank will maximize profit by setting $D = 15$, yielding profit equal to 10. Note that under this arrangement the firm's return, given by the left-hand side of (1), is 5 and so, since this exceeds the manager's effort cost of 1, the firm will accept this contract.

On the other hand, the bank could choose $35 \geqslant D > 15$, but then it knows the firm will choose project 2. This means that the bank's profit is

$$(4/5)(0) + (1/5)(D) < 10 \tag{3}$$

Hence this strategy results in lower profit for the bank.

We see then that the profit-maximizing policy for the bank is to set $D = 15$ and have the firm select project 1.[2] But, with this contract, the firm gets a surplus of 4 from the transaction (expected return equal to 5 minus effort cost equal to 1). Hence in the second-best there will be credit rationing in equilibrium: the firms that do not receive the loan will be strictly worse off than the firm that does get the loan. To put it another way, the firms will fall over each other trying to be the lucky one to get the bank's funds.

This example captures the main aspects of the SW moral hazard theory of credit rationing. When the firm's choice of project is unobservable, an increase in interest rate, here represented by D, has two effects. One is to increase the bank's receipts, which is of course favorable to the bank. The second is to lead to a change in the firm's choice of project – in the above example this occurs at $D = 15$, but with more than two projects it can occur at several values of D or even continuously. This second effort may cause the bank's expected return to fall (it does in the above example) and this may more than offset the first effect. As a result, when there is an excess demand for loans, the bank may choose to ration customers rather than make the loan 'more expensive'. Hence rationing can be an equilibrium phenomenon.

Let me turn to a discussion and some criticisms of this theory. First, I think that the model, as it stands, is not completely satisfactory. A major problem is the treatment of bankruptcy. The assumption made is that in states where the firm goes bankrupt, i.e. $R \leqslant D$, the return R is paid to the bank. This is curious since R is meant to be observed only by the firm. Somehow it is being assumed that bankruptcy causes variables which are ordinarily private information to become public information. Now there could be something in this idea, given that bankrupt firms may be subject to thorough examination as part of the process of going into receivership. However, the assumption certainly needs to be backed up by a much more detailed and elaborate analysis of the bankruptcy process than is to be found in the SW papers.[3]

Moreover, even if we accept the assumption that R becomes observable in bankrupt states, the SW analysis must be modified. The point is that if R

is publically observable in certain states, then contingent contracts which make debt payments in these states a function of R can be written. In fact, in the simple example above, the first-best can be achieved in this way! Simply set $D > 40$, so that the firm goes bankrupt in every state. Then R is always publically observable and the first-best contract, in which the firm hands over all its profit except for £1, can be implemented. And, of course, this involves no credit rationing.

Now the idea that a contract is written which requires the firm to go bankrupt in every state is obviously absurd. The reason presumably is that bankruptcy is costly. This simply reinforces my previous point that the bankruptcy process – both in terms of its benefits and its costs – needs to be modelled more carefully.

What are likely to be the results of a more careful modelling of this process? First, as long as bankruptcy provides information about R, even if it is a costly process, contracts which make the firm's repayment partly contingent on R can and generally will be written. Such contracts, which contain certain profit-sharing features, do not have the simplicity (or even perhaps realism) of the SW debt contracts, and they are also more difficult to analyze. Analyze them one must, however, unless one is just going to rule them out on the grounds of complexity.

Secondly, these more complicated contracts, although they will surely not achieve the first-best, are *less* likely to generate credit rationing in equilibrium than the SW debt contracts, although it is by no means impossible that they will do so. The reason is that, when D can depend on R, there are more degrees of freedom in the contract, and this makes it easier for the bank to make the loan 'more expensive' at the same time as not upsetting incentives.

A simple example will illustrate this. Suppose the firm's manager has a von Neumann–Morgenstern utility function $U(I, p)$ where p stands for the project chosen and I is his remuneration (we allow the manager now to be risk averse, i.e. U may be concave). For each p, let $F(R; p)$ be the distribution function of the firm's return, given the choice of project p, and suppose that p can be represented by a real number. As in SW, suppose that the bank does not observe p, but, due to bankruptcy or for some other reason, it does observe R sometimes, so remuneration I can depend on R to some extent. In the extreme case where R is always (costlessly) observable, I can be chosen to be any function of R, and we are in the principal-agent world of, say, Holmstrom (1979).

In this extreme case, suppose the optimal second-best contract calls for a particular project, p^*, to be implemented. Then the bank must ensure that

$$\frac{d}{dp}\left[\int U(I(R), p)dF(R; p)\right] = 0 \quad \text{at } p = p^* \tag{4}$$

$$\int U(I(R), p^*)dF(R; p^*) \geq \bar{U} \tag{5}$$

where $\bar{U}$ is the manager's expected utility if he does not borrow from this bank. (5) says that the manager will be prepared to sign the contract, while (4) says that the manager's first-order conditions are satisfied at p^*. Under certain concavity conditions concerning the distribution functions F (see Rogerson (1985)), (4) is a sufficient condition for p^* to be chosen and we suppose that this is the case from now on.

Now the question of whether there is credit rationing turns on whether (5) holds with equality at the optimum. To put it another way, if there is inequality in (5), so that the manager is getting some surplus, the bank would like to 'pull down' the function $I(R)$ so as to increase its profits, but the question is whether it can do this at the same time as satisfying (4). It is intuitively clear that the more realizations of R there are, and hence the more possible remuneration levels $I(R)$ there are, the more likely it is that the bank can achieve this. To look at it slightly differently, the bank is trying to solve two equations and the more variables it has at its disposal the more likely it will be able to do this. (In the example analyzed previously, the reason for the credit rationing was that the bank had only one degree of freedom, D, and that was not enough to satisfy (4) and (5) with equality.)

It should be stressed that the number of degrees of freedom is not the only issue here. First, even if R takes on many values, it may be impossible to satisfy (4) and (5) with equality if I 'hits a corner'. For example, the way for the bank to increase profit without upsetting incentives may be, say, to reduce $I(R_1)$, $I(R_3)$ and $I(R_{17})$, but this may be impossible because some of these I's are already zero and the manager cannot be paid a negative amount. Secondly, in a more complicated model, p might be multidimensional. This increases the number of first order conditions (4) which must be satisfied, hence using up more degrees of freedom (and, more generally, the first-order conditions may have to be supplemented by second-order conditions). In spite of this second problem, it is shown in Grossman and Hart (1983) that if U is additively or multiplicatively separable, (5) will hold with equality at the second-best optimum, whatever the dimensionality of p, as long as there are no corners. Hence under these conditions, there will be no credit rationing in equilibrium.

The above discussion is for the extreme case where R is observable in every state and hence $I(\cdot)$ can be arbitrary function. Of course, if R is observable only in certain states, $I(\cdot)$ will be constrained, which is like reducing the number of variables the bank has to work with. Under these conditions, credit rationing is more likely, but it is still less probable than in the SW case where the bank has only the single instrument D at its disposal.

It should be evident from this discussion that I do not think that a careful modelling of bankruptcy will necessarily destroy the credit rationing result. Nor will the result necessarily be upset if additional degrees of freedom are available to the bank for other reasons. An important variable at the bank's disposal, for example, is the amount of collateral that the firm must provide, a variable set equal to zero in Stiglitz and Weiss (1981). Some authors (e.g. Bester (1985)) have argued that allowing variable collateral as well as variable interest rates will eliminate rationing in equilibrium. As SW show in the paper in this volume, however, this is not true in general (the present paper, though, is still open to the criticism that contracts which make D a function of R in bankruptcy states, although apparently feasible, are ruled out). The point essentially is that however many degrees of freedom are allowed, a sufficiently complicated model can be constructed such that the degrees of freedom are insufficient for the bank to be able to eliminate the firm's surplus without upsetting incentives. This is particularly true if, following SW, we enrich the model to include adverse selection as well as moral hazard. For example, suppose there are two types of potential customers, serious ones who invest the funds £F diligently and crooks who take the money and run off to Brazil (a similar assumption may be found in Jaffee and Russell (1976)). Assume that the bank cannot distinguish between these customers ex ante. Then if the bank tries to eliminate excess demand for loans by 'pulling down' the $I(\cdot)$ function, this will deter the serious customers, but not the crooks (who are not going to pay anything back anyway). The bank may therefore prefer to ration so as to keep both types in its pool. Of course, this is a case where collateral could be an excellent screening device, leading possibly to the elimination of the rationing.

Let me conclude. Economists have found it extremely difficult to derive equilibrium theories of rationing, and Joe Stiglitz and Andy Weiss deserve considerable credit for coming up with one of the few models which has at least a chance of success. My feeling though is that they have shown the *possibility* not the *probability* of credit rationing. Whether rationing will occur in a particular model depends on a delicate balance between the number of degrees of freedom at the bank's disposal and the number of the agent's decision variables or characteristics the bank is trying to control or screen for. More work at both the theoretical and empirical levels is required before we can assess the significance of the Stiglitz–Weiss theory or, for that matter, the empirical importance of credit rationing itself.

NOTES

* I would like to acknowledge helpful conversations with Martin Hellwig, Joe Stiglitz and Andy Weiss.

1 Hence there are informational asymmetries between the parties. Since these only materialize after the contract is signed, they are not of the adverse selection variety, but rather have the character of moral hazard.

2 With $D = 15$, the firm is exactly indifferent between the projects. We suppose that, in this case, if the bank asks the firm nicely, the firm will be prepared to choose project 1. An alternative assumption is that the bank sets D slightly below 15, in which case the firm strictly prefers 1.

3 The beginning of an analysis along these lines may be found in Gale and Hellwig (1985).

REFERENCES

Bester, H. (1985). 'Screening Versus Rationing in Credit Markets with Imperfect Information.' *American Economic Review*, **75**, 850–855.

Gale, D. and M. Hellwig (1985). 'Incentive-Compatible Debt Contracts: The One Period Problem.' *Review of Economic Studies*, **52**, 647–664.

Grossman, S. and O. Hart (1983). 'An Analysis of the Principal-Agent Problem.' *Econometrica*, **51**, 7–45.

Holmstrom, B. (1979). 'Moral Hazard and Observability.' *Bell Journal of Economics*, **10**, 74–91.

Jaffee, D. and T. Russell (1976). 'Imperfect Information and Credit Rationing.' *Quarterly Journal of Economics*, **90**, 657–666.

Keeton, W. R. (1979). *Equilibrium Credit Rationing*. Garland, New York.

Rogerson, W. (1985). 'The First-Order Approach to Principal-Agent Problems.' *Econometrica*, **53**, 1357–1368.

Stiglitz, J. E. and A. Weiss (1981). 'Credit Rationing in Markets with Imperfect Information.' *American Economic Review*, **71**, 393–410.

Weiss, A. (1980). 'Job Queues and Layoffs in Labor Markets with Flexible Wages.' *Journal of Political Economy*, **88**, 526–538.

6 Competitive banking in a simple model

LUCA ANDERLINI*

I Introduction

In general the assets of the banking system (the liabilities of the borrowers) are less liquid than its liabilities (the assets of the depositors). This is an obvious claim, and almost every textbook on the matter will include the transformation of illiquid assets into more liquid liabilities amongst the reasons for the very existence of a banking system. Some headway has recently been made in the modelling of this process (Diamond and Dybvig (1983), Smith (1984)). There are two key features which are common to all theoretical models of liquidity transformation. The depositors are unsure as to when they will want to withdraw, and production technology is such that early disinvestment is penalized; production takes time.

This paper also makes use of these two features. Its aim is precisely that of gaining further insight into the liquidity transformation process and its consequences. The specification of consumers which I use is more complex than that used in previous models in this line. The consequences are far reaching and I contrast the findings of this paper with results previously obtained in the concluding section.

The combination of an illiquid technology with consumers' 'desire for flexibility'[1] is enough to create the need for a financial intermediary with illiquid assets and more liquid liabilities. It is interesting that this is so without the introduction of any uncertainty in the technology. The banking system, transforming illiquid assets into more liquid ones for its depositors, provides a Pareto-superior equilibrium for the economy. Precisely this transforming role, however, opens the possibility of another 'bad' equilibrium: the bank run. If the liquidity transformation is ruined by a bank run, the resulting situation can be worse than the equilibrium for the economy without banks. This necessary 'instability' of the banking system seems to provide a good argument in favour of its regulation. I conjecture that there are regulations which will guarantee that the banking system as modelled in this paper will always work smoothly. This is the subject of my current research. Preliminary results seem to indicate that the richer structure of the present model makes the prevention of runs a much more complex problem than in simpler models in this line (Diamond and Dybvig (1983)).

For the sake of simplicity, I consider a finitely lived economy throughout the paper. This is completely inessential, and all the results of the paper also hold in a model where generations, all identical to the one I consider, overlap.

The paper is organized as follows. The model is set up in Section II. Section III analyzes the equilibrium of the model without a banking sector. The bank contract and its main features are examined in Section IV. In Section V a game setting for the bank contract is provided. The analysis of the equilibria of the banking game explains how bank runs can happen in the model. Section VI analyzes the competitive process amongst banks and Section VII contains some concluding remarks.

II The model

II.1 Technology

There is a single homogeneous good in the model. The production technology, which all agents have access to, is linear. To model the illiquidity of investment in the technology I make a distinction between the beginning of each time period, which is also the end of the previous one, and its mid-point. I make three assumptions about the technology.

Assumption II.1 Timing. Inputs for the technology have to be provided at the beginning of each period while consumption takes place at the mid-point.

Assumption II.2 Linearity. An amount $x \geq 0$ of the good invested in the technology at the beginning of period t will yield either a 'high' return Rx ($R > 1$) at the beginning of $t + 1$, or a 'low' one Lx ($L < 1$) if output is collected at the mid-point between t and $t + 1$.

Assumption II.3 No storage. Unless it is used as an input for the production technology, the good does not survive storage from one period to the next.

This is a crude but convenient way to model the illiquidity of physical investment in a world in which production takes time.

II.2 Consumers

Consumers form a continuum and they are ex-ante identical. They live

$N > 2$ periods and are endowed with one unit of the good at $t = 1$ and none thereafter. Their utility function is of the form

$$\sum_{t=1}^{N} \delta_t U(c_t)$$

where c_t, consumption at date t, is a non-negative scalar, and $U(\cdot): R_+ \to R$ is a strictly concave and increasing, bounded below, once continuously differentiable function satisfying $U'(x) \to +\infty$ as $x \to 0$. The discount rates form a stochastic process which I now make explicit. Let $\{\theta\}_{t=1}^{N-1}$ be a collection of i.i.d. random variables each taking M strictly positive values $\theta^1 < \theta^2 < \ldots < \theta^M$ with probability $\pi_1 > 0; \ldots; \pi_M > 0$ respectively.[2] Then

$$\delta_t = \begin{cases} 1 & \text{if } t = 1 \\ \delta_{t-1}\theta_{t-1} & \text{if } 1 < t \leqslant N \end{cases}$$

This stochastic process is identical and independent across consumers. So, because of the continuum hypothesis, π_i also represents the proportion of consumers observing the realization θ^i for δ_t. Consumers observe the realization of their δ_t at the beginning of the tth period. These realizations are private information and are not observable by any other agent in the model. Finally consumers are assumed, in each period, to maximize expected utility subject to the appropriate resource and informational constraints. These are set out in detail below.

III Equilibrium without banks

Since the realizations of each consumer's discount rates are private information, it is impossible for agents to write contracts for future delivery of the good contingent upon these realizations.

The information available to consumers is the same at the beginning and at the mid-point of each period. This has two important consequences: the facility allowing for early collection of a low output is never used since it is dominated by short-term storage, and markets can be assumed to open at the beginning of each period only. This implies immediately that, given the linear technology, arbitrate conditions determine the prices on the futures markets uniquely. The price at t of one unit of the good available at $t' > t$ must be $R^{(t-t')}$ units of current consumption good. These prices ensure that consumers will always be indifferent between trading consumption ahead and operating the technology. Hence there is no loss of generality in assuming that the competitive equilibrium for the model entails no trade at all.

Further characterization of the competitive equilibrium without banks calls for an analysis of the dynamic optimization problem that agents face. Let $(\Omega; \Gamma; \mu)$ be the probability space underlying the sequence of random variables $\{\theta_t\}_{t=1}^{N-1}$. Let then $(t = 1;\ldots; N)^3$ $\mathbf{h}_t = (\theta_1;\ldots; \theta_t)$ and Γ_t be the sub-σ-field generated by $\mathbf{h}_t$. Since consumers observe the realization of θ_t at the beginning of t, their behaviour can be summarized as follows: choose two sequences of random variables $\mathbf{c}_t$ and $\mathbf{w}_t$ so as to solve

$$
\text{Problem III.1}
\begin{cases}
\max E\left\{\sum_{t=1}^{N} \delta_t U(\mathbf{c}_t)\right\} \\
\text{s.t. } \mathbf{w}_{t+1} \leqslant R(\mathbf{w}_t - \mathbf{c}_t) \text{ for all } t \\
\mathbf{c}_t \text{ and } \mathbf{w}_{t+1}\ \Gamma_t\text{-measurable} \\
\mathbf{c}_t \geqslant 0;\ \mathbf{w}_t \geqslant 0 \text{ for all } t \\
\mathbf{w}_1 = 1
\end{cases}
$$

Problem III.1 is a standard stochastic dynamic programming one. Establishing the existence of a solution and its main properties only involves standard arguments. This is why the following is stated without proof (cf. Gale (1983), Chap. 2, part 2 and Mathematical Appendix).

Theorem III.1 Problem III.1 has a unique solution. Let this be $c_t(\mathbf{h}_t)$; $w_{t+1}(\mathbf{h}_t)$. Also define

$$
\text{Problems III.2}
\begin{cases}
H_{N-1}(w_{N-1}; \theta_{N-1}^i) = \max U(c_{N-1}) + \theta_{N-1}^i U(c_N) \\
\text{s.t. } c_N + Rc_{N-1} \leqslant Rw_{N-1} \\
c_N \geqslant 0 \quad c_{N-1} \geqslant 0
\end{cases}
$$

and let $c'_N(w_{N-1}; \theta_{N-1})$, $c'_{N-1}(w_{N-1}; \theta_{N-1})$ and $H_{N-1}(w_{N-1}; \theta_{N-1})$ be the random variables defined by the solution to the above. Define recursively $(t = N-2;\ldots; 1 \text{ and } w_1 = 1)$

$$
\text{Problems III.3}
\begin{cases}
H_t(w_t; \theta_t^i) = \max U(c_t) + \theta_t^i E[H_{t+1}(w_{t+1}; \theta_{t+1})] \\
\text{s.t. } w_{t+1} + Rc_t \leqslant Rw_t \\
w_{t+1} \quad c_t \geqslant 0
\end{cases}
$$

and let $c'_t(w_t; \theta_t)$, $w'_{t+1}(w_t; \theta_t)$ and $H_t(w_t; \theta_t)$ be the random variables defined by the solutions to the above problems. Define lastly $c'_1(\mathbf{h}_1) = c'_1(1; \theta_1)$ and $w'_2(\mathbf{h}_1) = w'_2(1; \theta_1)$ and by successive substitutions let $w'_{t+1}(\mathbf{h}_t) = w'_{t+1}[w'_t(\mathbf{h}_{t-1}); \theta_t]$ and $c'_t(\mathbf{h}_t) = c'_t[w'_t(\mathbf{h}_{t-1}); \mathbf{h}_t]$. Then $c_t(\mathbf{h}_t) = c'_t(\mathbf{h}_t)$ for $t = 1;\ldots; N$ and $w_{t+1}(\mathbf{h}_t) = w'_{t+1}(\mathbf{h}_t)$ for $t = 1;\ldots; N-2$. And finally, the solution to problem III.1 satisfies $c_t(h_t) > 0$ for all t.

Viewed from the beginning of each period, consumers' preferences are not affected by the realization of past θ_t's. Theorem III.1 simply says that as a consequence of this, consumption and investment decisions taken at t are solely a function of the amount of the good available to each consumer w_t

and the relevant available information θ_t. Having established the recursive nature of the solution to problem III.1 will be essential in Section IV below.

IV The bank deposit contract

In the equilibrium of the model described in Section III, consumers face privately observable risks. As a consequence of unobservability, simple competitive markets are unable to provide consumers with any insurance against the fluctuations of their future discount rates. Yet, owing to the absence of aggregate uncertainty, some insurance against such fluctuations can be provided: a particular insurance contract can be constructed which induces the consumers to 'reveal' truthfully the realizations of their discount rates in each period. I call the institution providing this insurance contract 'the bank'.

For the remainder of this section and in Section V below it is assumed that there is only one such institution which maximizes consumers' welfare subject to a resource constraint as in the definition of the optimal bank contract below. This assumption is dropped in Section VI where competition amongst banks is analyzed. There the competitive process is seen to lead to the offering of bank contracts which are optimal in the sense specified below (Definition IV.3). I now establish that the bank contract exists and that all consumers prefer it to what they can achieve operating the technology individually. Imagine initially that all consumers are required to deposit their endowment with the bank when they are born, and that the bank can observe the realizations of consumers' discount rates. The bank can then announce two sets of non-negative discrete functions

$$q_1(\theta_1; 1); q_2(\theta_2; b_2); \ldots; q_{N-2}(\theta_{N-2}; b_{N-2});$$

$$q_{N-1}(\theta_{N-1}; b_{N-1}); q_N(\theta_{N-1}; b_{N-1}) \tag{1}$$

$$b_2(\theta_1; 1); b_3(\theta_2; b_2); \ldots; b_{N-1}(\theta_{N-2}; b_{N-2})$$

The functions $q_t(\cdot)$ are to be interpreted as possible withdrawals at t given the balance b_t at the beginning of t and the realization θ_t. The functions $b_{t+1}(\cdot)$ are to be interpreted as balances for the beginning of $t+1$ resulting from actions taken at t. They could be rewritten as $b_{t+1}[q_t(\theta_t; b_t); b_t]$.

Because of the continuum hypothesis the resource constraint for the bank is an average one. Given the temporary assumption of observability of consumers' discount rates it is natural to stipulate that functions of the kind (1) are said to be resource feasible for the bank if they satisfy ($b_1 = 1$)

$$E[Rq_t(\mathbf{h}_t) + b_{t+1}(\mathbf{h}_t)] \leqslant RE[b_t(\mathbf{h}_{t-1})] \quad t = 1; \ldots; N-2$$

$$E[Rq_{N-1}(\mathbf{h}_{N-1}) + q_N(\mathbf{h}_{N-1})] \leqslant RE[b_{N-1}(\mathbf{h}_{N-2})] \tag{2}$$

where the functions $q_t(h_t)$ and $b_{t+1}(h_t)$ are obtained from (1) substituting forward as usual.

The bank on the other hand is not able to observe consumers' discount rates. Hence if functions like (1) are announced the bank will have to accept that a consumer aged t with a balance of b_t is free to choose amongst the M pairs

$$[q_t(\theta_t^1; b_t); b_{t+1}(\theta_t^1; b_t)]; \ldots; [q_t(\theta_t^M; b_t); b_{t+1}(\theta_t^M; b_t)]$$

As in all problems of incentive-compatibility, there is no loss of generality in imagining consumers 'reporting' the realization of their θ_t's to the bank. Reported realizations can of course be different from the true ones, but only in the case in which all consumers report truthfully the realizations of their discount rates does the resource constraint (2) makes sense. More notation is needed to analyze the problem.

The reported value of θ_t is indicated by θ_t'. Actions at t can only depend upon the information available at t. When this needs to be made explicit let $\theta_t'(\cdot): \Phi^t \to \Phi$ (where Φ is the common support of the random variables θ_t), defining $\theta_t'(h_t)$, represent this dependence. S_t denotes the space of all such measurable functions $\theta_t'(\cdot)$. Let now $_t r_{t+s}(h_{t+s}) = [\theta_t'(h_t); \ldots; \theta_{t+s}'(h_{t+s})]$ and analogously define $_t h_{t+s} = (\theta_t; \ldots; \theta_{t+s})$ and $_t \delta_{t+s} = \prod_{i=t-1}^{t+s-1} \theta_i$. For the sake of compactness in the notation let also $_t \delta_{t-1} = 1$.

An agent aged $1 \leqslant z \leqslant N-2$ faces the following problem. Discount rates are known up to δ_{z+1}, and past declarations determine a balance at the beginning of z and b_z. Given h_z he will report a value θ_z' and make plans on how to report future values of the θ_t's contingent upon their realizations. From (1), by successive substitutions, obtain present and future withdrawals as a function of b_z and present and future declarations. That is a set of functions $q_z(\theta_z'; b_z); \ldots; q_{N-1}(\theta_z'; \ldots; \theta_{N-1}'; b_z); q_N(\theta_z'; \ldots; \theta_{N-1}'; b_z)$. Then let

$$\delta_{z+1} Q_z(\theta_z'; b_z)$$

$$= \max E\left\{ \sum_{t=z+1}^{N} \delta_{z+1} \cdot {}_{z+2}\delta_t U\left[q_t[{}_{z+1} r_t({}_{z+1} h_t; h_z); b_{z+1}(b_z; \theta_z')]\right]\right\}$$

$$\theta_{z+1}(\cdot) \in S_{z+1}$$

$$\cdot$$

(3)

$$\cdot$$

$$\theta_{N-1}(\cdot) \in S_{N-1}$$

$\delta_{z+1} Q_z(\theta_z'; b_z)$ represents the maximum expected utility from $z+1$ onwards which a consumer starting z with a balance of b_z and observing h_z can achieve through any admissible set of declaration policies, as a function of his declaration at z, θ'_z. At $t = N - 1$ there is no uncertainty left for the consumers. Hence the analogue of the $Q_z(\cdot)$ functions for $t = N - 1$ can be simply defined as:

$$\delta_N Q_{N-1}(\theta'_{N-1}; b_{N-1}) = \delta_N U[q_N(\theta'_{N-1}; b_{N-1})] \tag{4}$$

At any $t = 1; \ldots; N - 1$, consumers will then choose to declare a value θ'_t such that

$$\delta_t U[q_t(\theta'_t; b_t)] + \delta_{t+1} Q_t(\theta'_t; b_t)$$

is maximized. Dividing through by δ_t one can define the optimal declarations $\theta^*_t(\theta_t; b_t)$ as the sets of values solving the problems

$$\max_{\theta'_t \in \Phi} U[q_t(\theta'_t; b_t)] + \theta_t Q_t(\theta'_t; b_t) \tag{5}$$

This unavoidably complex set-up justifies the following:

Definition IV.1 A set of withdrawal and balance functions as in (1) are sequentially incentive-compatible iff for all $t = 1; \ldots; N - 1$

$$\theta_t \in \theta^*_t(\theta_t; b_t) \text{ for all } (\theta_t; b_t)$$

It is now possible to state the main result of the paper. This takes the form of Theorems IV.1 and IV.2 below.

Theorem IV.1 There exists a set of withdrawal and balance functions which

i)   are sequentially incentive-compatible
ii) are resource feasible for the bank
iii) are preferred at $t = 1$ by all agents to what they can achieve operating the technology individually, that is

$$E\left\{ \sum_{t=1}^{N} \delta_t U[q_t(\mathbf{h}_t)] \,\Big|\, h_1 \right\} > E\left\{ \sum_{t=1}^{N} \delta_t U[c_t(\mathbf{h}_t)] \,\Big|\, h_1 \right\} \text{ for all } h_1$$

Proof See Appendix.

Definition IV.2 A set of withdrawal and balance functions enjoying properties i), ii) and iii) is called a viable bank contract.

The next definition has a two-fold justification. It identifies a set of bank contracts which enjoy two important properties. Firstly they meet an efficiency requirement subject to the resource and incentive-compatibility constraints. Secondly, as proved in Section VI below, these contracts constitute a competitive equilibrium for the bankers' market according to a familiar definition.

Definition IV.3 A set of withdrawal and balance functions such that, for all h_1,

$$E\left\{\sum_{t=1}^{N} \delta_t U[q_t(\mathbf{h}_t)] \,\middle|\, h_1\right\}$$

is maximized subject to

i) the withdrawal and balance functions are resource feasible for the bank
ii) the withdrawal and balance functions are sequentially incentive-compatible
iii) $Rq_1(h_1) + b_2(h_1) \leqslant R$ for all h_1

is called an optimal bank contract.

Since the constraint iii) imposed in the definition of the optimal bank contract is more stringent than the one of resource feasibility for the bank, it is not obvious that an optimal bank contract is necessarily viable. The theorem below, however, answers the question affirmatively.

Theorem IV.2 The optimal bank contract is unique and viable.

Proof See Appendix.

Theorems IV.1 and IV.2 say that a new equilibrium is possible for the model. Imagine a bank offering a viable bank contract at $t = 1$ and make the following four assumptions.

Assumption IV.1 Mid-point. When a bank offers a bank contract, withdrawals are only allowed at the mid-point of each period.

Assumption IV.2 No post-dated cheques. Futures markets in bank withdrawals are prohibited.

Assumption IV.3 Expectations. When a bank offers a viable bank contract all consumers expect it to honour its present and future commitments with probability one.

Assumption IV.4 Willingness to be truthful. When reporting the realizations of their θ_t's if the set of optimal reported values (as defined in (5)) contains untrue values as well as the true one, consumers always report the truth.

Assumptions IV.1 and IV.2 together with the no storage assumption II.3 rule out the reopening of markets in any period after consumers have withdrawn from the bank. Assumption IV.1 does not prevent consumers from enjoying the consumption of the good they withdraw because of the timing assumption II.1. Assumptions IV.3 and IV.4 ensure that when a viable bank contract is offered all consumers always report the truth and hence that the bank's resource constraint is never violated. By property iii) of viable bank contracts all consumers will be willing to deposit their initial endowments. So if a viable bank contract is offered at $t = 1$, a new, ex-ante Pareto-superior, equilibrium is obtained. The bank contract in itself constitutes a complete description of the new equilibrium.

To conclude this section I want to point out an interesting property of the viable and optimal bank contract. It implies non-linear pricing in terms of interest rates. The following is self-explanatory.

Definition IV.3 Consider the viable and optimal bank contract. The (gross) interest rate earned during t by a depositor aged $t = 1; \ldots; N - 2$ is

$$Z_t(\theta_t; b_t) = b_{t+1}(\theta_t; b_t) \cdot [b_t - q_t(\theta_t; b_t)]^{-1}$$

and for $t = N - 1$

$$Z_{N-1}(\theta_{N-1}; b_{N-1}) = q_N(\theta_{N-1}; b_{N-1}) \cdot [b_{N-1} - q_{N-1}(\theta_{N-1}; b_{N-1})]^{-1}$$

The theorem below then formalizes the claim.

Theorem IV.3 Consider the optimal and viable bank contract. For all $t = 2; \ldots; N - 1$ and for all b_t, there exists a pair $i \neq j$ $(i; j = 1; \ldots; M)$ such that

$$Z_t(\theta_t^i; b_t) \neq Z_t(\theta_t^j; b_t)$$

Proof See Appendix.

V The banking game

V.1 Embedding the bank contract in a game

Assumption IV.3 that consumers always expect the bank to honour its commitments is pretty unreasonable. If a fraction of positive measure of consumers deviates from truth-telling behaviour, the bank may not have enough of the good available to service all demands for withdrawals. The need for consumers to take into account what other depositors are doing is evident. A general result can be obtained without fully specifying a bankruptcy rule for the bank.

Consider a viable bank contract. To make explicit the dependence of each consumer's pay-off on other consumers' actions define the (identical and independent across consumers) random variables[4]

$$\mathbf{g}(\theta_t'; b_t; M_t) = \begin{cases} q_t(\theta_t'; b_t) \text{ with probability one if} \\ M_t = \{E[q_t(\mathbf{h}_t)]; \ldots; E[q_1)\mathbf{h}_1)]\} \\ \mathbf{g}_t \text{ such that } E[\mathbf{g}_t | \theta_t'; b_t; M_t] \leqslant q_t(\theta_t'; b_t) \\ \text{if } M_t \neq \{E[q_t(\mathbf{h}_t); \ldots; E[q_1(\mathbf{h}_1)]\} \end{cases} \tag{6}$$

where M_t represents the sequence of attempted withdrawals up to t. This defines a pay-off rule postulating that if up to t average attempted withdrawals have been regular (i.e. 'as if' every depositor had been reporting the truth), then the bank will honour its commitment to pay upon request according to the reported θ'_t with probability one. If average attempted withdrawals deviate from their normal value at or before t, the pay-off from declaring θ'_t is a random variable (which can be degenerate of course) with an expected value no greater than in case of regular withdrawals. Full specification of the pay-off rules would involve full specification of a bankruptcy rule for the bank. For the moment the $g_t(\cdot)$ are any random variables satisfying (6).

As in Section IV, at each date $1 \leqslant t \leqslant N-1$ depositors choose a value θ'_t to report in the current period and a set of reporting policies $\theta'_{t+1}(\cdot); \ldots; \theta'_{N-1}(\cdot)$ for future periods. In this section they make their choice as Nash players, taking other consumers' actions and plans as given.

Assume that consumers with an identical history always behave in an identical way. If a truthful option is in the optimal set of actions then assumption IV.4 on the willingness to be truthful is sufficient to guarantee this. If not, any arbitrary rule guaranteeing this can be imagined to apply. Notice then that a set of functions $\theta'_t(\cdot)$ can be interpreted as both contingent reporting plans for a given consumer and distributions of reported realizations across consumers.

Consider now the model in period $1 \leqslant z \leqslant N-1$ and let $b'_z(h_{z-1}) = b_z[r_{z-1}(h_{z-1})]$ represent the distribution of balances across depositors at the beginning of z, and B_z be the space of all possible distributions of balances at z. Given $b'_z(\cdot)$ and each consumer's present reported value and reporting plans define, for each $t \geqslant z$

$$\tilde{q}_t(\cdot): B_z \times S_z \times \ldots \times S_t \to R_t \text{ defining } \tilde{q}_t = E\{q_t[_zr_t(_z\mathbf{h}_t); b'_z(\mathbf{h}_{z-1})]\} \tag{7}$$

as attempted withdrawals at t. Actual realized withdrawals at t could be defined on the basis of attempted withdrawals and the pay-off rules (6). In the notation just established one has

$$M_t = [\tilde{q}_1; \ldots; \tilde{q}_t]$$

so that, again taking everything that happened before $1 \leqslant z \leqslant N-1$ (including $\tilde{q}_1; \ldots; \tilde{q}_{z-1}$) as given one can let for all $t \geqslant z$

$$_zM_t(\cdot): B_z \times S_z \times \ldots \times S_t \to R^t_+ \text{ defining}$$
$$_zM_t(\cdot) = [\tilde{q}_1; \ldots; \tilde{q}_{z-1}; \tilde{q}_z(\cdot); \ldots; \tilde{q}_t(\cdot)] \tag{8}$$

This defines for each period $t \geqslant z$ the sequence of average realized withdrawals up to $t-1$ and attempted withdrawals at t as determined by the state of the model at z and actions and plans from z to t.

Analogously to the functions (3) used to define sequential incentive-compatibility let $1 \leqslant z \leqslant N - 2$

$$\delta_{z+1} P_z[\theta'_z; b'_z(h_{z-1}); \theta'_z(\cdot); \ldots; \theta'_{N-1}(\cdot); b'_z(\cdot)]$$

$$= \max E\left\{ \sum_{t=z+1}^{N} \delta_{z+1} \cdot {}_{z+2}\delta_t U[\mathbf{g}_t[_{z+1}r_t(_{z+1}\mathbf{h}_t; h_z); b_{z+1}(b'_z(h_{z-1}); \theta'_z); {}_zM_t(\cdot)]] \right\}$$

$$\theta_{z+1}(\cdot) \in S_{z+1} \tag{9}$$

.

.

$$\theta_{N-1}(\cdot) \in S_{N-1}$$

and for $z = N - 1$ let

$$\delta_N P_{N-1}[\theta'_{N-1}; b'_{N-1}(h_{N-2}); \theta'_{N-1}(\cdot); b'_{N-1}(\cdot)]$$

$$= E\{\delta_N U[\mathbf{g}_N(\theta'_{N-1}; b'_{N-1}(h_{N-2}); {}_{N-1}M_N(\cdot))]\} \tag{10}$$

Definitions (9) and (10) are the exact analogues of (3) and (4), except that here the effect of other depositors' actions and plans through the pay-off rules and the withdrawal mappings ${}_zM_t(\cdot)$ is taken into account. Finally let $\theta_z^{**}[\theta_z; b'_z(h_{z-1}); \theta'_z(\cdot); \ldots; \theta'_{N-1}(\cdot); b'_z(\cdot)]$ be the set of θ'_z solving

$$\max_{\theta'_z \in \Phi} E\{ U[\mathbf{g}_z[\theta'_z; b'_z(h_{z-1}); {}_zM_z(\cdot)]] \}$$

$$+ \theta_z P_z[\theta'_z; b'_z(h_{z-1}); \theta'_z(\cdot); \ldots; \theta'_{N-1}(\cdot); b'_z(\cdot)] \tag{11}$$

Since $\theta_z^{**}(\cdot)$ is the set of optimal θ'_z declarations for an agent starting at z with $b'_z(h_z)$ taking as given all other agents' present declarations and plans for the future, as well as everything that happened before z, this set-up prompts the following

Definition V.1 Given $b'_z(\cdot)$ and $\tilde{q}_1; \ldots; \tilde{q}_{z-1}$, a set of functions $\theta'_z(\cdot); \ldots; \theta'_{N-1}(\cdot)$ constitutes a sequential Nash equilibrium for the banking game starting at $1 \leqslant z \leqslant N - 1$ iff, for all $t \geqslant z$ and all h_t,

$$\theta'(h_t) \in \theta_t^{**}\{\theta_t; b_t[_zr_t(h_t); b'_z(h_{z-1})]; \theta'_z(\cdot); \ldots; \theta'_{N-1}(\cdot); b'_z(\cdot)\}$$

The main result of this section amounts to a formalization in a multi-period model of the claim that if an allocation is incentive-compatible then there must be a contract structure which implements it as a Nash equilibrium. A preliminary result is needed.

Lemma V.1 Consider the viable and optimal bank contract. Then for all

$1 \leqslant z \leqslant N - 1$ and b_z

$$\delta_{z+1} Q_z(\theta'_z; b_z) = E \left\{ \sum_{t=z+1}^{N} \delta_{z+1} \cdot_{z+2} \delta_t U[q_t[_{z+1} \mathbf{h}_t; b_{z+1}(b_z; \theta'_z)]] \right\}$$

Proof See Appendix (Lemma A.6).

Lemma V.1 says that if depositors expect the bank to honour its commitments with probability one and the optimal contract is offered, then starting from any balance and any current declaration in a given period, they cannot do better for themselves than plan to report their true characteristics in all following periods.

The above mentioned result in Nash equilibria is stated as

Theorem V.1 Consider the viable and optimal bank contract and a given $1 \leqslant z \leqslant N - 1$. Let $b'_z(h_{z-1}) = b_z(h_{z-1})$ (if $z = 1$ let $b'_1 = 1$) and $\tilde{q}_1 = E[q_1(h_1)];$ $\ldots; \tilde{q}_{z-1} = E[q_{z-1}(h_{z-1})]$ be given. Then the set of truthful functions

$$\theta'_z(h_z) = \theta_z \text{ for all } h_z; \; \theta'_{N-1}(h_{N-1}) = \theta_{N-1} \text{ for all } h_{N-1}$$

constitute a sequential Nash equilibrium for the banking game starting at z.

Proof From truthfulness and the given past history of regular withdrawals clearly it must be that $M_t = \{E[q_1(\mathbf{h}_1)]; \ldots; E[q_t(\mathbf{h}_t)]\}$ for all $t \geqslant z$. Then from (6)

$$\mathbf{g}_t(\theta'_t; b_t; M_t) = q_t(\theta'_t; b_t) \text{ for all } t \geqslant N \text{ and } b_t$$

by the definition of $P_t(\cdot)$, and by Lemma V.1 this implies that for all $t \geqslant z+1$ and h_t (if $t = z$ the notation changes in an obvious way)

$$P_t\{\theta'_t; b_t[_z r_{t-1}(h_{t-1}); b'_z(h_z)]; \theta'_t(\cdot); \ldots; \theta'_{N-1}(\cdot); b_t[_z r_{t-1}(\cdot); b'_z(\cdot)]\} = Q_t[\theta'_t; b_t(h_{t-1})]$$

These two equalities in turn directly yield, for all $t \geqslant z$ and h_t

$$\theta_t^{**}\{\theta_t; b_t[_z r_{t-1}(h_{t-1}); b'_z(h_{z-1})]; \theta'_t(\cdot); \ldots; \theta'_{N-1}(\cdot); b_t[_z r_{t-1}(\cdot); b'_z(\cdot)]\}$$
$$= \theta_t^*[\theta_t; b_t(h_{t-1})]$$

By sequential incentive-compatibility of viable bank contracts the last equality implies that, for all $t \geqslant z$ and h_t

$$\theta_t \in \theta_t^{**}\{\theta_t; b_t[_z r_{t-1}(h_{t-1}); b'_z(h_{z-1})]; \theta'_t(\cdot); \ldots; \theta'_{N-1}(\cdot); b_t[_z r_{t-1}(\cdot); b'_z(\cdot)]$$

which proves the theorem.

V.2 Multiple Nash equilibria bank runs

Theorem V.1 does not claim uniqueness of equilibrium. Multiplicity of equilibria turns out to be crucial in the explanation of bank runs. The results obtained on this matter are, predictably, extremely sensitive to the specification of different bankruptcy rules. The following rule has been called the 'sequential service constraint' (Diamond and Dybvig (1983)): *in every period, agents attempting to withdraw from the bank are served in full at random until the bank runs out of assets.*

To formalize the sequential service constraint a definition of the bank's assets in each period is needed. Consider the beginning of a period $1 \leqslant z \leqslant N - 1$, and the viable and optimal bank contract. Assume that the distribution of balances $b_z'(\cdot)$ is 'as if' all consumers had been truthful up to $z - 1$. That is let $b_z'(h_{z-1}) = b_z(h_{z-1})$ for all h_{z-1}. The bank knowing its future commitments will invest an amount $E[b_z(\mathbf{h}_{z-1})] - E[q_z(\mathbf{h}_z)]$, and will store until the mid-point (when the withdrawal requests are presented), an amount $E[q_z(\mathbf{h}_z)]$ in order to cover withdrawals. Because of assumption II.2 stipulating the low return L for early disinvestment, the total liquidation value of the bank's assets at the mid-point of z is

$$A_z = E[q_z(\mathbf{h}_z)] + L \cdot E[b_z(\mathbf{h}_{z-1}) - q_z(\mathbf{h}_z)] \tag{12}$$

To model the effects of the sequential service constraint I assume that the $g_t(\cdot)$ random variables satisfy (*in addition* to (6))

$$\text{if } \tilde{q}_1 = E[q_1(\mathbf{h}_1)]; \ldots; \tilde{q}_{t-1} = E[q_{t-1}(\mathbf{h}_{t-1})]$$

$$\text{then } \mathbf{g}_t(\theta_t'; b_t; M_t) = \begin{cases} q_t(\theta_t'; b_t) & \text{with prob. } p_t = \min(1; A_t \cdot \tilde{q}_t^{-1}) \\ 0 & \text{with prob. } 1 - p_t \end{cases} \tag{13}$$

and

$$\text{if there exists a } z < t \text{ for which } \tilde{q}_z \geqslant A_z$$

$$\text{then } g_t(\theta_t'; b_t; M_t) = 0 \text{ with prob. } 1 \tag{14}$$

Specification (13) says that if attempted withdrawals are regular up to $t - 1$ and are equal to $\tilde{q}_t > A_t$ at t then only a fraction $A_t \cdot \tilde{q}_t^{-1}$ of requests can be serviced and that this is done randomly. Depositors can be imagined to join randomly a queue at the bank, and the bank to be constrained to service depositors sequentially until all its assets have been liquidated. Specification (14) more simply stipulates that if in any period the bank is forced to liquidate all its assets, it will be unable to service any withdrawal requests in any of the subsequent periods.

Notice that (6), (13) and (14) still do not constitute a full specification of the bank's actions when withdrawals deviate from normal. Many intermediate cases in which $E[q_t(\mathbf{h}_t)] < \tilde{q}_t < A_t$ are possible. Full specification would greatly complicate the analysis. What I have introduced, however, is enough to prove

Theorem V.2 Consider the optimal and viable bank contract and $1 \leqslant z \leqslant N - 1$. Let $\tilde{q}_1 = E[q_1(\mathbf{h}_1)]; \ldots; \tilde{q}_{z-1} = [q_{z-1}(\mathbf{h}_{z-1})]$ and $b'(h_z) = b_z(h_z)$ for all h_z. Assume that the pay-off rules $\mathbf{g}_t(\cdot)$ satisfy the sequential service constraint. That is, assume they satisfy (13) and (14) as well as (6). Then, if L is sufficiently low, in addition to the truthful functions of Theorem V.1 the following constitute a sequential Nash equilibrium for the banking game starting at z

$$\theta'_z(h_z) = \theta'_z \in \Phi \text{ such that } q_z[\theta'_z; b_z(h_{z-1})] \text{ is maximized}$$

and any functions

$$\theta'_{z+1} \in S_{z+1}; \ldots; \theta'_{N-1} \in S_{N-1}$$

Such an equilibrium is called a bank run.

Proof From the Appendix (Theorem A.2) for all h_{z-1}

$$\max_{\theta_z \in \Phi} q_z[\theta'_z; b_z(h_{z-1})] > E\{q_z[\theta_z; b_z(h_{z-1})]\}$$

and hence if the declarations distribution is as above

$$\tilde{q}_z > E[q_z(\mathbf{h}_z)]$$

For L sufficiently low this implies

$$\tilde{q}_z > A_z$$

So by (14) $P_z(\cdot)$ simply does not vary with any of its arguments. Hence whatever the distribution of future declarations $\theta_z^{**}[\theta_z; b_z(h_{z-1})]$ is by definition the set of $\theta'_z \in \Phi$ maximizing

$$E\{U[\mathbf{g}_z[\theta'_z; b_z(h_{z-1}); M_z]]\}$$

and this by (13) directly implies the theorem.

The bank run Nash equilibrium described in Theorem V.2 is one in which depositors 'panic' about the bank. They all think that the bank will not be able to honour its future commitments, and as a result they attempt to withdraw as much as possible immediately. This indeed forces the bank to liquidate all its assets and hence prevents it from being able to honour its future commitments: a 'bad' Nash equilibrium.

The possibility of a bank run occurring is in no way connected with the actual financial state of the bank. It can, exactly as in the pioneering article by Diamond and Dybvig (1983), be caused by anything that causes depositors to panic: a bad economic forecast, or even sunspots (Azariadis (1981)). The illiquidity of physical investment and the agents' desire for flexibility determining the characteristics of the viable and optimal bank contract are sufficient to generate runs if agents panic.

Theorem V.2 states that if up to any period z average realized withdrawals are regular and if the sequential service constraint is in operation then a run on the bank is always possible at z. But if one takes the position that outcomes must match anticipations further questions immediately arise.

Imagine that runs are caused by a sunspot variable and that depositors anticipate correctly their probability. Then, starting from the first period, their behaviour will be affected by such an anticipation. They could clearly even decide not to deposit their endowment at the bank despite the dominance property iii) of viable bank contracts (Theorem IV.1). The assumption in Theorem 5.2 that up to $z - 1$ average realized withdrawals are regular evidently ignores this possibility.

I have no formal answer to the question of the effect of depositors anticipating runs with positive probability on the sequential Nash equilibria of the banking game. I conjecture that the key to tackling successfully this problem is giving consumers the choice of depositing only part of their endowment. This would provide them with at least partial insurance against bank runs.

VI Competitive equilibrium

Two interesting questions stem from the non-uniqueness result of the previous section: the effects of the anticipation of runs, and whether there exist bankruptcy rules which rule out runs altogether. The analysis of these questions would logically precede the problem analyzed in this section. In analyzing competition amongst banks however I shall ignore this problem and assume again that agents expect the bank to honour its commitments with probability one. In the light of Theorem V.2 this assumption does not contradict familiar equilibrium concepts. If all depositors expect the bank to honour its commitments with probability one, by sequential incentive-compatibility they will all reveal truthfully their discount rates. By doing so they will enable the bank to honour its commitments in every period and hence to fulfill their expectations. Given this expectations assumption each consumer's expected utility from buying a bank contract is a well defined quantity once the contract is specified.

Imagine now that agents are free to engage actively in banking. They are, in other words, free to offer bank contracts in exchange for deposits in competition with other bank contracts being offered. To analyze the outcome of this process I make the following three assumptions.

Assumption VI.1 Nash behaviour. Bank contracts are offered taking the existing set of bank contracts on offer as given.

Assumption VI.2 No parallel activity.[5] Bank contracts which do not require the deposit of the full initial endowment are prohibited.

Assumption VI.3 Identical declarations. Agents observing identical realizations of their discount rates always report identical values for such realizations.

In addition to the above three I also postulate that assumptions IV.1 (Mid-point), IV.2 (No post-dated cheques), IV.3 (Expectations) and IV.4 (Willingness to be truthful) hold.

In Section IV I pointed out that assumptions IV.1–IV.4 rule out the reopening of markets at any date $t > 1$. In an exactly analogous way they rule out the possibility of any depositor 'changing banks' after depositing at the beginning of $t = 1$. The competition for depositors only takes place at $t = 1$.

Consider now an arbitrary bank contract. Because of the identical declarations assumption VI.3 there is no loss of generality in assuming that each of the optimal declarations sets $\theta_t^*(\theta_t; b_t)$ contains only one element. Let $\theta_t^*(h_t)$ be obtained from these by substituting forward. Let also $h_t^*(h_t) = [\theta_t^*(h_t); \ldots; \theta_1^*(h_1)]$. These are, contingent upon the realized h_t, the declarations that agents buying the contract make. Suppose now that only agents having observed h_1 in a particular set, say E, buy the contract in question at the beginning of $t = 1$. In calculating average withdrawals in each period the bank offering such a contract will have to consider both the declaration policies $h_t^*(h_t)$ and the particular subset of agents buying the contract. This prompts the following

Definition VI.1 Suppose that only agents such that $h_1 \in E$ buy a given bank contract. Then the contract is said to make non-negative profit iff for all $t = 1; \ldots; N - 2$ it satisfies ($b_1 = 1$)

$$E\{Rb_t[h_{t-1}^*(\mathbf{h}_{t-1})] - Rq_t[h_t^*(\mathbf{h}_t)] - b_{t+1}[h_t^*(\mathbf{h}_t)] \,|\, h_1 \in E\} \geq 0 \qquad (15)$$

and for $t = N - 1$

$$E\{Rb_{N-1}[h_{N-2}^*(\mathbf{h}_{N-2})] - Rq_{N-1}[h_{N-1}^*(\mathbf{h}_{N-1})]$$
$$- q_N[h_{N-1}^*(\mathbf{h}_{N-1})] \,|\, h_1 \in E\} \geq 0 \qquad (16)$$

In analyzing competition amongst banks one cannot restrict attention to bank contracts which satisfy the sequential incentive-compatibility requirement. For this reason in Definition VI.1 the sequences of optimal declarations $h_t^*(\cdot)$ are used rather than the actual realizations h_t. This however causes a further problem. Two, or more, bank contracts which differ only in their 'labelling' could be on offer. In other words, bank contracts which after taking into account depositors' declarations are identical could be offered. To take into account this possibility I state

Definition VI.2 Consider two bank contracts $q_t(\cdot)$ and $q_t'(\cdot)$. Let also $h_t^*(\cdot)$

and $h_t^{*\prime}(\cdot)$ be the declaration sequences which they respectively cause. Imagine now that contract $q_t(\cdot)$ is bought by agents such that $h_1 \in E$ and contract $q_t'(\cdot)$ is bought by agents such that $h_1 \in E'$, and that $E' \cap E$ is not empty. Then the two contracts are said to be substantially different iff there exists t and $h_1 \in E' \cap E$ such that for some h_t

$$q_t[h_t^*(h_t)] \neq q_t'[h_t^{*\prime}(h_t)] \tag{17}$$

A definition of competitive equilibrium can now be given. This is, except for the fact that the possibility of relabelling of contracts is excluded, completely analogous to the one often used in the analysis of competitive insurance markets (Rothschild and Stiglitz (1976)). In view of the Nash behaviour assumption VI.1 this is

Definition VI.3 A set C of bank contracts constitutes a (Nash) competitive equilibrium for the banking sector iff, when agents choose contracts maximizing expected utility,

a) all contracts in C make non-negative profit,
b) there is no contract, substantially different from all contracts in C, which if offered would make non-negative profit.

Finally, the following supports the use of the optimal bank contract, rather than any viable one, throughout the analysis of the banking game.

Theorem VI.1 The optimal and viable bank contract constitutes a competitive equilibrium for the banking sector.

Proof See Appendix.

VII Conclusions

In this paper the banking system transforms illiquid assets into more liquid ones. The latter are preferred by consumers because of their desire for flexibility. There is another interesting way to view the matter. In the equilibrium of the economy without banks there are missing markets because of the unobservability of discount rates. Contracts contingent upon the realization of the discount rates are not available. The truthful competitive equilibrium with a banking system provides an allocation which is better for all agents than the one without banks. It does not however provide the agents with the fully optimal allocation: the one they would achieve if there were no missing markets, that is if the realizations of the discount rates were observable. The sequential incentive-compatibility constraint 'bites'. This is in contrast with the result obtained by Diamond and Dybvig (1983) in their pioneering paper on the liquidity transformation process. In their model agents live three periods and *either* want to consume when aged 2 *or* when aged 3. This extreme assumption makes the allocation achieved by competitive markets when discount rates are observable incentive-compatible. Hence the banking sector is able to provide it. The fact that in the present model agents want to consume in every period yields this important difference in the two results.

The more complex set-up on the consumers' side which I used in this paper also makes it more difficult to rule out untruthful equilibria for the banking game. A simple bankruptcy rule which they call 'suspension of convertibility' excludes the possibility of untruthful equilibria in the Diamond and Dybvig model. In the present model if a bank is allowed to stop servicing withdrawals before it has to liquidate early any investment it clearly will not go bankrupt. However, this suspension of convertibility mechanism in the present model would not rule out untruthful equilibria for the banking game. One of the reasons for this is the richer dynamic structure of the present model. For a competitive bank that just breaks even an excess of liquidity is as bad as a liquidity squeeze. Roughly speaking, this is because the only way the bank has to increase its liquidity is to fail to invest enough in the technology. Hence a bank trying to increase its liquidity during t may not be left with enough resources to cover depositors' balances at the beginning of $t + 1$.

In addition to particular bankruptcy rules it is also natural to ask what are the effects of the presence of a lender of last resort or of deposit insurance schemes. Together with the effects of the anticipation of runs on both the banking game and the competitive equilibrium for the bankers' market these questions evidently merit further research.

Finally, Theorem VI.1 on the competitive equilibrium for the banking sector owes everything to the assumption of ex-ante identical consumers. Rothschild and Stiglitz (1976) have shown in the context of insurance markets that if agents are not ex-ante identical a competitive (Nash) equilibrium need not exist. I conjecture that this also holds true for the present model. This further 'instability' of the banking system in a model like the one by Diamond and Dybvig developed by Smith (1984) produces the rationale for an interest rate ceiling regulation. In general such non-existence results seem to constitute a further argument for the regulation of banks.

APPENDIX

Here I establish the existence and main features of the viable and optimal bank contract and prove Theorem VI.1. A number of technical lemmas are needed first.

Lemma A.1 Dominance. Let $V(\cdot): R_+ \to R$ be a bounded below, strictly increasing and concave, continuous function. Let also $U(\cdot): R_+ \to R$ be a function as set out in Section II.2. Consider then the two problems

Problem A.1
$$\begin{cases} \max \sum_{i=1}^{M} \pi_i[U(c_{1i}) + \theta^i V(c_{2i})] \\ \text{s.t. } Rc_{1i} + c_{2i} \leqslant Rw \text{ for all } i \\ c_{1i} \geqslant 0 \quad c_{2i} \geqslant 0 \text{ for all } i \end{cases}$$

and

Problem A.2
$$\begin{cases} \max \sum_{i=1}^{M} \pi_i[U(q_{1i}) + \theta^i V(q_{2i})] \\ \text{s.t. } \sum_{i=1}^{M} \pi_i(Rq_{1i} + q_{2i}) \leqslant Rw \\ U(q_{1i}) + \theta^i V(q_{2i}) \geqslant U(q_{1j}) + \theta^i V(q_{2j}) \text{ for all } i \neq j \\ q_{1i} \geqslant 0 \quad q_{2i} \geqslant 0 \text{ for all } i \end{cases}$$

Let now $(c_{11}^*; c_{12}^*; \ldots; c_{1M}^*; c_{21}^*; \ldots; c_{2M}^*)$ and $(q_{11}^*; q_{12}^*; \ldots; q_{1M}^*; q_{21}^*; \ldots; q_{2M}^*)$ be the arrays solving Problems A.1 and A.2 respectively. Define finally

$$G(w) = \sum_{i=1}^{M} \pi_i[U(c_{1i}^*) + \theta^i V(c_{2i}^*)]$$

and

$$D(w) = \sum_{i=1}^{M} \pi_i[U(q_{1i}^*) + \theta^i V(q_{2i}^*)]$$

Then if for all i $c_{1i}^* > 0$ and $c_{2i}^* > 0$

$$D(w) > G(w) \text{ for all } w > 0$$

Proof Problem A.1 is a standard one and there is no need to prove it has a solution. The opportunity set of Problem A.2 is evidently compact. It is also non-empty since the solution to Problem A.1 belongs to it. Hence by continuity of the objective function Problem A.2 has a solution. Notice now that, for all i, $(c_{1i}^*; c_{2i}^*)$ must solve

Problems A.3
$$\begin{cases} \max U(c_{1i}) + \theta^i V(c_{2i}) \\ \text{s.t. } Rc_{1i} + c_{2i} \leqslant w \\ c_{1i} \geqslant 0 \quad c_{2i} \geqslant 0 \end{cases}$$

otherwise an immediate contradiction of their maximality for Problem A.1 is obtained. By strict concavity of the objective function each one of

Problems A.3 has a unique solution. This together with the assumption that $c_{1i}^* > 0$, $c_{2i}^* > 0$ for all i is enough to establish that

$$U(c_{1i}^*) + \theta^i V(c_{2i}^*) > U(c_{1j}^*) + \theta^i V(c_{2j}^*) \text{ for all } i \neq j \tag{A.1}$$

Since $(c_{11}^*; \ldots; c_{1M}^*; c_{21}^*; \ldots; c_{2M}^*)$ belongs to the opportunity set of Problem A.2 to prove the Lemma it is enough to establish that $(c_{11}^*; \ldots; c_{1M}^*; c_{21}^*; \ldots; c_{2M}^*)$ does not solve Problem A.2. Suppose then that the Lemma is false and so assume that $(c_{11}^*; \ldots; c_{1M}^*; c_{21}^*; \ldots; c_{2M}^*)$ solves Problem A.2. From the inequalities (A.1), given two indices $i \neq j$, one can assume without loss of generality that

$$c_{1i}^* > c_{1j}^* \Leftrightarrow U'(c_{1i}^*) < U'(c_{1j}^*) \tag{A.2}$$

Choose then two real numbers $\delta_i < 0$ and $\delta_j > 0$ such that

$$\pi_i \delta_i + \pi_j \delta_j = 0 \tag{A.3}$$

and

$$c_{1i}^* + \delta_i > c_{1j}^* + \delta_j \tag{A.4}$$

Define next

$$\Delta U_i = U(c_{1i}^* + \delta_i) - U(c_{1i}^*) < 0$$
$$\Delta U_j = U(c_{1j}^* + \delta_j) - U(c_{1j}^*) > 0 \tag{A.5}$$

applying the mean value theorem, there exist $f_i \in (c_{1i}^* + \delta_i; c_{1i}^*)$ and $f_j \in (c_{1j}^*; c_{1j}^* + \delta_j)$ such that

$$\pi_i \Delta U_i + \pi_j \Delta U_j = \pi_i \delta_i U'(f_i) + \pi_j \delta_j U'(f_j) \tag{A.6}$$

but from (A.4) it must also be the case that

$$U'(f_i) < U'(f_j) \tag{A.7}$$

Combining (A.3), (A.6), and (A.7) one finally has

$$\pi_i \Delta U_i + \pi_j \Delta U_j > U'(f_i)(\pi_i \delta_i + \pi_j \delta_j) = 0 \tag{A.8}$$

Now, by (A.1) and (A.3) and, for δ_i and δ_j sufficiently small it is feasible in Problem (A.2) to increase c_{1j}^* by δ_j and to decrease c_{1i}^* by δ_i. By (A.8) this also increases expected utility and so $(c_{11}^*; \ldots; c_{1M}^*; c_{21}^*; \ldots; c_{2M}^*)$ cannot solve Problem A.2. This is enough to establish Lemma 1.

Lemma A.2 Continuity. The quantity $D(w)$ is a continuous function of w.

Proof Standard results ensure that the claim is true provided that the opportunity set of Problem A.2 is both upper- and lower-hemicontinuous in w. Let $F(w)$ be the opportunity set of Problem A.2 given w. If $\tilde{q}$ represents the array $(q_{11}; \ldots; q_{1M}; q_{21}; \ldots; q_{2M})$, $F(w)$ can be concisely written as

$$F(w) = \{\tilde{q} \in R_+^{2M} \mid w - h(\tilde{q}) \geqslant 0; \bar{m}(\tilde{q}) \geqslant 0\} \tag{A.9}$$

where $h(\cdot): R_+^{2M} \to R_+$ is linear and continuous and increasing in all the components of $\tilde{q}$ and $\bar{m}(\cdot): R_+^{2M} \to R^{M \times M}$ is continuous in all its components with respect to all the elements of $\tilde{q}$.

To prove upper-hemicontinuity one needs to show that given any two non-negative sequences $w^k \to w^0$ and $\tilde{q}^k \to \tilde{q}^0$ such that $\tilde{q}^k \in F(w^k)$ for all k then $\tilde{q}^0 \in F(w^0)$. Suppose then to have two such sequences and that $\tilde{q}^0$ does not belong to $F(w^0)$. Then by definition, it must be

$$\text{either } w^0 - h(\tilde{q}^0) < 0 \tag{A.10}$$

or (for at least one component) $\bar{m}(\tilde{q}^0) < 0$.

Since $\tilde{q}^k \to \tilde{q}^0$, by continuity of $h(\cdot)$ and $\bar{m}(\cdot)$, for k sufficiently large it must be

$$\text{either } w^0 - h(\tilde{q}^k) < 0$$
$$\text{or (for at least one component) } \bar{m}(\tilde{q}^k) < 0 \tag{A.11}$$

If the second of the inequalities in (A.11) obtains one already has a contradiction of $\tilde{q}^k \in F(w^k)$ for all k. If $w^0 - h(\tilde{q}^k) < 0$ obtains, from $w^k \to w^0$, for k sufficiently large, it must be

$$w^k - h(\tilde{q}^k) < 0 \tag{A.12}$$

which again contradicts $\tilde{q}^k \in F(w^k)$ for all k. This establishes upper-hemicontinuity.

To prove lower-hemicontinuity one needs to show that for any given non-negative sequence $w^k \to w^0$ and any $\tilde{q}^0 \in F(w^0)$ there exists a sequence $\tilde{q}^k$ converging to $\tilde{q}^0$ and such that $\tilde{q}^k \in F(w^k)$ for all k. To verify that such a sequence can always be constructed I distinguish two cases:

Case 1 For the given $\tilde{q}^0$ it holds

$$w^0 - h(\tilde{q}^0) > 0 \tag{A.13}$$

Then since $w^k \to w^0$ for k' large enough

$$w^k - h(\tilde{q}^0) \geqslant 0 \text{ for all } k \geqslant k' \tag{A.14}$$

so that a sequence equal to any $\tilde{q}^k \in F(w^k)$ for $k < k'$ and such that $\tilde{q}^k = \tilde{q}^0$ for all $k \geqslant k'$ has the desired properties.

Case 2 For the given $\tilde{q}^0$ it holds

$$w^0 - h(\tilde{q}^0) = 0 \tag{A.15}$$

Let $\tilde{q}^{0\prime} \in F(w^0)$ be any arbitrary element of $F(w^0)$ such that $\tilde{q}^{0\prime} \neq \tilde{q}^0$ for at least one component. Let also $\gamma^k \rightarrow 0$ be a sequence for which $\gamma^k \in (0; 1)$ for all k finite. For each given γ^k construct an array $\tilde{q}^k = (q^k_{11}; \ldots; q^k_{1M}; q^k_{21}; \ldots; q^k_{2M})$ as follows: each component of $\tilde{q}^k$ satisfies

$$U(q^k_{1i}) = \gamma^k U(q^0_{1i}) + (1 - \gamma^k) U(q^0_{1i}) \text{ for all } i$$

$$V(q^k_{2i}) = \gamma^k V(q^0_{2i}) + (1 - \gamma^k) V(q^0_{2i}) \text{ for all } i \tag{A.16}$$

From the strict concavity of $U(\cdot)$ and $V(\cdot)$ and the fact that $h(\cdot)$ is linear and increasing in all its arguments for the $\tilde{q}^k$ defined above it must be

$$w^0 - h(\tilde{q}^k) > 0 \tag{A.17}$$

Moreover the fact that $\gamma^k \rightarrow 0$ implies $\tilde{q}^k \rightarrow \tilde{q}^0$ by (A.16). By inspection of the non-linear constraints in Problem A.2 which $\bar{m}(\cdot)$ represents it is possible to verify that since $\tilde{q}^{0\prime} \in F(w^0)$ and $\tilde{q}^0 \in F(w^0)$ it is also true that

$$\bar{m}(q^k) \geqslant 0 \text{ for all } k \tag{A.18}$$

By (A.17), and since $w^k \rightarrow w^0$, for k' large enough it will be

$$w^k - h(\tilde{q}^k) \geqslant 0 \text{ for all } k \geqslant k' \tag{A.19}$$

Hence a sequence equal to any $\tilde{q}^k \in F(q^k)$ for $k < k'$ and as defined in (A.16) for $k \geqslant k'$ satisfies $\tilde{q}^k \rightarrow \tilde{q}^0$ and $\tilde{q}^k \in F(w^k)$ for all k.

Since these are the desired properties this is sufficient to establish lower-hemicontinuity and hence Lemma 2.

Lemma A.3 Monotonicity. The quantity $D(w)$ is a strictly increasing function of w.

Proof Weak monotonicity is almost obvious. By inspection of the constraints of Problem A.2 if $\tilde{q} \in F(w)$ and $w' > w$ then $\tilde{q} \in F(w')$, so that $D(w)$ must be non-decreasing in w. Suppose then that the Lemma is false. Then there exist $w'' > w'$ such that

$$D(w'') = D(w') \tag{A.20}$$

Let now $\tilde{q}''$ and $\tilde{q}'$ be the arrays solving Problem A.2 for the w'' and w' levels of w respectively. Since $\tilde{q}' \in F(w'')$ (A.20) implies that $\tilde{q}'$ solves Problem A.2 at the w'' level of w. But then one can replace the first m elements of $\tilde{q}'$ by $\tilde{q}'_{11} + \Delta_1; \ldots; q'_{1M} + \Delta_M$ where the $\Delta_i > 0$ satisfy

$$\sum_{i=1}^{M} \pi_i \Delta_i = w'' - w' \tag{A.21}$$

and, for all i and j

$$U(q'_{1i} + \Delta_i) - U(q'_{1i}) = U(q'_{1j} + \Delta_j) - U(q'_{1j}) \tag{A.22}$$

By inspection of the constraints of Problem A.2 the new array, satisfying

(A.21) and (A.22), does not violate any constraints at the w'' level of w. Also the new array is better than $\bar{q}'$ and so $\bar{q}'$ cannot solve Problem A.2 at the w'' level of w. This contradiction establishes the Lemma.

Corollary A.1 Weak inequality. In the solution to Problem A.2 the constraint

$$\sum_{i=1}^{M} \pi_i(Rq_{1i} + q_{2i}) \leqslant Rw$$

is satisfied with equality.

Proof If not construct a new array exactly as in the proof of Lemma A.3 and obtain a contradiction.

Lemma A.4 Concavity. The quantity $D(w)$ is a strictly concave function of w.

Proof More explicit notation is needed. Let $\bar{q}(w) = [q_{11}^*(w); \ldots; q_{1M}^*(w); q_{21}^*(2); \ldots; q_{2M}^*(w)]$ represent a solution to Problem A.2 given w. Suppose now that the Lemma is false. Then there exist $w' \neq w''$ such that for some $\gamma \in (0; 1)$

$$\gamma D(w') + (1-\gamma)D(w'') \geqslant D[\gamma w' + (1-\gamma)w''] \tag{A.23}$$

Let now q'_{1i} and q'_{2i} be real numbers which respectively solve, for all i

$$U(q'_{1i}) = \gamma U[q_{1i}^*(w')] + (1-\gamma)U[q_{1i}^*(w'')]$$
$$V(q'_{2i}) = \gamma V[q_{2i}^*(w')] + (1-\gamma)V[q_{2i}^*(w'')] \tag{A.24}$$

and let also $\bar{q}' = [q'_{11}; \ldots; q'_{1m}; q'_{21}; \ldots; q'_{2m}]$. By Lemma A.3 one knows that $\bar{q}(w') \neq \bar{q}(w'')$. Also by Corollary A.1, for all w

$$\sum_{i=1}^{M} \pi_i[Rq_{1i}^*(w) + q_{2i}^*(w)] = Rw$$

Hence, by strict concavity of $U(\cdot)$ and $V(\cdot)$ it must be

$$\sum_{i=1}^{M} \pi_i[Rq'_{1i} + q'_{2i}] < \gamma w' + (1-\gamma)w'' \tag{A.25}$$

By construction (cf. (A.24)) one also has

$$\sum_{i=1}^{M} \pi_i[U(q'_{1i}) + \theta^i V(q'_{2i})] = \gamma D(w') + (1-\gamma)D(w'') \tag{A.26}$$

Distinguish now two cases:

Case 1 The inequality (A.23) is strict. By (A.25) $\bar{q}' \in F[\gamma w' + (1-\gamma)w'']$, and by (A.26) $\sum_{i=1}^{M} \pi[U(q'_{1i}) + \theta^i V(q'_{2i})] > D[\gamma w' + (1-\gamma)w'']$, which is a contradiction.

Case 2 The inequality (A.23) is weak. Then $\sum_{i=1}^{M} \pi_i[U(q'_{1i} + \theta^i V(q'_{2i})] = D[\gamma w' + (1-\gamma)w'']$ and this together with (A.25) contradicts Corollary A.1.

Corollary A.2 Uniqueness. The solution to Problem A.2 is unique.

Proof In the proof of Lemma A.4 set $w' = w''$ and assume that there exist $\tilde{q}'(w) \neq \tilde{q}''(w)$ and construct a new array exactly as in (A.24). This by (A.25) immediately contradicts Corollary A.1 as in Case 2 of the proof of Lemma A.4.

Lemma A.5 Interior solution. Consider Problem A.1. Assume as usual that both $U(\cdot)$ and $V(\cdot)$ are bounded below, strictly increasing and concave and continuous. Also as in Section II.2, let $U(\cdot)$ be once continuously differentiable and assume $U'(x) \to +\infty$ as $x \to 0$. In addition assume that there exists a continuous, strictly increasing and concave function $H(\cdot): R_+ \to R$ such that

$$H(0) = V(0) \text{ and } H(x) \leqslant V(x) \text{ for all } x > 0 \qquad (A.27)$$

Let also c_{1i}^{**}, c_{2i}^{**} be the solutions to the problems

$$
\text{Problems A.4} \quad
\begin{cases}
\max U(c_{1i}) + \theta^i H(c_{2i}) \\
\text{s.t. } Rc_{1i} + c_{2i} \leqslant Rw \\
c_{1i} \geqslant 0 \quad c_{2i} \geqslant 0
\end{cases}
$$

and assume that $H(\cdot)$ is such that

$$c_{1i}^{**} > 0 \quad c_{2i}^{**} > 0 \text{ for all } i \qquad (A.28)$$

Then in the solution to Problem A.1 one has

$$c_{1i}^* > 0 \quad c_{2i}^* > 0 \text{ for all } i$$

Proof Suppose the Lemma is false and recall that c_{1i}^*, c_{2i}^* solve Problems A.3 for all i. Distinguish now two cases, at least one of which must hold if the Lemma is false.

Case 1 There exists i for which

$$c_{1i}^* = w \text{ and } c_{2i}^* = 0 \qquad (A.29)$$

By (A.26) this implies

$$U(c_{1i}^*) + \theta^i V(c_{2i}^*) = U(c_{1i}^*) + \theta^i H(c_{2i}^*) \qquad (A.30)$$

also, by (A.28) and (A.29) one has (recall that the solutions to Problems A.4 are all unique by strict concavity)

$$U(c_{1i}^{**}) + \theta^i H(c_{2i}^{**}) > U(c_{1i}^*) + \theta^i H(c_{2i}^*) \qquad (A.31)$$

From the inequality in (A.27), (A.31) and (A.30) direclty imply

$$U(c_{1i}^{**}) + \theta^i V(c_{2i}^{**}) > U(c_{1i}^*) + \theta^i V(c_{2i}^*) \qquad (A.32)$$

and (A.32) evidently contradicts the assumption of maximality of c_{1i}^*, c_{2i}^*.

Case 2 There exists i for which

$$c_{1i}^* = 0 \text{ and } c_{2i}^* = Rw$$

Let now $\delta_1 > 0$ and $\delta_2 < 0$ be two small real numbers such that

$$R\delta_1 + \delta_2 = 0 \tag{A.33}$$

Let also

$$c_{1i}' = c_{1i}^* + \delta_1 \text{ and } c_{2i}' = c_{2i}^* + \delta_2 \tag{A.34}$$

The change in utility obtained by varying c_{1i} and c_{2i} as in (A.34) is:

$$\Delta_i = U(\delta_1) - U(0) + \theta^i [V(c_{2i}') - V(c_{2i}^*)] \tag{A.35}$$

Applying the mean value theorem to $U(\cdot)$ there exists $f_i \in (0; \delta_1)$ such that

$$\Delta_i = U'(f_i)\delta_1 + \theta^i [V(c_{2i}') - V(c_{2i}^*)] \tag{A.36}$$

Dividing (A.36) through by δ_1 and using (A.33) one has

$$\Delta_i > 0 \text{ iff } U'(f_i) + \theta^i R [V(c_{2i}') - V(c_{2i}^*)](-\delta_2)^{-1} > 0 \tag{A.37}$$

Now, by concavity, finiteness, and continuity of $V(\cdot)$ the expression

$$[V(c_{2i}') - V(c_{2i}^*)](-\delta_2)^{-1} \tag{A.38}$$

is not only a continuous function of δ_2 but converges to a finite limit for $\delta_2 \to 0$ as long as c_{2i}^* is in the interior of the domain of $V(\cdot)$ (cf. Rockafellar (1970), Theorem 24.1, pp. 227–228). But then since $U'(x) \to +\infty$ as $x \to 0$, for δ_1 and δ_2 small enough it must be that

$$U'(f_i)\theta^i R [V(c_{2i}') - V(c_{2i}^*)](-\delta_2)^{-1} > 0 \tag{A.39}$$

This implies, by (A.37), that the change in c_{1i}, c_{2i} is utility improving. By (A.33) it is also budget feasible and hence it cannot be that $c_{1i}^* = 0$ and $c_{2i}^* = Rw$. This concludes the proof of Lemma A.5.

Sufficient preliminary results have now been established to construct a candidate for the viable and optimal bank contract. Define

$$\textit{Problem A.5} \begin{cases} V_{N-1}(b_{N-1}) = \max \sum_{i=1}^{M} \pi_i [U(q_{N-1i}) + \theta_{N-1}^i U(q_{Ni})] \\[2mm] \text{s.t. } \sum_{i=1}^{M} \pi_i (Rq_{N-1i} + q_{Ni}) \leqslant Rb_{N-1} \\[2mm] U(q_{N-1i}) + \theta_{N-1}^i U(q_{Ni}) \geqslant U(q_{N-1j}) + \theta_{N-1}^i U(q_{Nj}) \\[1mm] \qquad\qquad\qquad\qquad\qquad\qquad\qquad \text{for all } i \text{ and } j \\[2mm] q_{N-1i} \geqslant 0 \quad q_{Ni} \geqslant 0 \text{ for all } i \end{cases}$$

and let $q_{N-1}(\theta_{N-1}; b_{N-1})$ and $q_N(\theta_{N-1}b_{N-1})$ be the random variables defined by the array solving Problem A.5. Define also recursively $t = N-2; \ldots; 2$

Problems A.6
$$
\begin{cases}
V_t(b_t) = \max \sum_{i=1}^{M} \pi_i[U(q_{ti}) + \theta_t^i V_{t+1}(b_{t+1i})] \\[2mm]
\text{s.t. } \sum_{i=1}^{M} \pi_i(Rq_{ti} + b_{t+1i}) \leqslant Rb_t \\[2mm]
U(q_{ti}) + \theta_t^i V_{t+1}(b_{t+1i}) \geqslant U(q_{tj}) + \theta_t^i V_{t+1}(b_{t+1j}) \\[2mm]
\hspace{6cm} \text{for all } i \text{ and } j \\[2mm]
q_{ti} \geqslant 0 \quad b_{t+i} \geqslant 0 \text{ for all } i
\end{cases}
$$

and let $q_t(\theta_t; b_t)$ and $b_{t+1}(\theta_t; b_t)$ be the random variables defined by the arrays solving Problems A.6. Lastly define for all $i = 1; \ldots; M$

Problems A.7
$$
\begin{cases}
V_1(1; h_1) = \max U(q_{1i}) + \theta_1^i V_2(b_{2i}) \\[1mm]
\text{s.t. } Rq_{1i} + b_{2i} \leqslant R \\[1mm]
q_{1i} \geqslant 0 \quad q_{2i} \geqslant 0
\end{cases}
$$

and let $q_1(\theta_1; 1)$ and $b_2(\theta_1; 1)$ be the random variables defined by the solutions to Problems A.7. The random variables defined through Problems A.5–A.7 will turn out to be the unique, optimal and viable bank contract.

Remark A.1 Problems A.5–A.7 are all well-defined and have a solution.

Proof Since the opportunity sets of Problems A.5–A.7 are all non-empty and compact by inspection, recursive application of the continuity Lemma A.2 is enough to guarantee the claim.

Remark A.2 The $V_t(\cdot)$ value functions defined in Problems A.5–A.7 are all continuous, strictly monotonic and concave.

Proof Recursive application of Lemmas A.2 (continuity), A.3 (monotonicity) and A.4 (concavity) is enough to guarantee the claim.

Remark A.3 The contract defined through problems A.5–A.7 is resource feasible for the bank.

Proof This is obvious by inspection of the constraints imposed in Problems A.5–A.7.

Remark A.4 The contract defined through Problems A.5–A.7 is unique.

Proof By Remark A.2, all the $V_t(\cdot)$ $t = N-1 \ldots 2$ functions satisfy the assumptions of Corollary A.2 and so does $U(\cdot)$. The solutions to Problems A.7 are unique by standard arguments and this is enough to prove the claim.

The following, when the contract defined through Problems A.5–A.7 will be proved to be viable and optimal, will constitute proof of Lemma V.1.

Lemma A.6 Consider the contract defined through Problems A.5–A.7 and define $Q_t(\theta'_t; b_t)$ $(t = 1; \ldots; N-2)$ as in (3). Then for each given z

$$Q_z(\theta'_z; b_z) = E\left\{ \sum_{t=z+1}^{N} {}_{z+2}\delta_J U[q_t[{}_{z+1}\mathbf{h}_t; b_{z+1}(b_z; \theta'_z)]] \right\} \qquad (A.40)$$

Proof By construction the $Q_z(\cdot)$ functions satisfy the recursive relation $(2 \leqslant z \leqslant N-1)^6$

$$Q_{z-1}(\theta'_{z-1}; b_{z-1}) = E\{U[q_z[\theta^*_z(\theta_z; b_z(\theta'_{z-1}; b_{z-1}))] \\ + \theta_z Q_z[\theta^*_z(\theta_z; b_z(\theta'_{z-1}; b_{z-1})); b_z(\theta'_{z-1} b_{z-1})]\} \qquad (A.41)$$

I now prove that the Lemma is true for $z = N-2$, and the rest of the proof will follow by induction using (A.41). By (4) for all b_{N-1}

$$Q_{N-1}(\theta^i_{N-1}; b_{N-1}) = U[q_N(\theta^i_{N-1}; b_{N-1})] \qquad (A.42)$$

also by the constraints imposed in Problem A.5

$$U[q_{N-1}(\theta^i_{N-1}; b_{N-1})] + \theta^i_{N-1}U[q_N(\theta^i_{N-1}; b_{N-1})] \\ \geqslant U[q_{N-1}(\theta^j_{N-1}; b_{N-1})] + \theta^i_{N-1}U[q_N(\theta^j_{N-1}; b_{N-1})] \\ \text{for all } i,j \text{ and } b_{N-1} \qquad (A.43)$$

From (A.43) it follows immediately that

$$\theta^i_{N-1} \in \theta^*_{N-1}(\theta^i_{N-1}; b_{N-1}) \text{ for all } i \text{ and } b_{N-1} \qquad (A.44)$$

and hence by the definition of $V_{N-1}(\cdot)$ in Problem A.5 it follows that for all θ'_{N-2} and b_{N-2}

$$Q_{N-2}(\theta'_{N-2}; b_{N-2}) = V_{N-1}[b_{N-1}(\theta'_{N-2}; b_{N-2})] \qquad (A.45)$$

By an identical argument, using the recursive relation (A.41) and the constraints imposed in Problems A.7 it follows that for all $t = N-2; \ldots; 2$ if

$$Q_t(\theta'_t; b_t) = V_{t+1}[b_{t+1}(\theta'_t; b_t)] \text{ for all } \theta'_t \text{ and } b_t \qquad (A.46)$$

then

$$Q_{t-1}(\theta'_{t-1}; b_{t-1}) = V_t[b_t(\theta'_{t-1}; b_{t-1})] \text{ for all } \theta'_{t-1} \text{ and } b_{t-1} \qquad (A.47)$$

Hence by induction I have proved that the equalities (A.47) hold for all $t = 2 \ldots N-1$. This, noticing that by construction it is, for $z = 1; \ldots; N-2$

$$V_{z+1}[b_{z+1}(\theta'_z; b_z)] = E\left\{ \sum_{t=z+1}^{N} {}_{z+2}\delta_t U[q_t[{}_{z+1}\mathbf{h}_t; b_{z+1}(b_z; \theta'_z)]] \right\} \qquad (A.48)$$

is clearly enough to prove the Lemma.

Corollary A.3 Consider any contract

$$q_1(\theta_1; 1); \ldots; q_{N-2}(\theta_{N-2}; b_{N-2}); q_{N-1}(\theta_{N-1}; b_{N-1}); q_N(\theta_{N-1}; b_{N-1})$$
$$b_2(\theta_1; 1); \ldots; b_{N-1}(\theta_{N-2}; b_{N-2})$$

which is sequentially incentive-compatible. Let then

$$S_{N-1}(b_{N-1}) = E\{U[q_{N-1}(\theta_{N-1}; b_{N-1})] + \theta_{N-1} U[q_N(\theta_{N-1}; b_{N-1})]\} \quad (A.49)$$

and recursively ($t = N - 2; \ldots; 1$)

$$S_t(b_t) = E\{U[q_t(\theta_t; b_t)] + \theta_t S_{t+1}[b_{t+1}(\theta_t; b_t)]\} \quad (A.50)$$

then, for all i, j and b_{N-1}

$$U[q_{N-1}(\theta_{N-1}^i; b_{N-1})] + \theta_{N-1}^i U[q_N(\theta_{N-1}^i; b_{N-1})]$$
$$\geqslant U[q_{N-1}(\theta_{N-1}^j; b_{N-1})] + \theta_{N-1}^i U[q_N(\theta_{N-1}^j; b_{N-1}]) \quad (A.51)$$

and for all $t = 1; \ldots; N - 2$ and all i, j and b_t

$$U[q_t(\theta_{N-1}^i; b_t)] + \theta_t^i S_{t+1}[b_{t+1}(\theta_t^i; b_t)]$$
$$\geqslant U[q_t(\theta_t^j; b_t)] + \theta_t^i S_{t+1}[b_{t+1}(\theta_t^j; b_t)] \quad (A.52)$$

Proof Suppose the claim is false and let z be the largest t for which either (A.51) or (A.52) is violated. Then from Lemma A.6 it must be that

$$Q_z(\theta_z'; b_z) = S_{z+1}[b_{z+1}(\theta_{z+1}^1; b_z)] \quad (A.53)$$

But then violation of one of the constraints (A.51) or (A.52) immediately contradicts sequential incentive-compatibility by the definition of $\theta_z^*(\cdot)$, and this is enough to prove the claim.

It is now possible to prove

Lemma A.7 The contract defined through Problems A.5–A.7 is sequentially incentive-compatible.

Proof By Lemma A.6 for $t = 1 \ldots N - 1$ and for all b_t

$$Q_t(\theta_t'; b_t) = V_{t+1}[b_{t+1}(\theta_t'; b_t)]$$

so that $\theta_t^*(\theta_t; b_t)$ is the set of θ_t' solving

$$\max_{\theta_t' \in \Phi} U[q_t(\theta_t'; b_t)] + \theta_t V_{t+1}[b_{t+1}(\theta_t'; b_t)]$$

but from the constraints imposed in Problems A.6 it then follows immediately that for $t = 2; \ldots; N - 1$ and for all θ_t and b_t

$$\theta_t \in \theta_t^*[\theta_t; b_t]$$

For $t = 1$ notice that in Problems A.7 it was required that for all θ_1

$$Rq_1(\theta_1; 1) + b_2(\theta_1; 1) \leqslant R$$

so that if it were not true that

$$\theta_1 \in \theta_1^*[\theta_1; 1] \text{ for all } \theta_1$$

maximality of $q_1(\theta_1; 1)$, $b_2(\theta_2; 1)$ would be contradicted. This concludes the proof of Lemma A.7.

Proof of Theorem IV.1 To prove that the contract defined through the solutions to Problems A.5–A.7 has all the claimed properties it only remains to show that for all h_1

$$E\left\{\sum_{t=1}^{N} \delta_t U[q_t(\mathbf{h}_t)] \middle| h_1\right\} > E\left\{\sum_{t=1}^{N} \delta_t U[c_t(\mathbf{h}_t)] \middle| h_1\right\} \tag{A.54}$$

This is because such a contract has already been proved to be sequentially incentive-compatible (Lemma A.7) and is by construction resource feasible for the bank (Remark A.2). Consider Problems III.2 and A.5. The dominance Lemma A.1 then clearly guarantees that for all $b_{N-1} > 0$

$$V_{N-1}(b_{N-1}) > E[H_{N-1}(b_{N-1}; \theta_{N-1}^i)] \tag{A.55}$$

Consider then, for a given $t = N - 2; \ldots; 2$, Problems III.3 and A.6. Since the opportunity set of Problems A.6 contains the solution to Problems 3.3 it is immediate that

$$\begin{aligned} &\text{if } V_{t+1}(b_{t+1}) > E[H_{t+1}(b_{t+1}; \theta_{t+1})] \text{ for all } b_{t+1} > 0 \\ &\text{then } V_t(b_t) > E[H_t(b_t; \theta_t)] \text{ for all } b_t > 0 \end{aligned} \tag{A.56}$$

The inequalities (A.55) and (A.56) recursively imply that, for all b_2

$$V_2(b_2) > E[H_2(b_2; \theta_2)] \tag{A.57}$$

This last inequality, since the opportunity sets of Problems A.7 and III.3 for $t = 1$ are identical, implies that for all h_1

$$V_1(1; h_1) > H_1(1; h_1) \tag{A.58}$$

which directly implies (A.54).

Proof of Theorem IV.2 In view of the proof of Theorem IV.1 and Remark A.4 it is enough to prove that the contract defined through Problems A.5–A.7 is optimal. This, using Corollary A.3 is obvious by standard recursive techniques and I omit the details.

Lemma A.8 Consider the value functions $V_t(\cdot)$ $t = 2; \ldots; N-2$ defined by

Problems A.5 and A.6. Define also

$$
\text{Problems A.8} \quad
\begin{cases}
G_t(b_t) = \max \sum_{i=1}^{M} \pi_i[U(x_{ti}) + \theta_t^i V_{t+1}(x_{t+1 i})] \\
\text{s.t.} Rx_{ti} + x_{t+1 i} \leqslant Rb_t \text{ for all } i \\
x_{ti} \geqslant 0 \quad x_{t+1 i} \geqslant 0 \text{ for all } i
\end{cases}
$$

Then for all $t = 2; \ldots; N-1$ and for all $b_t > 0$

$$V_t(b_t) > G_t(b_t) \tag{A.59}$$

Proof I prove this by showing that the dominance Lemma A.1 can be applied. In order to do so one needs to show that in the solution to Problems A.8, for all $t = 2; \ldots; N-2$ and for all i

$$x_{ti} > 0 \quad x_{t+1 i} > 0 \tag{A.60}$$

Notice now that in order to solve Problems A.8 $x_{ti}, x_{t+1 i}$ must solve, for all i and for all $t = 2; \ldots; N-2$

$$
\text{Problems A.9} \quad
\begin{cases}
\max U(x_{ti}) + \theta_t^i V_{t+1}(x_{t+1 i}) \\
\text{s.t.} \ Rx_{ti} + x_{t+1 i} \leqslant Rb_t \\
x_{ti} \geqslant 0 \quad x_{t+1 i} \geqslant 0
\end{cases}
$$

Consider now the value functions of Problem III.1, $H_t(\cdot)$. By construction and as in the proof of Theorem IV.1 for all $t = 2; \ldots; N-2$, and for all $b_t \geqslant 0$

$$V_t(0) = E[H_t(0; \theta_t)] \text{ and } V_t(b_t) \geqslant E[H_t(b_t; \theta_t)] \tag{A.61}$$

By the interior property of the solution to Problem III.1 and by (A.61) the functions $E[H_t(b_t; \theta)]$ satisfy all the hypotheses of Lemma A.5 for all $t = 2; \ldots; N-2$. Hence (A.60) must hold and this is enough to prove the Lemma.

Lemma A.9 For the optimal and viable bank contract it holds: for all $t = 2; \ldots; N-1$, and for all b_t, there exist $i \neq j$ such that

$$Rq_t(\theta_t^i; b_t) + b_{t+1}(\theta_t^i; b_t) \neq Rq_t(\theta_t^j; b_t) + b_{t+1}(\theta_t^j; b_t) \tag{A.62}$$

and for all b_{N-1} there exist $i \neq j$ such that

$$Rq_{N-1}(\theta_{N-1}^i; b_{N-1}) + q_N(\theta_{N-1}^i; b_{N-1})$$

$$\neq Rq_{N-1}(\theta_{N-1}^j; b_{N-1}) + q_N(\theta_{N-1}^j; b_{N-1}) \tag{A.63}$$

Proof Suppose (A.63) is not true and that there exists a b_{N-1} for which the array $[q_{N-1}(\theta_{N-1}^i; b_{N-1}); q_N(\theta_{N-1}^i; b_{N-1})]$ is feasible for Problems III.2 when $w_{N-1} = b_{N-1}$. This contradicts the already established dominance property

$$E[H_{N-1}(b_{N-1}; \theta_{N-1})] < V_{N-1}(b_{N-1}) \text{ for all } b_{N-1} > 0 \qquad \text{(A.64)}$$

Hence (A.63) must hold. Suppose now that (A.62) is false. Then using the resource constraint of Problem A.6 there exist a t and b_t such that

$$Rq_t(\theta_t^i; b_t) + b_{t+1}(\theta_t^i; b_t) \leqslant Rb_t \text{ for all } i \qquad \text{(A.65)}$$

From (A.65) the array $[q_t(\theta_t^i; b_t); b_{t+1}(\theta_t^i)]$ is then feasible for the appropriate Problem A.8. But this contradicts the dominance property (A.59) established in Lemma A.8. This concludes the proof of Lemma A.9.

Proof of Theorem IV.3 If the Theorem is false for $t = N - 1$, through simple algebra, it must be that there exists b_{N-1} such that for all i and j

$$\begin{aligned} Rq_{N-1}(\theta_{N-1}^i; b_{N-1}) + q_N(\theta_{N-1}^i; b_{N-1}) \\ = Rq_{N-1}(\theta_{N-1}^j; b_{N-1}) + q_N(\theta_{N-1}^j; b_{N-1}) \end{aligned} \qquad \text{(A.66)}$$

which contradicts (A.63) of Lemma A.9. Analogously, if the Theorem is false for any $t = 2; \ldots; N - 2$ a contradiction of (A.62) of Lemma A.9 is obtained.

Theorem A.2 For the optimal and viable bank contract, given any $t = 2; \ldots; N - 1$ and b_t it is

$$\max_{\theta_t' \in \Phi} q_t(\theta_t; b_t) > E[q_t(\theta_t; b_t)] \qquad \text{(A.67)}$$

Proof By Corollary A.1 the optimal bank contract must satisfy, for all $t = 1; \ldots; N - 2$ and for all b_t

$$RE[q_t(\theta_t; b_t)] + E[b_{t+1}(\theta_t; b_t)] = b_t \qquad \text{(A.68)}$$

Suppose now that (A.67) is false for some $t = 2; \ldots; N - 2$. Then there exists $t = 2; \ldots; N - 2$ and b_t such that

$$q_t(\theta_t^i; b_t) = E[q(\theta_t; b_t] \text{ for all } i \qquad \text{(A.69)}$$

For the optimal bank contract by construction it is also, for all $t = 1; \ldots; N - 2$ and for all b_t

$$\begin{aligned} U[q_t(\theta_t^i; b_t)] + \theta_t^i V_{t+1}[b_{t+1}(\theta_t^i; b_t)] \\ \geqslant U[q_t(\theta_t^j; b_t)] + \theta_t^i V_{t+1}[b_{t+1}(\theta_t^j; b_t)] \text{ for all } i,j \end{aligned} \qquad \text{(A.70)}$$

Simple algebra, and monotonicity of $U(\cdot)$ and $V_{t+1}(\cdot)$, show that the inequalities (A.70) imply

$$q_t(\theta_t^i; b_t) = q_t(\theta_t^j) \Leftrightarrow b_{t+1}(\theta_t^i; b_t) = b_{t+1}(\theta_t^j; b_t) \qquad \text{(A.71)}$$

Combining (A.71), (A.69) and (A.68) one finally obtains that if (A.63) is false for some $t = 2; \ldots; N - 2$, then there exists b_t for which for all i

$$q_t(\theta_t^i; b_t) = E[q_t(\theta_t; b_t)]; \quad b_{t+1}(\theta_t^i; b_t) = E[b_{t+1}(\theta_t; b_t)] \qquad \text{(A.72)}$$

The equalities (A.72) contradict (A.62) of Lemma A.9 and this establishes that (A.67) must be true for $t = 2; \ldots; N - 2$. The proof for $t = N - 1$ is, mutatis mutandis, identical and so I omit it.

The following is needed in order to prove Theorem VI.1. From now on all the assumptions made at the beginning of Section VI are supposed to hold.

Lemma A.10 Consider any bank contract

$$q_1(\theta_1; 1); \ldots; q_{N-2}(\theta_{N-2}; b_{N-2}); q_{N-1}(\theta_{N-1}; b_{N-1}); q_N(\theta_{N-1}; b_{N-1})$$

$$b_2(\theta_1; 1); \ldots; b_{N-1}(\theta_{N-2}; b_{N-2}) \tag{A.73}$$

and let $h_1^*(h_1); \ldots; h_{N-1}^*(h_{N-1})$ be the optimal declaration functions which the contract yields. Then the contract (obtained by successive substitutions as usual)

$$\hat{q}_t(h_t) = q_t[h_t^*(h_t)] \quad t = 1; \ldots; N - 1$$

$$\hat{q}_N(h_{N-1}) = q_N[h_{N-1}^*(h_{N-1})] \tag{A.74}$$

$$\hat{b}_t(h_{t-1}) = b_t[h_{t-1}^*(h_{t-1})] \quad t = 2; \ldots; N - 1$$

is sequentially incentive-compatible.

Proof Let $\hat{Q}_t(\cdot)$ and $Q_t(\cdot)$ be the maximum expected utility functions from $t + 1$ onwards defined in (3) and (4) for contracts $[\hat{q}_t(\cdot); \hat{b}_t(\cdot)]$ and $[q_t(\cdot); b_t(\cdot)]$ respectively. From (A.74) and (3) some manipulation yields that, for all $t = 1; \ldots; N - 1$, and for all θ_t' and b_t

$$\hat{Q}_t(\theta_t'; b_t) = Q_t(\theta_t'; b_t) \tag{A.75}$$

From the definition of sequential incentive-compatibility IV.1 and the equalities (A.75) the Lemma then follows immediately and I omit the details.

Proof of Theorem VI.1 By construction the optimal and viable bank contract makes non-negative profit. So (a) is satisfied. Suppose now that the optimal bank contract is on offer and (b) is not true. Then there must exist a contract $[q_t'(\cdot); b_t'(\cdot)]$ substantially different from $[q_t(\cdot); b_t(\cdot)]$ (the optimal bank contract) with the following properties. Let $h_t^{*\prime}(h_t)$ be the optimal declaration functions yielded by the contract $[q_t'(\cdot); b_t'(\cdot)]$, then there exists E (subset of $h_{11}; \ldots; h_{1M}$) such that for all $h_1 \in E$

$$E\left\{ \sum_{t=1}^{N} \delta_t U[q_t'[h_t^{*\prime}(\mathbf{h}_t)]] \,\big|\, h_1 \right\} \geqslant E\left\{ \sum_{t=1}^{N} \delta_t U[q_t(h_t)] \,\big|\, h_1 \right\} \tag{A.76}$$

and $[q_t'(\cdot); b_t'(\cdot)]$ makes non-negative profit given $h_1 \in E$. Construct now a new contract as

$$\hat{q}_t(h_t) = q_t'[h_t^{*\prime}(h_t)] \tag{A.77}$$

and

$$\hat{b}_t(h_{t-1}) = b_t'[h_{t-1}^*(h_{t-1})]$$ (A.78)

By Lemma A.10 the new contract is sequentially incentive-compatible. Let also

$$R\hat{b}_{N-1}(h_{N-2}) = E[R\hat{q}_{N-1}(\theta_{N-1}; h_{N-2}) + \hat{q}_N(\theta_{N-1}; h_{N-2})]$$ (A.79)

and recursively $(t = 2; \ldots; N-2)$

$$R\hat{b}_t(h_{t-1}) = E[R\hat{q}_t(\theta_t; h_{t-1}) + \hat{b}_{t+1}(\theta_t; h_{t-1})]$$ (A.80)

The contract $[\hat{q}_t(\cdot); \hat{b}_t(\cdot)]$ is clearly also sequentially incentive-compatible. Hence by Corollary A.3 and by construction ((A.79) and (A.80)) it satisfies all the constraints of Problems A.5 and A.6. By assumption $[q_t'(\cdot); b_t'(\cdot)]$ is substantially different from the optimal bank contract. Hence, from (A.77) and Definition VI.2 there exists t and $h_1 \in E$ such that for some h_t

$$\hat{q}_t(h_t) \neq q_t(h_t)$$ (A.81)

Let now $\tilde{E}$ be the non-empty subset of $(h_{11}; \ldots; h_{1M})$ for which (A.81) obtains. Then by uniqueness of the optimal bank contract, and since $[\hat{q}_t(\cdot); \hat{b}_t(\cdot)]$ satisfies all the constraints of Problems A.5 and A.6, it must be that if (A.76) holds then

$$R\hat{q}_1(h_1) + \hat{b}_2(h_1) > R \text{ for all } h_1 \in \tilde{E}$$ (A.82)

and since it clearly must also be

$$R\hat{q}_1(h_1) + \hat{b}_2(h_1) = R \text{ for all } h_1 \in E - \tilde{E}$$ (A.83)

the $[\hat{q}_t(\cdot); \hat{b}_t(\cdot)]$ contract cannot make non-negative profit and so neither can $[q_t'(\cdot); b_t'(\cdot)]$. This contradiction establishes the theorem.

NOTES

* I would like to thank Margaret Bray who patiently read and commented upon many earlier versions of the paper. Partha Dasgupta, Frank Hahn and Tim Kehoe also offered me helpful comments. The responsibility for the opinions expressed and any remaining errors is, of course, solely mine.
1 This terminology is due to Gale (1982), pp. 192–194. The form of consumers' utility function which I use below is also almost directly borrowed from Gale ((1983), Chap. 2, part 2), although here it serves a different purpose.
2 Throughout this paper random variables and their realizations are denoted by the same symbol; the former in bold type.
3 Even though there are only $N-1$ random variables in the collection, it is

notationally convenient to define N history random variables by setting $h_N = h_{N-1}$.

4 The notation used here will become improper when the argument of $g_t(\cdot)$ is a random variable itself. This, however, does not create any ambiguity and facilitates the exposition.

5 The assumption of no parallel activity VI.2 above is an extreme one. I use it here because it avoids great technical and notational complication of the analysis. However, notice that a bank can always mimic what single consumers can achieve individually. This suggests that, if Definition VI.1 below is suitably modified, the main result of this section should also hold true without the assumption of no parallel activity.

6 The use of the set $\theta_z^*(\cdot)$ as an argument of the function $q_z(\cdot)$ must be interpreted as any element of $\theta_z^*(\cdot)$.

REFERENCES

Azariadis, C. (1981). 'Self-Fulfilling Prophecies.' *Journal of Economic Theory*, **25**, 380–396.

Diamond, D. W. and P. H. Dybvig (1983). 'Bank Runs, Deposit Insurance and Liquidity.' *Journal of Political Economy*, **91**, 401–419.

Gale, D. (1982). *Money: in Equilibrium*. Cambridge University Press, Cambridge.

Gale, D. (1983). *Money: in Disequilibrium*. Cambridge University Press, Cambridge.

Hammond, P. J. (1979). 'Straightforward Individual Incentive Compatibility in Large Economies.' *Review of Economic Studies*, **46**, 263–282.

Hurwicz, L. (1972). 'On Informationally Decentralized Systems.' Chap. 14 (pp. 297–336) in *Decision and Organization*, C. B. McGuire and R. Radner eds. North Holland Publishing Company, London.

Rockafellar, R. I. (1970). *Convex Analysis*. Princeton University Press, Princeton.

Rothschild, M. and J. E. Stiglitz (1976). 'Equilibrium in Competitive Insurance Markets: An Essay in the Economics of Imperfect Competition.' *Quarterly Journal of Economics*, **90**, 629–649.

Smith, B. D. (1984). 'Private Information, Deposit Interest Rates, and the "Stability" of the Banking System.' *Journal of Monetary Economics*, **14**, 293–317.

COMMENT DAVID C. WEBB

Modelling the behaviour of banks and equilibrium in the banking sector is an important and as yet underdeveloped area of research in economics. The paper by Diamond and Dybvig (1983) is proving to be something of a watershed in this area. The current paper by Luca Anderlini is an interesting extension of their model. My discussion will be divided into three main parts: in part I I review the basis problem essentially by outlining the Diamond–Dybvig analysis; in part II I review the main contributions of the Anderlini paper; in part III I comment on some important unresolved problems which in my opinion warrant research.

I The Diamond–Dybvig model

Diamond and Dybvig show that a bank offering an ordinary deposit contract can provide allocations superior to those of simple exchange markets. However, an undesirable property of the equilibrium with bank deposits is that the bank may be subject to runs. The main assumptions of their analysis are:

A.1 Consumer-investors face privately observed risks. They receive a given endowment at date t. At date $t+1$ they find out whether they are type 1 who only care about consumption at date $t+1$ or type 2 who care only about consumption at date $t+2$. This private risk is not directly insurable because it is not publicly verifiable.

A.2 The technology is safe, it transforms an unit input at date t into an output of $L = 1$ at date $t+1$ and $R > 1$ at date $t+2$. Selling costs of early liquidation of investments would do the same job as this assumption. There is unproductive private storage but this is only useful between dates $t+1$ and $t+2$ because the technology does at least as well over the first period.

A.3 A bank is a simple deposit-investment organisation. It transforms illiquid assets into liquid ones with a smoother pattern of returns. For the bank to perform this function efficiently requires confidence and no panics. If there is a panic withdrawal the bank is forced to liquidate assets at a loss. This means that the bank may liquidate all of its assets even though not all depositors withdraw.

Here I present an informal summary of the main results in the Diamond–Dybvig paper. Consumer-investors do not initially know what type they are going to be but learn their type at date $t+1$. However, the technology is only productive over two periods. The lack of observability of agents' types rules out Arrow–Debreu markets because this would require claims that depend upon non-verifiable private information. Assuming a fixed known proportion of each type of consumer-investor they show that it is possible to achieve an optimal (incentive-compatible) insurance contract. This involves each type of consumer depositing its entire endowment in the bank and receiving a bank deposit, with the bank's assets being investments in the technology. The incentive compatibility of the ordinary deposit contract means that on observing its type, agents do not have an incentive to lie, which means behaving like the other type. Because the optimal contract is incentive-compatible, there necessarily exists a contract structure which implements it as a (pure strategy) Nash equilibrium and hence the demand deposit is a contract that will work.

In this equilibrium banks provide insurance by providing liquidity, guaranteeing a reasonable return when the investor cashes in before maturity which is required for optimal risk sharing. However, it is precisely this feature of the uninsured bank deposit contract which makes the bank susceptible to runs. In other words the uninsured bank deposit contract has multiple Nash equilibria (with different levels of confidence), one of which is a bank run. To show this they assume that in the event of a rush to withdraw the demand deposit satisfies a sequential servicing constraint which means that the pay off to a depositor depends (at random) only on his place in line. By joining such a queue, in a run, a type 2 consumer expects to do better than if he left his money in the bank.

I will leave a discussion of deposit insurance and suspension of convertibility to part III.

II The Anderlini model

The basic motivation of the Anderlini model is exactly the same as in the Diamond–Dybvig model. However, it does provide an interesting generalisation of their model. I begin by outlining the important changes in assumptions that he makes:

A'.1 Consumer-investors have finite lives of duration $N > 2$. They receive an initial endowment and wish to consume in the middle of each period. However, at each date the consumer's discount rate is the outcome of an i.i.d. stochastic process (identical across consumers). The realisation of the discount rates is private information observed at the beginning of each period by the consumer and by no other agent.

A'.2 The technology is safe but yields a high return per unit invested of $R > 1$ if operated for a period and a lower return per unit invested of $L < 1$ if operated for half a period. There is no unproductive storage.

A'.3 This is the same as A.3.

The superiority of a bank deposit contract over the outcome in which consumers operate the technology individually follows for the same reasons as in the Diamond–Dybvig model, so that the bank contract is an insurance contract. The contract problem is examined in Theorem IV.1 which shows that there exist withdrawal and balance functions which are sequentially incentive-compatible, resource feasible for the bank and preferred by all consumers to operating the technology on their own. Moreover, it is shown in Theorem IV.2 that the optimal contract is unique and viable if the bank earns non-negative profits. Unlike Diamond and Dybvig who assume a contract form and then prove that it is incentive compatible, Anderlini constrains contracts to be incentive-compatible and then derives the optimal contract. The contract which solves this problem is an ordinary demand deposit. It should be noted that the assumption of a continuum of consumers is used in these theorems to express the bank's feasibility and profit constraints in average terms, so that the bank is effectively risk neutral.

Anderlini then, in Section V, examines a banking game. Here, he shows in the spirit of Diamond and Dybvig that, if an allocation is incentive-compatible, there must be a contract structure which implements it as a (sequential) Nash equilibrium. It turns out that this equilibrium is not unique and one of the Nash equilibria is a bank run. Again the bank has a sequential servicing constraint which means that it randomly services deposits if it cannot meet all requests for withdrawals. If it loses all of its deposits it is closed.

III Bank runs and the insights of these models

In both the Diamond–Dybvig and Anderlini models there is no risk in the bank's portfolio other than that induced by consumer behaviour. If outcomes match anticipations then a run will not occur, since no one would deposit anticipating a run. In both models agents will deposit some of their endowment (all in the cases studied) in the bank provided the probability of the run is sufficiently small. However, neither model explains why a run ever occurs. Diamond and Dybvig suggest that a bad earnings report for the bank, a run on another bank, or a negative government forecast can cause a run. But all of these explanations require that there is some uncertainty about the returns on the bank's assets, yet the assumption of a safe technology precludes this. These analyses in their current form rely on sunspot generation of consumer expectations which are not explained by the models.

I now turn to suggestions for eliminating runs. One possibility is suspension of convertibility of deposits into currency. This is credible and works in the Diamond–Dybvig model. When the proportion of types is known the bank deposit contract with suspension of convertibility will achieve optimal risk sharing. However, if the proportion of types is stochastic this is not so but the allocation is still superior to that of the contract without suspension. In Anderlini's model suspension of convertibility proves more problematical. In particular, for how long must suspension be in place to eliminate the problem of the run? Presumably what is required to establish credibility is that the deposit contract is modified to include a suspension clause which penalises depositors in some way for engaging in a run. This is only suggestive and requires more thought.

In both models deposit insurance can avert the problem of a run and preserve optimal risk sharing. The disadvantage of private insurance schemes is that they must hold reserves, or find some other way of precommiting funds to make promises to depositors credible. Therefore it can be argued that the government may have a natural advantage here since because of the power of taxation it has no need to hold reserves. But if the private scheme held reserves in the form of government bonds then it would be backed by an equivalent demand on tax payers. However, there may be some cost here in distorting the bank's portfolio.

Anderlini's paper provides a useful extension of the Diamond–Dybvig model. However, neither paper addresses some important issues. I will list these as a set of questions:

1 What are the effects of introducing risk into the bank's portfolio and allowing the bank to choose from a range of investments? What then is the appropriate form of contract between the bank and its depositors? If there is still the possibility of a bank run does suspension of convertibility or deposit insurance improve matters? Note here that there is now a moral hazard associated with deposit insurance.
2 What are the implications of allowing consumers to diversify their portfolios between banks or by holding securities directly?
3 Does the structure of the banking industry have implications for its efficiency? For example, are concentrated banking systems more or less efficient at providing liquidity through risk sharing than less concentrated systems? What is the role of the bank's stockholders?
4 With many banks, what is the role of a bankers' market? There are many aspects to this question, but we may ask to what extent banks borrowing and lending amongst themselves leads to cooperative behaviour and thereby stabilises the model? Can this market provide insurance for depositors? There are of course many additional questions.
5 How do banks develop credible policies? Here there is a role for investigating bank reputation.
6 What is the role of the central bank as lender of last resort and provider of confidence in the banking system?

These questions are all suggested by reading these papers which I feel underlines the real interest of this area of research. My feeling is that unless we model the environment in which banks actually operate we cannot expect to understand their behaviour and the role of regulation.

INTERNATIONAL FINANCE

7 A cost of capital approach to the taxation of foreign direct investment income

JULIAN ALWORTH*

I Introduction

Most economists approach the subject of the taxation of foreign investment in an asymmetric fashion. On the one hand, when describing the company tax systems which exist in various countries they are extremely taxonomical and specific. On the other hand, the effects of the tax system itself are analysed in highly stylised models of the economy in which the institutional character of the specific tax provisions is completely lost. In many respects this characterisation of the literature is one which might equally well have applied to many studies of domestic company tax systems in the 1960s. As a result of these deficiencies in the analysis of international tax environments, there is a substantial degree of unawareness of the manner in which tax considerations might affect the financial decisions of multinational companies.

This paper represents a clear break from the approaches mentioned above. It has two objectives. The first is to suggest a framework in which to analyse the various tiers of company taxes that bear on international direct investment income. The general classification chosen resembles that developed at length in King (1977) and applied to the examination of the corporate tax systems of several countries in King and Fullerton (1984). This approach permits a straightforward comparison of different types of double tax agreements as well as the examination of alternative systems of integrating the taxation of corporations with that of dividends.

The second objective of this paper is to examine the effect of these alternative systems of double taxation relief on the financial policy of multinational companies. The approach taken here to this question differs in several respects from previous contributions (see for example Adler (1979), Horst (1977) or Senbet (1979) on this subject). Firstly, the effects of taxation are examined under the Modigliani–Miller assumptions. Whilst for almost all tax systems this implies that firms choose financial policies

185

that are corner solutions if all individuals pay personal income taxes at the same rate, such an approach highlights the precise nature of the most important incentives present in the tax system. It also allows for other possible types of equilibria, analogues to those presented in Miller (1977) and Auerbach and King (1982). The second major departure from previous studies is that explicit account is taken of the effects of different types of company tax systems in the home and host country on the financial policies followed by multinational companies. The explicit recognition of these taxes is particularly important since the benefits of double taxation relief at the corporate level are in some countries (for example the UK) almost entirely offset by the tax treatment of dividend distributions. In addition, the financial effects on foreign investment of alternative systems of integrating company taxes are often a major consideration for determining which system of integration is chosen for integrating taxes domestically. Finally, this paper examines the incentives which company tax systems provide for pricing intra-company loans at non-market rates. Since such intra-company flows represent a large portion of the financing of affiliates by head offices and their pricing has been the source of much litigation with the tax authorities, inattention to the 'transfer pricing' problem in the context of the financial decisions of multinational companies has been a major drawback of previous studies.

Before turning to the description of the model in the following sections it is important to examine one effect of taxation on financial decision-making in an international context which is not considered explicitly by this paper. Taxation affects the legal status of the manner in which investments are undertaken. Whilst such effects in the domestic case generally reduce to the issue of whether a firm should incorporate or not, a wider set of decisions needs to be taken in the international sphere. Where should the owners of the firm reside given that a parent company is established in a particular jurisdiction and vice versa? Should the foreign affiliate be a branch or a subsidiary? Where should the head office locate given the location of the affiliate and vice versa?

It is clear that if individuals and companies were able to choose freely their country of residence, all these questions would have to be solved simultaneously, and that it might even be possible to have multiple optimal combinations of locational choice compatible with the same after-tax profit profile. As mobility across tax and legal jurisdictions grows, there can be little doubt that these types of considerations are increasingly going to affect the decision-making of firms.

There may, however, be limitations on such full optimisation. The most important are likely to be of a managerial nature. There is also the possibility that the authorities may attempt to limit the scope for such movements by changing jurisdiction rules, for example, by taxing individuals on the basis of citizenship, or by prohibiting the emigration of company head offices to other tax jurisdictions.

II Systems of company taxation and double taxation relief

II.1 A simple definition

The taxation of company investment income arising overseas can be represented by a framework analogous to that developed in King (1977). In fact under the assumption employed throughout this paper that the company consists of only a head office and an affiliate[1] – either a branch or a wholly-owned subsidiary – the two general tax variables which are used to characterise systems of company taxation and double taxation relief for foreign investment bear a striking resemblance to the tax variables used to classify domestic tax systems.

The first parameter, τ^*, is the tax rate on company income Y of the affiliate as defined by the tax statutes.[2] By analogy with its domestic counterpart it is defined as the rate of tax which would apply if no profits were distributed by the affiliate. The value of τ^*, however, depends on the tax systems in the two jurisdictions. In the host country profits are taxed at a rate τ_a. In the home country profits are taxed at a rate τ_h but the ultimate tax liability depends, sometimes in a complicated manner, on the form of relief given on taxes paid abroad and, as we shall see below, in some cases on the system of taxation of dividend repatriations in the host country.

The second parameter, θ^*, is concerned with the measure of discrimination between retentions in the foreign affiliate and distributions to the final shareholder of the parent company. In the domestic case a similar 'tax discrimination variable' denoted by θ is defined as the opportunity cost of retaining earnings within the corporate sector in terms of net dividends foregone, where the net dividends D are those a shareholder would receive after paying all company and personal taxes. Hence θ equals the additional dividends after company and personal taxes. Under a classical system of corporation tax, such as that in the United States, $\theta = (1-m)$ where m is the marginal personal tax rate of a shareholder. In the international case, θ^* is more complex since it applies to two levels of distributions and depends on the manner in which these two distributions are taxed. The first distribution is from the affiliate to the parent. As we shall show in the next sub-section, under some, but not all, systems of double taxation relief the value of θ^* will depend on the opportunity cost of retaining earnings in the affiliate θ_a, defined as the additional potential income which the parent company would receive if the affiliate distributed a unit of retained earnings. In the simplest case of a classical system and a withholding tax (w) on dividend payment $\theta_a = 1 - w$. If taxation of profits Y is deferred until dividends are repatriated, the value of θ^* will also depend in a complicated fashion on the taxation of profits in both countries, τ_a and τ_h.

The second level of distributions (D_h) is from the parent to the ultimate shareholder. The opportunity cost of retaining earnings in the parent company θ_h is defined in a similar fashion as for the affiliate, i.e. as the additional potential income the shareholder in the home country would receive if the parent company distributed a unit of retained earnings. Analytically the additional tax liability incurred in this case is the same as that for domestic companies although in practice the taxes on distributions to shareholders from foreign earnings are often different from those on income generated domestically. From the definition of θ^*, we know that if one unit of dividends is distributed by the affiliate and passed on to the ultimate shareholder, θ^* is received by the shareholder and $(1 - \theta^*)$ is shared by the tax authorities of the two countries. This entails (see Alworth (1987) for a more detailed derivation) that the additional tax per unit of net dividends (D_h) is given by $(1 - \theta^*)/\theta^*$. Hence, the total tax liability (T) on company income in the two countries is given by

$$T = \tau^* Y + (1 - \theta^*)D_h/\theta^*$$

In addition, from the definition of τ^* and θ^*, it is clear that $(1 - \tau^*)\theta^*$ is the maximum amount that shareholders can receive after payment of all taxes.

II.2 Alternative systems of double taxation relief

The values taken by τ^* and θ^*, namely the manner in which τ_a, τ_h, θ_a and θ_h interact, depend to a large extent on the system of double tax relief adopted by the home country and on the systems of company taxation in both countries.[3]

The principal forms of double tax relief are as follows:

(a) Credit system without deferral
(b) Credit system with deferral
(c) Exemption
(d) Deduction system without deferral
(e) Deduction system with deferral

With very few exceptions, the first three methods apply at present in various countries to foreign corporation taxes. Table 7.1 shows the type of tax relief provisions which exist in western Europe, Canada, Japan and the

Table 7.1. *Systems of double taxation relief in various countries*

Credit without deferral	Credit with deferral	Exemption
Austria[1] (*b*; *DTA*)	Austria[2] (*s*; *DTA*)	Belgium (*b*; *p*; *DTA*)
Canada (*b*)	Belgium (*s*)	France (*b*; *s*)
Denmark (*b*)	Canada (*s*)	Italy (*b*), for local
Finland (*b*; *DTA*)	Denmark (*s*; *DTA**)	income tax
Germany (*b*; *DTA*)	Finland (*s*)	Liechtenstein (*b*)
Ireland (*b*)	Germany (*s*)	Netherlands (*b*; *p*; *s*)
Italy (*b*; *DTA*), against	Greece (*s*)	Norway (*b*; *p*; *DTA*)
corporate income tax	Ireland (*s*)	Switzerland (*b*; *DTA*)[3]
Japan (*b*)	Italy (*s*), against	
Luxembourg (*s*)	corporate income tax	
United Kingdom (*b*)	Japan (*s*)	
United States (*b*)	Luxembourg (*b*; *DTA*)[4]	
	Norway (*s*)	
	Spain (*b*; *s*)	
	Sweden (*s*), against the	
	national income tax	
	Switzerland[5] (*s*; *p*)	
	United Kingdom (*s*)	
	United States (*s*)	

Source: Own adaptation from information contained in Frommel (1975) and Adams and Whalley (1977) as well as Inland Revenue and Price Waterhouse various issues. The systems are those in force in 1982.

Notation: *s* = subsidiaries only; *b* = branches only; *DTA* = under all or most double tax agreements provides for full exemption; *p* = partial; *DTA** = exemption under some double tax agreements.

Notes:

[1] There are no explicit legal provisions for unilateral double taxation relief but relief may be granted by Minister of Finance upon application in the form of a credit or an exemption.

[2] Dividends received from a foreign company are exempt from Austrian taxation when there is at least a 25 per cent shareholding.

[3] In the absence of a double tax treaty, income enters into the Swiss corporation's taxable profit net of foreign taxes.

[4] Taxes paid abroad in excess of the tax credit are deductible as expenses.

[5] There is no credit for foreign income taxes, but certain double tax treaties provide for a credit against Swiss income taxes of the unrelieved portion of foreign withholding taxes on dividends.

United States for corporation and dividend taxes. Although at present the two latter methods apply only to wealth taxes and withholding taxes on interest income in certain countries, they are discussed here since they have been at times suggested as a way of providing double tax relief for corporation taxes. The remaining part of this section examines the manner in which these different systems operate in terms of the parameters discussed in the introduction.

(a) *Credit without deferral*

Many countries, including the United Kingdom and the United States, allow taxes paid in the host country as a credit against the tax liability in the home country. If there is no deferral, profits earned by the foreign branch or subsidiary are consolidated with those of the parent and all eligible taxes, including withholding taxes on dividends, levied in the host country are allowable as credits.[4] Therefore, the overall burden on the foreign investment in this case is determined only by the tax system in the home country so that

$$\tau^* = \tau_h \quad \text{and} \quad \theta^* = \theta_h$$

Taxes in the host country do not affect the foreign investment decision.

In practice, limitations are generally imposed on the extent to which foreign taxes can be credited against home country taxes on foreign income. This limitation takes the form of setting a ceiling equal to τ_h on foreign taxes which are creditable. The limitation of positive tax revenue in the home country implies that if foreign tax rates are higher than domestic taxes, i.e. $(1-\tau_h) > (1-\tau_a)\theta_a$, a company will have excess credits, or in the jargon, that there is an 'overspill'.[5] Under these circumstances, only taxes on dividend distributions will be levied in the home country. The tax parameters will therefore take the value of

$$\tau^* = \tau_a \quad \text{and} \quad \theta^* = \theta_h\theta_a$$

(b) *Credit with deferral*

As can be seen from Table 7.1, undoubtedly the most common system of affording double tax relief on the income of subsidiaries is to defer taxation until earnings are repatriated to the parent. This deferral of taxation follows from the jurisdictional rule that a foreign subsidiary is a company established as a separate entity, even if it is wholly owned by the parent, and this legal principle is analogous to that which applies in most countries to the taxation of groups of affiliated companies resident within the same tax jurisdiction.

The exact tax base employed in the home country depends on whether dividends net of foreign taxes or dividends 'grossed up' by the amount of underlying company taxes paid, i.e. $1 - \theta_a(1 - \tau_a)$, are assumed to have been repatriated. At present most tax systems adopt the latter system for computing both the taxable income and the allowable credit and we shall consider only this case in what follows. In the United States, however, net dividends constituted the tax base on all foreign earned income of subsidiaries until 1962. After that date and until 1976 this system continued to apply to foreign income earned in less-developed countries.

Under the 'gross-up' system, and in the absence of 'excess credits'[6], the values of the parameters are given by (after some manipulation)

$$\tau^* = \tau_a \quad \text{and} \quad \theta^* = \theta_h(1-\tau_h)/(1-\tau_a)$$

Hence, the deferral provision implies that if $\tau_h > \tau_a$ companies have an incentive to avoid repatriating profits in order to escape the excess liability which they would incur on such distributions from their affiliate. This potential loss of revenue for the home country tax authorities and implicit incentive towards foreign investment has led many, especially in the United States,[7] to argue for the abolition of the deferral provision.

Three types of arguments can be presented to support the continuation of deferral. Firstly, unlike branches, which are legally part of the parent company, subsidiaries are separate entities. Abolishing deferral would amount in practice to the consolidation into the parent company's balance sheet of all foreign participation in which share ownership exceeded a certain percentage. Paradoxically this could lead to an unwarranted 'tax insolvency' if domestic operations did not generate sufficient income and the dividend payout ratio of the affiliate were constrained at too low a value in respect of the tax liability on foreign operations in the home country. The latter would be likely to occur if some limitations on dividend payouts were enforced by host country authorities because of exchange control regulations.

A second argument against abolishing deferral is presented by Hartman (1977). He contends that the revenue gains to the US tax authorities would be minimal since retaliation in the form of higher tax rates by foreign countries' tax authorities would nullify possible revenue gains.[8]

Lastly, as we shall show below, it is important to realise that the reform of the taxation of foreign direct investment income needs to proceed closely in hand with that of the taxation of other capital flows. Given the increased internationalisation of financial markets and the enhanced possibilities for avoiding domestic regulations which this entails, the isolated abolition of deferral on the taxation of profits arising abroad would be of little use so long as firms could engage in forms of financing which might lead implicitly to the same benefits derived from deferral. In the next section we shall show that this argument does not hold true in most circumstances.

(c) *Exemption system*
Under this system the income of the affiliate is taxed either by the home or the host country but not by both. The profits may be exempt from tax in the

country in which the recipient resides (exemption on a destination basis). If the foreign income is exempt in the home country, the tax is said to be based on territoriality.[9] It is clear that the case of 'overspill' described above is equivalent to an exemption system so that the tax parameters are given by

$$\tau^* = \tau_a \quad \text{and} \quad \theta^* = \theta_h \theta_a$$

(d) *Deduction system without deferral*

Many taxes are allowable as deductions in determining the tax base for other taxes. For example, domestic companies are often allowed to deduct local taxes in determining taxable income for company taxes. However, at present the deduction system is not implemented by any country for foreign income taxes.

The reason for considering the deduction system is that it has been regarded as the optimal tax when the objective is to maximise national social welfare (Musgrave (1972), Feldstein and Hartmann (1980)). Indeed, in the United States, the taxation of foreign income according to this method was proposed and rejected in the late 1960s (the Burke–Hartke Bill; see Alworth (1987)). The parameterisation of this system is somewhat more complex because the deductions of foreign taxes act upon the domestic tax base, and hence the host and home country tax rates enter multiplicatively in the value of τ^*.

In the general case the tax variables take the following values (see Alworth (1987) for a full derivation):

$$\tau^* = \tau_a + [\tau_h(1-\tau_a)]/[\theta_a + \tau_h(1-\theta_a)]$$

and

$$\theta^* = \theta_h[\theta_a + \tau_h(1-\theta_a)]$$

It should be noted that the values of τ^* and θ^* simplify considerably if $\theta_a = 1$ (no foreign withholding taxes) to

$$\tau^* = \tau_a + \tau_h(1-\tau_a) \quad \text{and} \quad \theta^* = \theta_h$$

As in the case of repealing deferral, numerous institutional arguments (see Hufbauer *et al.* (1975)) can be made against the substitution of the credit system by one of deduction. In addition, since under the deduction system the tax rates on foreign investment exceed those on domestic investment, companies will have an incentive to transform their income from foreign investments into income subject to domestic tax rates. Two examples of how this might occur are back-to-back and parallel loans.[10]

(e) *Deduction with deferral*

If the deduction system were adopted, it is not likely that there would be allowance for deferral. However for the sake of completeness we shall consider this possibility. In this case our tax parameters would have values of

$$\tau^* = \tau_a$$

$$\theta^* = \theta_h \theta_a (1 - \tau_h)$$

If the firm retains profits abroad this system would be less burdensome for the multinational than the no deferral deduction system. It would, moreover, as we shall see, leave open a wider range of advantageous policies for avoiding tax.

Before concluding this section it is important to notice that tax authorities in both the host and home countries are also conscious of the problems which arise for the taxation of foreign direct investment from all systems of company taxation which allow for some form of dividend relief. On the one hand in the case of deferral (or exemption) and if $\theta_a > 1$ the possibility arises for companies to retain earnings at company tax rates lower than τ_a by setting up intermediary financial subsidiaries in countries adopting exemption systems (see below) through which to channel their profits. In practice these profits are reinvested in the affiliate at rates below those which would be possible for retentions. On the other hand, under certain types of dividend relief in the home country (i.e. $\theta_h > 1$) the home country authorities may find themselves providing tax credits for underlying company taxation which has not been paid in the case of overspill. The simple parameters described in this section and summarised in Table 7.2 clearly illustrate these possibilities. The following section examines the implications of these different tax systems for the financial policy of multinational companies.

III The financing decisions of multinational companies

Multinational companies can engage in a wide range of financial policies, summarised in Table 7.3, not available to companies operating in only one jurisdiction. The primary benefit for the multinational is the ability to segregate these financing decisions into different balance sheets and thereby to straddle jurisdictions in such a way as to minimise tax. An additional potential benefit from straddling jurisdictions is that multinationals can undertake inter-company financial transfers at internal prices that reflect capital cost minimising strategies rather than the real opportunity costs of other forms of financing. These advantages, however, should not be confused with the ability to tap sources of finance in different countries or in

Table 7.2. *Systems of double tax relief: values of* θ^*, τ^* *and* $\theta^*(1-\tau^*)$

General tax parameters	Systems of Double Tax Relief				
	Credit: no deferral	Credit: with deferral	Exemption[1]	Deduction: no deferral	Deduction: with deferral
θ^*	θ_h	$\theta_h\dfrac{(1-\tau_h)}{1-\tau_a}$	$\theta_h\theta_a$	$\theta_h[\theta_a+\tau_h(1-\theta_a)]$	$\theta_h\theta_a(1-\tau_h)$
τ^*	τ_h	τ_a	τ_a	$\dfrac{\tau_h+\tau_a\theta_a(1-\tau_h)}{\theta_a+\tau_h(1-\theta_a)}$	τ_a
$\theta^*(1-\tau^*)$[2]	$\theta_h(1-\tau_h)$	$\theta_h(1-\tau_h)$	$\theta_h\theta_a(1-\tau_a)$	$\theta_h\theta_a(1-\tau_h)(1-\tau_a)$	$\theta_h\theta_a(1-\tau_a)(1-\tau_h)$

Notes:
[1] And 'overspill', credit with or without deferral.
[2] Assuming full repatriation of dividends.

Table 7.3. *Financial policies of the binational firm**

Autonomous financial policies of affiliate
1 Borrow
  a. In the host country (currency)
  b. In the home country (not from the parent) or in the international financial market
2 Retain earnings
3 Issue shares to non-majority shareholders (i.e. not to parent)

Parent–dependent financial policies of affiliate
1 Borrow from parent

source of   ⎧ a. The parent issues shares
parent funds ⎨ b. The parent borrows
           ⎩ c. The parent retains earnings

2 Issue shares to parent

source of   ⎧ a. The parent issues shares
parent funds ⎨ b. The parent borrows
           ⎩ c. The parent retains earnings

* Only downstream financing from the parent to the affiliate is considered in the table. In addition to these possibilities, multinational companies have the option of raising finance in different currencies.

different markets (such as in the Euro-markets) since in theory companies operating in only one tax jurisdiction may also borrow abroad.

This section examines the effects of the tax systems described in Section I on some specific financial policies of the binational firm. As for a firm operating in only one tax jurisdiction, the basis for analysing the effects of the tax system on the financial behaviour of the binational firm is the capital market equilibrium condition. This condition states that in the absence of uncertainty the yield on investing in a firm deriving its income from abroad is equal to that on any particular asset purchased domestically.

In order to abstract from the inter-relations which might exist between the investment decisions of the parent and the subsidiary, the parent firm is taken merely as a source of funds for and a recipient of income from the affiliate. Since the parent only acts as a shell through which funds flow abroad it is, in effect, for all relevant purposes merely a holding company.[11] Under these circumstances, the instantaneous capital market equilibrium condition is given by

$$\rho V_a = D_h + (1 - z)\dot{V}_a \qquad (1)$$

where ρ denotes the net of personal tax discount rate for shareholders in the home country, V_a is the value of the foreign project to these shareholders, $\dot{V}_a = \partial V_a/\partial t$ are instantaneous capital gains, and z is the home country tax rate on accrued capital gains.

This capital market equilibrium condition can be used to derive the financial cost of capital for the firm under alternative policies. In order to do this, we shall assume that a number of restrictions hold:

(i) There is only one representative shareholder residing in the home country. This allows us to abstract from differences in tastes, information and marginal tax rates amongst shareholders within and across borders as well as the possibility of tax arbitrage due to personal taxes.

(ii) Borrowing and lending rates (r) are identical internationally unless otherwise stated and the supply of funds to the firm is perfectly elastic.

(iii) Exchange rates are fixed and set equal to unity. There is no inflation.

(iv) There are no transaction costs and there is no uncertainty.

(v) Tax rates are fixed.

(vi) The home country tax authorities accept the host country's definition of the tax base.

(vii) There is no 'tax exhaustion' in the host country.[12]

Our discussion of the financial policies of the binational firm will follow rather closely the method employed by King (1977) and Atkinson and Stiglitz (1980) which consist of making pairwise comparisons between various policies. Our discussion, however, will not be exhaustive in the sense that not all the possible financing strategies shown in Table 7.3 will be compared. Only the most important ones will be examined since the others can be discussed in a straightforward manner (see Alworth (1987)). Note surprisingly the results are in many instances reminiscent of those for domestic companies.

(a) *Borrowing and retentions*

The first pairwise comparison is between the most important financial policies followed by multinationals:

(i) direct long-term borrowing by the affiliate on the host country market;
(ii) retentions by the affiliate.

Our analysis proceeds by expanding the capital market equilibrium condition to account for the possibility of debt finance. From the flow-of-funds account of the firm, we know that dividends are by identity a residual of the real and financial policies of the firm. Hence, net dividends received by the individual shareholder in the home country, under the assumption that the firm either borrows or retains earnings to finance its investments, are equal to after-tax residual cash flows shown by

$$D_h = \theta^*[x_a - r(1 - \gamma^* \tau^*)B_a + \dot{B}_a] \tag{2}$$

In addition to the tax parameters introduced in Section I, γ^* is the proportion of interest payments that are tax deductible, x_a are cash flows net of deductions (including tax allowances) for depreciation, B_a is the stock of outstanding external borrowings of the affiliate, and $\dot{B}_a = \partial B_a/\partial t$ is the instantaneous change in the stock of external borrowings. For the remainder of this paper capital assets will be assumed to be infinitely durable so that x_a can be interpreted as earnings before interest and taxes (EBIT).

Combining (1) and (2) and rearranging we obtain expression (3):

$$\rho V_a + \theta^* r(1 - \gamma^* \tau^*)B_a = \theta^*(x_a + \dot{B}_a) + (1 - z)\dot{V}_a \tag{3}$$

This is a modified capital market condition relating post-tax financial charges (on the left) to post-tax earnings (right). If we let $b_a = B_a/(B_a + V_a)$ be the leverage ratio at the margin (3) can be written more simply as[13]

$$N(B_a + V_a) = Tx_a + (\dot{B} + \dot{V}) \tag{4}$$

where N is the financial cost of capital to the firm, given by

$$N = [\rho(1 - b_a) + \theta^* r(1 - \gamma^* \tau^*)b_a]/[(1 - b_a)(1 - z) + b_a \theta^*] \tag{5}$$

and T is equal to

$$T = \theta^*/[1 - b_a)(1 - z) + b_a \theta^*] \tag{6}$$

The differential equation (4) can be resolved so as to yield the value maximising objective of the firm as (7)

$$B_a + V_a = T \int_0^\infty e^{-Nt} x_a dt \tag{7}$$

As is readily seen from this expression the firm maximises its value $(B_a + V_a)$ by discounting EBIT at a cost of capital N. Thus, expression (7) is analogous to the valuation formula for domestic projects.[14]

The value of the firm depends on N and consequently on the sources of finance chosen by the firm. In order to focus attention on the effects of taxation on this particular choice we shall retain the Modigliani–Miller assumption that the firm is indifferent between debt or equity in the absence of taxation. This assumption implies that the tax system gives rise to corner solutions in the choice of financial policies, i.e. all investment is financed at the margin from only one source. For the two cases considered here – debt and retained earnings – a firm will be indifferent between these financial policies only if

$$\rho/(1-z) = r(1-\gamma^*\tau) \tag{8}$$

If this condition does not hold, the firm will choose to finance its investment either out of retentions or by debt but not by both. In addition, if the discount rate for shareholders' equity equals the interest rate at which firms borrow net of the personal tax rate (m) in the home country[15] $\rho = r(1-m)$, condition (8) becomes

$$(1-m)/(1-z) = 1 - \gamma^*\tau^* \tag{9}$$

The left-hand side of this expression is the same as that obtained by King (1977, p. 99) for a firm operating in only one country. This is not surprising since both the shareholder's discount rate and the capital gains tax rate are identical to those for a firm operating in only one tax jurisdiction. The values of γ^* and τ^* are, however, different since they depend on the tax deductibility of interest abroad and the taxation of profits according to foreign and domestic tax systems.

In order to simplify our analysis, we shall concentrate on the two polar cases where interest is deductible ($\gamma^* = 1$) and where interest is not deductible ($\gamma^* = 0$) in the host country.

(i) $\gamma^* = 1$. If interest payments are deductible against tax, the larger the value taken by τ^* the greater the incentive for external borrowing for given values of m and z. The actual value taken by τ^* depends on the system of double taxation relief. As we have seen in the previous section, all tax systems which allow deferral or whose tax rates are below those which exist in the host country ('excess credits') imply $\tau^* = \tau_a$ so that only three possible cases need to be considered:

(i.a) $\tau^* = \tau_h$
(i.b) $\tau^* = \tau_a$
(i.c) $\tau^* = [\tau_a + \tau_h(1-\tau_a)]/[\theta_a + \tau_h(1-\theta_a)]$

(i.a) If the tax rate on domestic profits is equal to that from foreign investment (τ_h), the financial policy of the multinational under a credit system with no deferral is the same as that followed by any company operating in the home country jurisdiction. For $(1-m) > (1-z)(1-\tau_h)$, the optimal policy is to borrow as much as possible, not only to finance investment but also to increase dividends and make capital repayments. Legal restrictions, however, often imply that such extreme corner solutions are in practice not feasible. As King (1977) has pointed out, many countries do not allow dividend distributions to exceed accumulated earnings.

If $(1-m) < (1-z)(1-\tau_h)$, the optimal policy is the exact opposite: finance investment from retained earnings and use any excess retentions to accumulate financial assets. Again it is likely that if this policy is pursued beyond a certain degree, the home country authorities will deem the affiliate to be a 'tax avoidance scheme'. The need for these restrictions is analogous to that for domestic companies precluding the accumulation of funds which are in excess of the 'needs of the business', especially in the case of closely held companies.

(i.b) The 'deferral', 'exemption', and 'excess credits' (overspill) cases are similar in that the foreign tax system determines the company tax liability on the foreign project. If $(1-m) < (1-z)(1-\tau_a)$, firms will accumulate earnings abroad, seeking possibly to do so in countries with very low tax rates. This is the common tax avoidance scheme associated with so-called 'tax havens'. A number of the advantages associated with tax havens have been decreased by provisions such as those under the 'Subpart F' of the US Internal Revenue Code. Under these provisions in certain cases if a subsidiary is believed to have accumulated earnings abroad for the sole purpose of avoiding tax in the United States, such earnings are deemed to be repatriated and taxed accordingly, i.e. there is no deferral.

Potentially with deferral, foreign and domestic projects may be financed differently if the signs for (9) and its domestic equivalent are reversed. If $\tau_h > (m-z)/(1-z) > \tau_a$ domestic projects will be financed by borrowing and foreign projects by retained earnings.

(i.c) The deduction system without deferral will always imply a higher taxation of foreign investments than domestic investments. The incentive to borrow will, ceteris paribus, always be higher under this system than any of the previous ones. Only in the unlikely case that $\tau_a = 0$ and $\theta_a = 1$ will the incentives be identical to those which would exist for home country investments. Hence, unless there are extremely high marginal personal tax rates, shareholders will prefer that companies borrow to finance their foreign investments. It is, therefore, likely that under a deduction system foreign affiliates would be very thinly capitalised relative to what they would be under other systems of double taxation relief.

(ii) $\gamma^* = 0$. If the foreign country disallows the deduction of interest, as might be the case under an expenditure or 'cash flow' corporation tax, the incentives to follow a financial policy of either debt or retentions depend only on the home country tax system. If $m > z$, it pays the firm to retain earnings abroad, and if $m < z$, the optimal policy is to borrow abroad. Neutrality holds only if $m = z$. As for domestic firms if marginal tax rates in the home country are progressive, the actual policy followed on the project depends on the distribution of share ownership and the relationship between the marginal tax rates on capital gains and other sources of personal income. Since in practice z never exceeds m, the firm would never borrow abroad.

(b) *Retentions and new share issues*

The second pairwise comparison is between:

(i) Issuing new shares at home to buy new shares of the affiliate which in future periods distributes dividends;
(ii) Retaining earnings in the affiliate.

Dividends received by home country shareholders for these two policies equal

$$D_h = \theta^*(x_a + \dot{S}_a) \tag{10}$$

where $\dot{S}_a = \partial S_a/\partial t$ are new share issues.

The capital market equilibrium condition can be written as

$$\rho V_a = \theta^* x_a + \theta^* \dot{S}_a + (1-z)(\dot{V}_a - \dot{S}_a) \tag{11}$$

where the last term of this expression is 'taxable capital gains'.[16]

If we let $e = \dot{S}_a/\dot{V}_a$ be the proportion of the increase in the outstanding total value of the firm accounted for by new share issues, the financial capital cost, N, equals

$$N = \rho/[e\theta^* + (1-e)(1-z)] \tag{12}$$

and

$$T = \theta^*/[e\theta^* + (1-e)(1-z)] \tag{13}$$

By analogy with our previous comparison a firm will issue new shares if

$$\theta^* > (1-z) \tag{14}$$

i.e. the capital gains tax charged on retaining a unit of foreign profits abroad is less than the additional taxation incurred by paying that unit out as dividends and financing new investments from the home country. While this condition is reminiscent of the similar choice facing domestic investments, there is an important distinction to be made. θ^* represents the opportunity cost of distributing a dividend from the affiliate to the parent *and* the home country shareholder.

Although the value of θ^* depends on the taxation of dividends in the home country, it is possible that the parent may choose not to distribute dividends to its shareholders but rather to reinvest abroad by purchasing shares of the affiliate without new share issues from its own shareholders. In this circumstance, the taxation of dividends in the home country becomes irrelevant for the financial policies followed by the firm and θ_h is in effect equal to $(1-z)$. Table 7.4 presents the relevant pairwise comparisons for (14) of alternative systems of double tax relief for the case in which $\theta_h = 1 - z$.

Table 7.4. *Critical values of* θ^*, *given* $\theta_h = 1 - z$, *for which new share issues by the affiliate* (*purchased by the parent*) *are preferred to retentions by the affiliate*

Credit; no deferral	Credit with deferral	Exemption	Deduction; no deferral	Deduction with deferral
Equal[1]	$\tau_a < \tau_h$[2]	$\theta_a > 1$[3]	$\theta_a > 1$[4]	$\theta_a(1 - \tau_h) > 1$

Notes:
[1] The firm is indifferent.
[2] Implies excess credits.
[3] Also cases with excess credits.
[4] Sufficient condition.

The interpretation of Table 7.4 is straightforward. The credit system without deferral is neutral between the two forms of retentions. The firm is indifferent between purchasing new shares from the affiliate or retaining earnings abroad. If there are 'excess credits', the condition for retentions abroad is the same as the one that holds under the exemption system. In these cases, affiliates operating in countries with high corporation taxes but which adopt considerable amounts of dividend relief (such as Germany) will distribute dividends and issue new shares. Indeed, the affiliates should go further and issue new shares in order to finance higher current dividends. In practice, this does not occur since the host country authorities often restrict such dividend distributions deemed to result from fraudulent transactions. Under credit with deferral, firms will prefer retentions by the affiliates unless there are excess credits, in which case the previous conclusions apply.

It is surprising that under the deduction system without deferral, the condition for issuing new shares is that $\theta_a > 1$. The reason for this result lies in the fact that repatriations will, through dividend relief in the host country, reduce aggregate tax liabilities. With the deduction system with deferral, the affiliate will never issue shares if $\tau_h > \tau_a$.[17]

The main result which is obtained in this section is surprising, though not counter-intuitive: if there is deferral (or an exemption system), it is likely that affiliates located in high-tax countries which provide dividend relief to subsidiaries and branches of foreign firms will issue shares. Hence dividend distributions and new share issues may occur simultaneously.

As we have seen, whether a firm chooses to finance its investment abroad by issuing shares in the home country will depend on the value taken by θ_h. If new share issues are the tax preferred policy, a sufficient condition for dividends to be received by shareholders and new share issues to occur in the home country is clearly $\theta_h > (1-z)$. This depends on the system of company taxation in the home country, and also on the system of double tax relief, since θ_h may not equal the opportunity cost of dividend distributions for home country earnings.

In most countries, $\theta^* < (1-z)$, especially if there are excess credits. In the latter case, there would be no tax revenue from foreign investment in the home country and any attempt to provide dividend relief for distributions from foreign earnings would imply a loss in revenue to the home country's tax authorities.[18]

(c) *Inter-company loans*

The possibility of inter-company loans adds a margin of discretion to the financial policy of the binational company which is not available to companies operating in only one tax jurisdiction.[19] Binational firms can use the differences in the tax systems of the countries in which they operate to minimise their overall tax liability by pricing their inter-company loans at 'non-market' prices. Indeed, unless bounds are placed on the interest rate which firms can charge on inter-company loans, the financial cost of capital is undefined.[20]

Let us consider first the case where the firm borrows or issues shares at home and lends to the affiliate. In this case the firm's cash flow equation is composed of two separate parts. The first comprises the earnings received from the affiliate net of the borrowing cost from the parent

$$\theta^*[x_a - r'(1-\gamma^*\tau^* + w_a)B_a + \dot{B}_a] \tag{15}$$

This expression differs from (2) in two respects. Firstly, the interest rate on intra-company borrowings r' need not coincide with the market rate r in the two countries. Secondly, allowance is made for the possibility that a withholding tax w_a is levied in the host country on borrowings from the parent company.

The second part of the cash flows generated from the foreign operations comes from the interest received by the parent from the affiliate net of the borrowing costs in the home country. This is given by

$$\theta[r'(1-\gamma'\tau_h + w')B_a - r(1-\gamma\tau_h)B] \tag{16}$$

where γ' is the percentage of the interest payments received from the affiliate for which the parent company is taxable, γ and w' are the percentages of interest payments and foreign withholding taxes which can be offset against home country corporation taxes and θ is the opportunity cost of retaining earnings on domestically generated profits.

The principal differences from the cases discussed previously concern the level of r' which is determined at the discretion of the firm. The level at which

Table 7.5. *Tax incentives for discretionary pricing under different forms of double taxation relief*

Values of $M = \theta^*(1-\tau^*+w_a)-\theta_h(1-\tau_h+w')$

Credit without deferral	0
Credit with deferral	$w'\theta_h[(1-\tau_h)/(1-\tau_a)-1]$
Exemption	$\theta_h[\theta_a(1-\tau_a+w_a)-(1-\tau_h+w')]$
Deduction without deferral	$\theta_h\theta_a(1-\tau_h)(1-\tau_a)-\theta_h(1-\theta_h+w'-w_a)$
Deduction with deferral	$\theta_h\theta_a(1-\tau_h)(1-\tau_a+w_a)-\theta_h(1-\theta_h+w')$

r' is set depends on the interaction between the tax parameters in expressions (15) and (16).[21]

In order to compute financial costs and examine these incentives more closely we shall set $B+V = B_a$ and $B/(B+V) = b$.[22] The value of N is then given by

$$N = [\rho(1-b)+\theta r(1-\gamma\tau_h)b]/\theta^* + \frac{r'M}{\theta^*} \qquad (17)$$

where

$$M = \theta^*(1-\gamma^*\tau^*+w_a)-\theta(1-\gamma'\tau_h+w') \qquad (18)$$

From expression (18) we can see that the decision over the mode of finance in the home country is independent of the interest rate charged on the inter-company loan. This is due to our assumption that the affiliate's level of gearing does not depend on that of the parent. The principal difference from the previous values of N concerns the element of discretion in the choice of r'. The value chosen for r' depends on M, which measures the tax advantage of shifting profits from the parent to the affiliate. If $M > 0$, the firm has an incentive to choose the lowest possible value of r' and repatriate earnings through dividend distributions. Conversely, if $M < 0$, the firm would choose the highest value of r' and repatriate earnings on the inter-company account.[23]

Table 7.5 presents the possible values of M for $\gamma^* = \gamma = \gamma' = 1$, $w_a = w'$ and $\theta = \theta_h$. The only method of double tax relief which would not create incentives is the credit system without deferral.[24] All other systems encourage either the raising of r' above or lowering of r' below the market interest rate r. For plausible values of the tax parameters, a system of credit with deferral and the deduction system with or without deferral, would provide for an incentive to raise r'. Under the exemption system r' should be lowered.

The policy implications of this table are clear. If firms have wide discretion in choosing the value of r', the optimal financial policy of the firm and the consequent discount rate will depend on the firm's ability to minimise tax. If the authorities choose double tax relief systems which encourage firms to determine r' in order to minimise their tax burden, changes in domestic company tax rates (for whatever other reasons they are adopted) will indirectly affect the pricing of intra-company loans. The credit without deferral system is the only method of tax relief which overcomes this very serious drawback.

IV Conclusion

The purpose of this paper has been to present a new approach for examining the effects of taxation on the financing and investment decisions of multinational companies. This approach can be interpreted as an extension and generalisation to the international setting of the 'cost of capital' approach already extensively developed in the domestic context. Further extensions such as the examination of dividend payout behaviour and the computation of effective tax rates for multinationals can be easily derived (see Alworth (1987)).

Some important policy conclusions do, however, emerge quite clearly from this study. The theoretical superiority in many circumstances of the credit with 'no-deferral' method of double taxation relief over other systems of double taxation is difficult to refute. Another factor to which this paper has drawn attention is the importance of host country tax systems, including personal taxes, on decisions concerning financial policies of multinationals. The results furthermore suggest that harsher or more lenient policies which attempt to affect the direction and size of 'real' international investment may be destined to fail if firms have sufficient leeway to adjust their financing patterns. Such policy prescriptions cannot work unless due account is taken of the multi-tiered nature of financial decisions taken by multinationals involving choices with regard to the country of production, the residence of the parent company and the legal form of the affiliate (branch versus subsidiary), in addition to the type of financing.

These results suggest that economists need to reconsider the possible effects of corporate taxes on foreign direct investment and especially to move away from models which regard such investments as a form of equity transfer.

NOTES

* This paper is a summary of Chapter 3 of my D.Phil. thesis. I wish to thank my examiners, M. King and C. Mayer, for very helpful discussions on the topics covered in this paper and for their encouragement. I am also grateful to René Capitelli, and especially Abraham Ravid, for helpful comments on a previous draft of this paper. The views expressed in this paper are my own and not necessarily the views of the Bank for International Settlements.

1 I have shown in Alworth (1987) that this assumption can be easily relaxed without any major changes to the analytical framework. It is also possible to allow for different methods of allocating reliefs for possible taxation ('per country' or 'overall').

2 The definition of profits for tax purposes does not generally coincide with the definition of economic income (see Samuelson (1964)). In the case of a multinational company it is likely that the definition of taxable income in the host country does not coincide with the definition of taxable income in the home country in which double taxation relief is being granted. In this case the value of τ^* may become a complicated function of Y in the two countries. This possibility is not examined in this paper although it would be easy to allow for this complication. See Alworth (1987), Chap. 4.

3 This paper does not describe the different systems of domestic company taxation in the host and home countries. For a description of domestic company tax systems see King (1977) and for the international implications Alworth (1987), Chap. 2. Furthermore, in individual countries company tax rates on domestic (τ), inward (τ_a) and outward (τ_h) investments may differ markedly.

4 One of the major issues under any system of double taxation relief, but especially the credit system, is which taxes are eligible for relief. This is probably one of the more contentious issues covered by double taxation relief treaties.

5 The question of excess credits and the problems of 'tax exhaustion' are not discussed in this paper.

6 If there are 'excess credits' the values of the tax parameters are the same as those applying in these circumstances for the no deferral case.

7 See Hufbauer et al. (1975).

8 For some different findings see Horst (1977).

9 We have seen already that the deferral system is partly territorial.

10 A back-to-back loan is a financial transfer from the parent to the affiliate which takes place through a financial intermediary, generally a bank. The parent company deposits funds with the intermediary, which in turn often lends to the affiliate. Both the lending and deposit rates are above the market rate. The spread between the deposit and market rates net of commission is the implicit repatriation of profits to the parent. Parallel loans consist of a parent company in one country extending credit to the affiliate of another company in return for a similar arrangement in another country.

11 The investment plans by an affiliate may entail an expansion or contrction of the parent company investment plans. The holding company assumption is analogous to assuming that the repercussions of these interconnected decisions are of second-order importance or do not exist.

12 See de Angelo and Masulis (1980), Mayer (1986) and Majd and Myers (1985) for the implications of tax losses on financial decisions.

13 The revised capital market equilibrium condition is the basis for expressing the

firm's objective as being the maximisation of the market value of shares and bonds. The maximisation of this objective need not correspond to that of shareholder equity though it proceeds from it. See Auerbach (1981).

14 See Auerbach (1981) for a similar derivation of the capital cost.

15 This assumption is valid if:

(a) capital markets in the host country are not 'segmented' by transaction costs for non-residents and foreign-owned firms. This condition also implies that there are no opportunities for profitable arbitrage;

(b) the tax system allows interest parity to hold. Evidence presented in Levi (1977) suggests that in the presence of taxes these assumptions do not often hold in practice.

16 We make use here of the approximation $\partial V = S \partial v + v \partial S$ where v is the share price and capital gains are taxed at accrual on the increase in the value of the shares (vS). Setting $v = 1$, we obtain that $\partial(vS) = \partial V - \partial S$. In the previous sub-section, this particular formulation was not necessary because there was no dilution of market value through new share issues.

17 $\theta_a(1 - \tau_a)$ is always less than or equal to one, i.e. tax liabilities cannot be negative.

18 France, which follows roughly the exemption method of 'double tax relief', does not allow the imputation credit to be extended to dividends deemed to have been received from abroad.

19 This does not mean that affiliates of a concern operating in only one tax jurisdiction do not make use of inter-company finance. The scope for reducing tax liabilities in one jurisdiction is in general very limited, though for specific firms under particular tax provisions there could be large tax savings. For example, if loss offsets are limited and accounts of affiliates are not consolidated with the parent, profits could be shifted from one affiliate to another in order to reduce total taxable income.

20 A number of more complex financial strategies are possible which make use of the differential treatment of dividends and interest payments amongst various units of the firm. The prime tax avoidance technique involves the use of 'conduits' or 'intermediary' firms which employ 'back-to-back' loans. Reduced rates available under double tax treaties may then be available through the establishment of a subsidiary in a conveniently located third country, the employment of a 'broker' bank located in a country which is neither that of the borrower or lender, or the use of an international bank as an 'escrow trustee' to handle all loans to foreign subsidiaries. All the complex institutional detail of these arrangements is not captured by the model described in this section. This binational model does, however, explain the incentives for use of these legal arrangements outside the direct parent subsidiary link. For a thorough description of the actual mechanics of these intermediary operations see Edwards-Ker (1975).

21 There is, however, the possibility that γ^* may equal zero if the interest payment is deemed to be a 'concealed dividend' by the host country tax authorities. In this case the value of γ' may be adjusted by the home country authorities. The Finnish authorities, for example, may disallow the deductibility of interest payments from the tax base if these payments are judged to be a distribution of earnings to the parent company. See Edwards-Ker (1975), Chap. 7.

22 We shall also assume that there are other sources of taxable income in the home country so that $\theta[r'(1 - \gamma^*\tau^* + w_a)B_a - r(1 - \gamma\tau)B]$ need not be positive.

23 We have expressly not referred to minimisation or maximisation since there may

be no minimum or maximum in the absence of any government control. Governments will generally impose severe constraints on the values of r'. In the absence of explicit bounds on these values, firms will choose a value of r' on the basis of potential penalties which the tax authorities might apply in the case of tax evasion. For a discussion of the limitations on transfer pricing see Rugman and Eden (1985).

24 In the case where there is no 'overspill'.

REFERENCES

Adams, J. D. R. and J. Whalley (1977). *The International Taxation of Multi-national Enterprises.* Institute for Fiscal Studies, London.

Adler, M. (1979). 'US Taxation of US Multinational Corporations: A Manual of Computation Techniques and Managerial Decision Rules.' In M. Sarnath and G. Szego (eds), *International Finance and Trade.* Balanger, Cambridge, Mass.

Alworth, J. S. (1987). *Finance and Investment Decisions of Multinationals: The Tax Aspects.* Basil Blackwell, Oxford.

Atkinson, A. B. and J. E. Stiglitz (1980). *Lectures on Public Economics.* McGraw-Hill, New York.

Auerbach, A. (1981). 'A Note on the Efficient Design of Investment Incentives.' *Economic Journal*, **91**, 217–23.

Auerbach, A. (1983). 'Taxation, Corporate Financial Policy and the Cost of Capital.' *Journal of Economic Literature*, **31**, 905–41.

Auerbach, A. and M. King (1982). 'Corporate Financial Policy with Personal and Institutional Investors.' *Journal of Public Economics*, **17**, 259–85.

DeAngelo, H. and R. Masulis (1980). 'Optimal Capital Structure under Corporate and Personal Taxation.' *Journal of Financial Economics*, **8**, 3–29.

Devereux, M. P. and C. P. Mayer (1984). *Corporation Tax: The Impact of the 1984 Budget.* Institute for Fiscal Studies, London.

Edwards-Ker, M. (1975). *International Tax Strategy.* In-Depth Publishing, London.

Feldstein, M. and D. Hartman (1980). 'The Optimal Taxation of Foreign Source Investment Income.' *Quarterly Journal of Economics*, **93**, 613–29.

Frommel, S. N. (1975). *Taxation of Branches and Subsidiaries in Western Europe, Canada and the U.S.* Kluwer, Deventer.

Hartman, D. (1977). 'Deferral of Taxes on Foreign Source Income.' *National Tax Journal*, **30**, 417–25.

Hartman, D. (1979). 'Foreign Investment and Finance with Risk.' *Quarterly Journal of Economics*, **43**, 213–33.

Horst, T. (1977). 'American Taxation of Multinational Companies.' *American Economic Review*, **67**, 376–89.

Hufbauer, G. C., W. Schmidt, N. Ture and D. T. Smith (1975). *U.S. Taxation of American Business Abroad.* American Enterprise Institute, Washington.

King, M. (1977). *Public Policy and the Corporation.* Chapman and Hall, London.

King, M. and D. Fullerton (1984). *The Taxation of Income from Capital: a Comparative Study of the U.S., U.K., Sweden and West Germany.* Chicago University Press, Chicago.

Levi, M. (1977). 'Taxation and "Abnormal" International Capital Flows.' *Journal of Political Economy*, **85**, 635–46.

McLure, C. E. (1980). *Must Corporate Income be Taxed Twice?* Brookings Institution, Washington.

Majd, S. and S. C. Myers (1985). 'Valuing the Government's Tax Claim on Risky Corporate Assets.' National Bureau of Economic Research Working Paper No. 1553.

Mayer, C. (1986). 'Corporation Tax, Finance and the Cost of Capital.' *Review of Economic Studies*, **53**, 93–112.

Miller, M. H. (1977). 'Debt and Taxes.' *Journal of Finance*, **32**, 261–75.

Musgrave, P. B. (1972). 'International Tax Division Base and the Multinational Corporation.' *Public Finance*, **27**, 394–413.

Rugman, A. M. and L. Eden (eds) (1985). *Multinationals and Transfer Pricing.* Croom-Helm, London and Sydney.

Samuelson, P. A. (1964). 'Tax Deductability of Economic Depreciation to Insure Invariant Valuations.' *Journal of Political Economy*, **72**, 604–606.

Senbet, L. (1979). International Capital Market Equilibrium and the Multinational Firm: Financing and Investment Policies.' *Journal of Financial and Quantitative Analysis*, **14**, 455–76.

Stiglitz, J. E. (1976). 'The Corporation Tax.' *Journal of Public Economics*, **5**, 303–11.

8 Costs to crossborder investment and international equity market equilibrium

IAN COOPER and EVI KAPLANIS*

I Introduction

The Sharpe–Lintner Capital Asset Pricing Model (CAPM), which is based upon mutual fund theorems applied to a single domestic capital market, suggests that with homogeneous expectations and opportunity sets, all investors will hold identical portfolios of risky assets. Aggregation of investors' portfolios to get a market equilibrium implies that all individuals will choose their portfolios from two funds: the market portfolio of risky assets and the risk free asset, or a zero beta portfolio if there is no riskless asset.

The CAPM cannot be extended into an international CAPM by simply extending the opportunity set to include the world market portfolio, since the international capital markets differ from the domestic capital markets in certain important aspects, such as different currency areas, different socio-economic systems, taxes and barriers to capital flows. Several international capital market models have been developed to capture these complexities of the international capital markets. Most of these models treat exchange risk as the prime factor making international capital market equilibrium different from domestic equilibrium.

For instance, Grauer, Litzenberger and Stehle (1976) assume that exchange risk is due to different stochastic national inflation rates, while on the other hand Solnik (1974), Sercu (1980) and Adler and Dumas (1983) assume that exchange risk stems from differences in consumption baskets between investors of different origin. With the exception of Adler and Dumas these models suggest that investors, regardless of their origin, would hold the world market portfolio of risky assets, which plays the same role as the market portfolio in the single market case. Casual empiricism, however, conflicts strongly with the implications of these models. These models cannot explain why investors' portfolios have a large bias towards domestic risky assets relative to the world market portfolio. This behaviour can be explained if investors of different domiciles have different expectations or different opportunity sets in terms of net returns; for instance, if taxes on foreign investment make it more costly for foreign investors than for domestic investors to hold risky assets in a particular capital market.

Some authors (Black (1974), Stulz (1981)), have sought to model a two country capital market equilibrium where there are barriers to crossborder investments, assuming that these barriers can be considered as a tax on net foreign investments. This tax, according to Black (1974), is intended to represent various kinds of barriers to international investment, such as the possibility of expropriation of foreign holdings, direct controls on the import or export of capital, reserve requirements on bank deposits and other assets held by foreigners, and restrictions on the fraction of a business that can be foreign owned. It is even intended to represent the barriers created by the unfamiliarity that residents of one country have with the capital markets of other countries. It is possible that the general effect of all these kinds of barriers will be similar to the effect of a tax on international investment.

In a similar spirit to Black's paper, Cooper and Lessard (1981) have developed an international capital market equilibrium which allows for differential taxes on foreign investment depending on the country of investment and the origin of the investor. They obtained unique solutions for the taxes under the extreme assumptions that taxes depend on the country of investment, or on the origin of the investor. This paper extends the international capital market equilibrium model developed by Cooper and Lessard (1981), obtains upper bounds and unique solutions for the taxes under alternative assumptions, and estimates empirically the level of these barriers to crossborder investment.

In Section II of the paper we develop the international capital market equilibrium model with barriers to crossborder investment to derive shadow prices of the barriers to crossborder investment under alternative assumptions. The subsequent two sections describe our empirical work: Section III describes the data and Section IV presents and discusses the empirical findings. Finally, Section V comprises the summary and the conclusions.

II An international capital market equilibrium model with barriers to crossborder investment

The barriers to crossborder investment are a mixture of measurable costs such as withholding taxes and safe custody fees, and intangibles such as the extra risk of expropriation and information-gathering costs suffered by foreign investors. Therefore it is extremely difficult to quantify these barriers in order to give an overall effective tax rate equivalent to the total cost.[1]

The alternative to quantifying the barriers directly is to derive estimates of these barriers from investors' observed portfolio behaviour. Assuming a uniform tax rate on foreign investment, Black's pricing relationship (Black (1974)) reduces to

$$E(R_i) - \bar{R} - \bar{t}_i = b_i[E(R_m) - \bar{R} - t_m] \tag{1}$$

where

R_i is the return on security i
$\bar{R}$ is a weighted average of the interest rates in the two countries
$\bar{t}_i$ is the weighted average of the tax rates applied to holdings of security i by the residents of the two countries
R_m is the world market portfolio return
t_m is the weighted average of the tax rates on all securities
b_i $= \mathrm{cov}(R_i, R_m)/\mathrm{var}(R_m)$

In order to estimate the barriers to foreign investment, Black suggests the construction of a portfolio with the minimum possible variance whose expected return is a combination of t and known quantities. Black shows that the estimator for t is the difference between the expected return of the minimum variance zero beta world portfolio of risky assets and a weighted average of the interest rates of the individual countries.

Black's assumption that all investors are faced with the same effective tax rates on foreign investment, regardless of their origin or the country of investment, is unrealistic. For instance a South African investor is faced with severe exchange controls which make it virtually impossible for him to invest overseas, while a US investor is free to invest in any foreign market.

Cooper and Lessard (1981) developed a model which takes into account the fact that the marginal effective tax rates on crossborder investment are different for each investor/foreign country pair.[2] They derive unique solutions for the marginal effective taxes under the following extreme alternative assumptions:

(i) the deadweight costs are determined only by the country in which the investor is investing.
(ii) the deadweight costs are determined only by the investor's domicile.

In this section we will extend the Cooper and Lessard model to obtain estimates of the marginal effective taxes under less extreme assumptions, and obtain upper bounds to these taxes in the absence of any specific assumptions such as assumptions (i) and (ii).

II.1 Assumptions

The derivation of efficient portfolios in a world where there are barriers to crossborder investment, which depend both on the domicile of the investor and the country he is investing in, is based on the following assumptions:

A.1 There are N countries indexed by n

A.2 Investors have homogeneous expectations about gross real returns on risky securities; they also have the same covariance matrix of the returns on these securities, and homogeneous risk aversion

A.3 Unlimited short sales are allowed with full proceeds

A.4 There is no domestic or international real risk free asset

A.5 The deadweight costs of any investor are expressed in the form of a tax which is proportional to his net investment in each foreign country

A.6 All investors consume the same bundle of goods and purchasing power parity holds for this bundle

A.7 Returns are normally distributed, so investors are mean-variance optimisers.

A tax on the value of net investment (A.5) seems consistent with costs which are approximately proportional to the net foreign investment, such as withholding taxes, safe custody fees and exchange controls in the form of non-interest bearing deposit requirements. A proportional tax on crossborder investments, however, provides an imperfect representation of barriers such as information-gathering costs which are likely to be fixed.

Exchange controls that prevent a net increase in the foreign portfolios such as the 'dollar premium' in the UK or the 'devise titre' in France have an impact on the covariance matrix as well as reducing the rate of return earned on foreign investment. Although the representation of these costs by a proportional tax on crossborder investment is incomplete, it should partially capture the essence of these barriers. Further examination of the effects of these barriers in particular is given in Brealey, Cooper and Kaplanis (1985) where we develop an international capital market equilibrium model with exchange controls such as the 'dollar premium pool' in the UK before 1979. Similarly, imperfections resulting from real exchange rate variations would affect both the covariance matrix and expected returns. Therefore a proportional tax on the value of foreign investment would again be incomplete in this respect.

Finally, the cost of expropriation risk is an increasing function of the aggregate foreign investment in a country. For a marginal investor, however, the cost of expropriation risk could be considered as a constant percentage reduction of the return assuming that his actions have a negligible effect on the aggregate foreign investment in a specific country.

In this model we use a framework in which there is no exchange risk since we want to focus on barriers to crossborder investment which take the form of taxes on the value of investor's foreign investment. Assuming that all investors consume the same bundle of goods for which purchasing power parity holds, this implies that the real purchasing power of a given amount of money wealth is not affected by the numeraire currency. Alternatively, the purchasing power parity assumption implies that the relative prices of the consumption goods included in the consumption bundle do not vary and as a result the currency in which investors express their utility function does not affect the consumption choice. Therefore, given assumption A.6 the model does not include exchange risk as a determinant of portfolios.

Since all investors have homogeneous expectations (A.2) and operate within a mean-variance framework (A.7), our analysis remains unaffected if we assume that there is only one investor with consensus attributes in each country.

The assumptions of unlimited short sales (A.3), and of the deadweight costs being proportional to the net foreign holdings of an investor (A.5), imply that an investor with a short position in foreign assets has a negative deadweight cost. In other words, investors with a short position in foreign assets will have a benefit equal to the deadweight cost paid by investors with a long position in these foreign assets. Although these assumptions are very strong and unrealistic if the equilibrium is such that some investors want to short foreign assets, they are neutral if in equilibrium no one wants to short foreign assets. Stulz (1981) modelled the barriers to international investment assuming that an investor incurs a deadweight cost proportional to the absolute value of his holdings of risky assets rather than the net value. In such a model an investor incurs a deadweight cost when he has short or long holdings in foreign risky assets. Although from this point of view Stulz's model is more realistic, he can only derive bounds to the portfolio holdings but not a closed form solution. Under our assumptions a closed form solution is obtained at the expense of a somewhat unrealistic assumption (A.5).

In the absence of index linked bonds, there exists no real risk free asset. Assets which are risk free in nominal terms are not risk free when transformed in real terms. As a result, the introduction of nominal borrowing and lending would add complications but would not offer any additional insight. Nominal bonds are not real risk free assets and thus they can be considered as part of the set of risky securities.

Given our assumption of negative costs on short positions, the existence of indexed bonds would be problematic. Such bonds would imply riskless arbitrage profits, since the returns of the risk free assets between any two countries would be perfectly correlated and there would be a subsidy on foreign borrowing. In other words, an investor would be able to generate unlimited profits by borrowing abroad and lending domestically and therefore taking advantage of the subsidy on foreign borrowing.

II.2 Equilibrium with barriers

Each investor is assumed to act as an expected return maximiser for a given level of variance (A.7). Therefore, the ith consensus investor's optimisation problem is:

$$\text{Max}(x_i'R - x_i'c_i)$$

subject to

$$x_i'Vx_i = v$$
$$x_i'I = 1$$

where

x_i	is a column vector, the nth element of which is x_{in}
x_{in}	is the proportion of individual i's total wealth invested in risky securities of country n
R	is a column vector of pre-tax expected returns
c_i	is a column vector, the nth element of which is c_{in}
c_{in}	is the deadweight cost to investor i of holding securities in country n
v	is a constant
V	is the variance/covariance matrix of the gross (pre-cost, pre-tax) returns of the risky securities
I	is a unity column vector.

The Lagrangean of the above maximisation problem is

$$L = (x_i'R - x_i'c_i) - (h/2)(x_i'Vx_i - v) - k_i(x_i'I - 1) \tag{2}$$

where h and k_i are Lagrange multipliers. Setting the derivative of the objective function with respect to x_i equal to zero we get

$$R - c_i - hVx_i - k_iI = 0 \tag{3}$$

Therefore the optimal portfolio for investor i is

$$x_i = (V^{-1}/h)(R - c_i - k_iI) \tag{4}$$

where

$$k_i = [I'V^{-1}R - I'V^{-1}c_i - h]/I'V^{-1}I$$

Investors hold the same two funds as they do without barriers, the world market portfolio and the minimum variance zero beta portfolio. In addition, they hold an additional fund specific to the individual investor, which is the fund with the minimum variance for a specified level of deadweight cost.

Given the individual portfolio holdings we can aggregate to get a world capital market equilibrium. The clearing condition for the model is

$$\sum W_i x_i = M \tag{5}$$

where

W_i is the proportion of world wealth owned by country i
M is a column vector, the ith element of which is M_i
M_i is the proportion of world market capitalisation in country i's market.

Substituting equation (4) in equation (5) we obtain

$$R - \sum W_i c_i - \sum W_i k_i I = hVM \tag{6}$$

By subtracting equation (6) from equation (3) we can eliminate R

$$hV(x_i - M) = (\sum W_i c_i - c_i) + I(\sum W_i k_i - k_i) \tag{7}$$

But

$$\sum W_i k_i - k_i = z'(c_i - \sum W_i c_i) \tag{8}$$

where

$$z = V^{-1} I / (I' V^{-1} I) \tag{9}$$

and z is the global minimum variance portfolio. Substituting equation (8) in equation (7) we obtain

$$hV(x_i - M) = (\sum W_i c_i - c_i) - z'(\sum W_i c_i - c_i) I \tag{10}$$

If deadweight costs are zero, then each investor holds the world market portfolio, since the right-hand side of (10) is zero (as long as investors have equal degrees of risk-aversion).

Consider the case when the covariance matrix, V, is diagonal with all variances equal to s^2 and the deadweight cost of any country/investor pair is equal to c, except for domestic investment where it is equal to zero. Then the portfolio holdings of investor i in country n are

$$x_{in} = M_n - (W_n c / hs^2), \quad i \neq n$$
$$x_{in} = M_n - (W_n c / hs^2) + (c / hs^2), \quad i = n \tag{11}$$

Equation (11) suggests that the larger the marginal deadweight cost, c, the greater should be the deviation of portfolio holdings from the world market portfolio. This deviation is negative for foreign investment and positive for domestic investment. In other words, investors would put a greater weight on domestic securities and less weight on foreign securities.

To understand the equivalent relationship in the case of non-uniform deadweight costs we express equation (7) as

$$p_i = q_i - z'q_iI$$

where

$$p_i = hV(x_i - M)$$
$$q_i = \sum M_j c_j - c_i \tag{12}$$

The nth equation of the system given by (12) can be re-written as

$$p_{in} = -c_{in} + b_n + a_i - d, \quad i \neq n \tag{13}$$
$$p_{in} = b_n + a_i - d, \quad i = n \tag{14}$$

where

$$a_i = z'c_i$$
$$b_n = \sum M_j c_{jn}$$
$$d = z' \sum M_i c_i$$

a_i can be interpreted as the weighted average marginal deadweight cost for investor i, b_n as the weighted marginal deadweight cost for investors investing in country n, and d as the world weighted average marginal deadweight cost.

For simplicity, consider again the case where the covariance matrix is diagonal with all variances equal to s^2. Equations (13) and (14) simplify to

$$hs^2(x_{in} - M_n) = -c_{in} + b_n + a_i - d, \quad i \neq n \tag{15}$$
$$hs^2(x_{in} - M_n) = b_n + a_i - d, \quad i = n \tag{16}$$

If the marginal deadweight cost, c_{in}, is large relative to the weighted average marginal deadweight cost for investor i, a_i, or the weighted average marginal deadweight cost for investors investing in country n, b_n, it is more likely that the right-hand side of equation (15) would be negative. In that case the left-hand side of (15) should also be negative, implying that investor i should be underweight relative to the market in securities of country n. Similarly, since there are no barriers for investor i when investing domestically, the right-hand side of equation (16) will be positive, and consequently he would be overweight relative to the market in domestic securities. These results suggest that portfolio choice depends on the relative size of these costs to the weighted average marginal deadweight cost of the investor or of the country of investment.

II.3 Unique solutions for the barriers

One way to estimate the magnitude of the barriers to crossborder investment is to estimate the deadweight costs, c_{in}, for all i and n, on the basis of the observable equilibrium parameters. These are the portfolio holdings, the covariance matrix, and the market proportions. Closer examination of equations (13) and (14) suggests that they are not enough to determine the marginal deadweight costs. The system is underidentified since there are $n \times (n-1)$ unknown variables but only $(n-1) \times (n-1)$ linearly independent equations. Appendix A gives a simple numerical example in order to illustrate the problem. We will now discuss the derivation of unique solutions for the deadweight costs under alternative specific assumptions which render the system identified.

Assume that the marginal deadweight cost of an investor i investing in country n, c_{in}, can be decomposed into two elements, the one depending on the origin of the investor and the other on country of investment:

$$c_{in} = e_i + f_n$$

where

e_i is the cost for investor i investing in any foreign country
f_n is the cost for any investor investing in country n.

Substituting in equation (13) gives

$$p_{in} = -M_n(e_n + f_n) - z_i(e_i + f_i) + g, \quad i \neq n \tag{17}$$

$$p_{ii} = (1 - z_i - M_i)(e_i + f_i) + g \tag{18}$$

where

$$g = \sum z_n M_n(e_n + f_n)$$

z_n is the nth element of the vector z

The decomposition of c_{in} reduces the number of unknowns from $n \times (n-1)$ to $2 \times n$ while the number of equations remains the same $(n-1) \times (n-1)$. One is unable to solve for the components of c since the terms e_i and f_i appear as a sum in all equations of the system. Furthermore, for $n \geqslant 3$ the system becomes overidentified and inconsistent.

Unique solutions for the elements e_i and f_i can be obtained by treating the foreign portfolio holdings of any investor as unknown. Equation (17) can be written as

$$h \sum_j V_{nj}(x_{ij} - M_j) = -M_n C_n - z_i C_i + g \qquad (19)$$

where

$$C_i = e_i + f_i$$
V_{ij} is the ijth element of V

Let

$$h V_{in} x_{ii} - h \sum M_j V_{nj} = Y_{in}$$

Then

$$Y_{in} = -M_n C_n - z_i C_i + g - h \sum_{j \neq i} x_{ij} V_{jn}, \quad i \neq n \qquad (20)$$

Similarly equation (18) can be rewritten as

$$Y_{ii} = (1 - z_i - M_i) C_i + g - h \sum_{j \neq i} x_{ij} V_{jn} \qquad (21)$$

Solving the system of equations (20) and (21) simultaneously we obtain a unique solution for C_i's and x_i's.

Therefore, decomposition of the deadweight costs is useful for deriving an estimate of the total costs related to a certain country, C_i. This is the sum of the cost imposed on domestic investors investing abroad and the cost imposed on foreign investors investing locally. In the absence of any short selling constraints, the empirical estimates for these costs may be unrealistic due to large short positions (see Appendix B).

We can derive unique solutions for c_{ij} under two sets of less realistic assumptions. If the weighted average marginal deadweight cost for any investor is the same and deadweight costs are determined by the country in which the investor is investing, then

$$a_i = a_j \quad \text{all } i, j$$

and

$$c_{jn} = -p_{jn} + p_{nn} \qquad (22)$$

Alternatively, if the weighted average marginal deadweight cost for investing in any country is the same and only the investor's domicile affects the level of the deadweight costs, then

$$b_i = b_j \quad \text{all } i, j$$

and

$$c_{jn} = -p_{jn} + p_{jj} \tag{23}$$

Therefore, the level of the implied deadweight costs in this case depends only on the investor's own portfolio choice.

A less extreme alternative is to assume that the cost of investor i investing in country j is equal to the cost of investor j investing in country i. Such a symmetry in deadweight costs could be the result of bilateral agreements on withholding taxes or geographical proximity. This assumption is not so extreme as the previous two since it assumes that both the investor's origin and the country he is investing in are determinants of the deadweight costs. Therefore

$$c_{in} = (-p_{ni} - p_{in} + p_{ii} + p_{nn})/2 \tag{24}$$

Note that the level of the deadweight costs in this case is equal to the average of the former two solutions given by equations (22) and (23).

In order to obtain unique solutions for the c_{in}'s, certain restrictive assumptions are required. The question that arises is: if these assumptions are not true, what is the highest possible value that c_{in} could take, under any other set of assumptions?

Assume that the marginal deadweight costs are always greater than or equal to zero, so that the domestic investor i never has a disadvantage relative to the foreign investor j as far as investment in country i is concerned

$$c_{ij} \geqslant 0$$

But

$$c_{ij} + c_{ji} = p_{ii} + p_{jj} - p_{ij} - p_{ji}$$

which implies that

$$c_{ij} \leqslant p_{ii} + p_{jj} - p_{ij} - p_{ji} \tag{25}$$

The constraint given by (25) is binding if there are no barriers for investing in country i. For instance, if there are no barriers for investing in country i the level of the deadweight costs for the ith investor investing in any country j is given by

$$c_{ij} = p_{ii} + p_{jj} - p_{ij} - p_{ji}$$

We have now completed the development of alternative models for estimating the levels of implied barriers to international investment from portfolio holdings and asset covariances. Subsequent sections provide empirical estimates of these barriers.

Table 8.1. *Capitalisation of the major stock markets*

Country	Value of domestic equities ($ bn)	Percentage of all equities
USA	1145.4	52.57
CAN	104.1	4.78
UK	176.8	8.12
BEL	7.8	0.36
FRA	37.5	1.72
GER	62.5	2.87
ITA	24.0	1.10
NET	20.0	0.92
SWI	40.8	1.87
JAP	402.7	18.48
AUS	57.8	2.65
HK	42.3	1.94
SAF	22.2	1.02
SIN	34.8	1.60
Total	2178.7	100.00

Source: Capital International Perspective.

III Description of data

We estimate the level of deadweight costs for the following countries: USA, Canada, UK, Belgium, France, Germany, Italy, Netherlands, Switzerland, Japan, Australia, Hong Kong, South Africa, and Singapore. The proportional market capitalisations of the fourteen stock markets, which are given in Table 8.1, are used as proxies for the proportional marketable wealth of these countries.

The covariance matrix of returns of these major stock markets, given in Table 8.2, based on monthly data from August 1978 to May 1982, is used as a proxy of the covariance matrix of returns on the total marketable wealth of these countries. The returns used to estimate this covariance matrix are real returns converted to a basket of goods having the same proportional international composition as Table 8.1. In other words, money returns are first converted to an exchange basket with the weights given in Table 8.1 and these are then deflated by a weighted inflation rate using the same weights. Finally, the logarithmic transformation is used to make the distribution of the returns closer to normal by converting the returns into their continuously compounded form.

The source for the stock market indices is the *Financial Times*, with the exception of the Japanese index which is from the Nomura Manual of

Table 8.2. *The covariance matrix of real equity returns for the period August 1978–May 1982*

	US	CAN	UK	BEL	FRA	GER	ITA	NET	SWI	JAP	AUS	HK	SAF	SNG
US	.021													
CAN	.020	.039												
UK	.014	.019	0.39											
BEL	.005	.002	.012	.026										
FRA	.009	.007	.009	.011	.046									
GER	.009	.008	.013	.008	.007	.014								
ITA	.003	.014	.020	.003	.004	.002	.091							
NET	.011	.006	.016	.015	.004	.014	.017	.034						
SWI	.011	.011	.017	.013	.008	.011	.004	.016	.021					
JAP	.006	.006	.011	.008	.003	.008	.006	.011	.009	.012				
AUS	.014	.021	.014	.002	.003	.005	.016	.006	.010	.007	.038			
HK	.007	.016	.018	-.004	-0.009	.004	.024	.016	.005	.007	.023	.116		
SAF	.007	.012	.000	-.002	.019	-.006	.009	-.012	-.001	-.001	.023	.022	.126	
SNG	.012	.013	.012	.003	-.007	.008	.007	.018	.009	.007	.019	.042	-.018	.077

Table 8.3. *Equity market indices used*

Country	Index
USA	S&P 500
UK	FTA All Share
France	GAC General
Italy	Milan Bourse
Switzerland	Swiss Bank Co
Australia	Joint All Ordinary
South Africa	Gold-Price Index
Canada	Toronto SE Industrial
Belgium	Brussels Bourse
Germany	Commerzbank
Netherlands	ANP-CBS Industrial
Japan	Tokyo New SE
Hong Kong	Hang Seng Bank
Singapore	Straits T. Industrial

Securities Statistics. These indices are commonly used as benchmarks by local investors (see Table 8.3). The consumer price indices for the OECD countries are from the *Main Economic Indicators* (OECD), for South Africa and Singapore from the *International Financial Statistics*, and for Hong Kong from *Hong Kong Yearbook*. The source of the exchange rates is Datastream, except for the South African financial rand which is from the *Financial Times*. Until February 1983, South Africa had a two-tier currency, the commercial rand and the financial rand. Since the purchase and sales of securities had to be effected through the financial rand market in this study we use the financial rand exchange rate. Belgium, also, has a two tier foreign exchange market, the official market and the free market. The authorities intervene in the official market to maintain the franc within the margin of the EMS. Purchases and sales of shares are made through the free market. Therefore in this chapter we use the free exchange rate, or in other words, the financial rate.

Data on portfolio holdings are more difficult to obtain. The US is the only country where such information on aggregate holdings with a breakdown of these holdings by country is available. For most of the other countries, some information on the proportion of assets held overseas is available but without any breakdown of these holdings. Table 8.4 gives a matrix of portfolio holdings that is consistent with the information available to us for the 14 countries examined. The data on which this table is based are available from the authors.

Table 8.4. *Portfolio holdings*

IO:	US	CAN	UK	BEL	FRA	GER	ITA	NET	SWI	JAP	AUS	HK	SA	SNG
CI:														
US	98.82	8.40	10.27	21.10	20.33	6.50	3.72	23.08	18.75	2.30	5.40	9.11	.00	1.60
CAN	.66	90.00	.93	1.92	1.85	.59	.34	2.10	1.70	.20	.50	.83	.00	.15
UK	.19	.30	80.00	3.26	3.14	1.00	.57	3.57	2.90	.40	.80	1.41	.00	.25
BEL	.01	.01	.03	60.00	.14	.04	.03	.16	.13	.00	.00	.06	.00	.01
FRA	.04	.06	.16	.69	62.00	.21	.12	.76	.61	.10	.20	.30	.00	.05
GER	.07	.11	.26	1.15	1.11	88.00	.20	1.26	1.02	.10	.30	.50	.00	.09
ITA	.03	.04	.10	.44	.43	.14	93.00	.48	.39	.00	.10	.19	.00	.03
NET	.02	.03	.08	.37	.36	.11	.07	56.50	.33	.00	.10	.16	.00	.03
SWI	.04	.07	.17	.75	.72	.23	.13	.82	65.00	.10	.20	.32	.00	.06
JAP	.08	.69	5.60	7.42	7.15	2.28	1.31	8.11	6.59	96.50	1.90	3.20	.00	.56
AUS	.01	.10	.80	1.07	1.02	.33	.19	1.16	.95	.10	90.00	.46	.00	.08
HK	.01	.07	.68	.78	.75	.24	.14	.85	.69	.10	.20	83.00	.00	.06
SA	.01	.04	.36	.41	.39	.13	.07	.45	.36	.00	.10	.18	100.00	.03
SNG	.01	.06	.56	.64	.62	.20	.11	.70	.57	.10	.20	.28	.00	97.00

Note: IO = Investor's origin; CI = Country of investment.

223

Since the portfolio holdings used in estimating the level of deadweight costs are not very accurate, we also undertake a sensitivity analysis in order to examine to what extent the deadweight costs are affected by misestimation of the portfolio holdings.

Finally, an estimate of the reward to risk ratio, h, is required for the estimation of the deadweight costs. This is assumed to be equal to 2.5 and constant across countries.[3]

IV Empirical results

One way of estimating the level of the barriers to foreign investment is to take the barriers at their face value. The problem with this method is that a large number of these barriers such as information-gathering costs and exchange controls are not quantifiable. In the context of the model discussed earlier in this chapter, one could estimate the shadow prices of the barriers to foreign investment given investors' portfolio holdings and the covariance matrix of equity returns.

Before we present our estimates of the barriers to foreign investment using the model developed in Section I, we discuss the quantifiable barriers such as withholding taxes and safe custody fees which would provide us with some priors about the level of the barriers.

IV.1 Withholding taxes and safe custody fees

Investors in foreign markets are taxed on dividend income both in the foreign country and in their home country. However, under double taxation treaties the tax payable in the foreign country is reduced, and investors are entitled to take a credit in their home country for the withholding tax they paid.

For example, a UK investor is subject to UK income tax on the gross amount of foreign dividends received but takes a foreign tax credit for the withholding tax paid to the source country. Therefore, if the withholding tax rate is lower than the UK income tax rate, the UK tax rate on the foreign dividend income will be limited to the difference between the two rates. However, if the foreign withholding tax rate is higher than the UK rate, the UK tax rate on foreign dividend income will be zero but the excess foreign credit cannot be deducted from UK source income. As a result for pension funds which are not subject to income tax in the UK, the foreign withholding tax is a deterrent to foreign investment. Assuming that the dividend yield of a pension fund foreign portfolio is 7 per cent and the foreign withholding tax on dividends is 15 per cent then the cost of the withholding tax deterrent is 1 per cent of the portfolio value per annum. In the absence of double taxation treaties, the withholding tax is a deterrent for any investor, independent of his tax position in his home country (see Table 8.5 for tax treaties).

Non-resident investors may require the evidence of ownership of their foreign securities to be held in safe custody. Such services are provided by banks or stockbrokers. Furthermore, banks offer other custodianship services such as collection of dividends, currency translation, etc. Some typical examples of safe custody fees charged by commercial banks are given in Table 8.6. These fees are very low; they vary from around 0.07 to 0.35 per cent of the foreign portfolio value per annum. Thus the quantifiable barriers, that is the withholding taxes on dividends and the safe custody fees, should be of the order of 1–2 per cent of the net foreign investment.

IV.2 Empirical estimates of the barriers to foreign investment

Although a linear tax on net crossborder investment is an imperfect representation of the barriers to foreign investment, we expect that our tax estimates will capture the effective deterrents to foreign investment. For instance, we would expect countries with minimal or no exchange controls to have relatively low deadweight costs, around 1–2 per cent, which could be interpreted as the shadow price of information-gathering costs, withholding taxes and safe custody fees. On the other hand strict exchange controls, in countries such as South Africa and Italy, are expected to give rise to higher barrier estimates if these restrictions are effective. The difference between the deadweight costs of countries with strict exchange controls and no exchange controls could be viewed as a proxy for the shadow price of the exchange controls.

The marginal benefit to an investor from international diversification is greater when his domestic market is highly volatile and has a low covariance with the other markets. Therefore the shadow price of barriers which restrict his foreign investment will be higher when his domestic market is more volatile and less correlated with the other markets. In other words, the deadweight costs estimates will be higher since the foregone marginal benefit from foreign investment is greater.

We will now discuss our estimate of the barriers to foreign investment based on the alternative assumptions discussed in Section III in the context of the actual restrictions imposed either by the investor's country or by the country of investment. Table 8.7 presents the estimates of the costs assuming that they are determined by the country of investment whilst in Table 8.8 we assume that the costs are determined by the country of origin

Table 8.5. *Withholding taxes on dividends*

Recipient:	AUS	BEL	CAN	FRA	GER	HK	ITA	JAP	NET	SNG	SAF	SWI	UK	US
AUS	—	15	10	15	15	0	30*	15	15	0	15*	35*	—	15
BEL	15	—	10	15	15	0	15	15	15	0	15*	15	—	15
CAN	15	15	—	15	15	0	30*	15	15	0	15	15	—	15
FRA	15	10	10	—	15	0	15	15	15	0	15*	15	—	15
GER	15	15	10	15	—	0	30	15	15	0	15	15	—	15
HK	30*	20*	25*	25*	15*	—	30*	20*	25*	40*	15*	35*	—	30*
ITA	30*	15	10	15	25	0	—	15	15	0	15*	15	—	15
JAP	15	15	10	15	15	0	15	—	15	0	15	15	—	15
NET	15	5	10	15	15	0	30	15	—	0	15	15	—	15
SNG	15	15	10	25*	15	0	30*	15	15	—	15*	15	—	30*
SAF	30*	20*	20	15	15	0	30*	20*	15	40*	—	7.5	—	15
SWI	15	20*	10	15	15	0	30*	15	15	0	7.5	—	—	15
UK	15	15	10	15	15	0	15	15	15	0	15	15	—	15
US	15	15	10	15	15	0	15	15	15	0	15	15	—	—

Note: *Non-treaty.

Table 8.6. *Safe custody fees*

Canada	1–5 per cent of total annual dividend
Italy	Lire 1500 per six months for every Lire 1 million of securities deposited, subject to a maximum fee of Lire 150,000 per six months
Japan	0.1 per cent per annum of the par value of the shares held

of the investor. The results of Table 8.9 are based on the symmetry assumption that the cost of an investor from country i investing in country j is equal to the cost of an investor from country j investing in country i. Finally, Table 8.10 gives the upper bounds of the deadweight costs given the covariance structure of returns and investors' portfolio holdings.

The symmetry that is observed between Tables 8.7 and 8.8, in the sense that Table 8.7 is approximately the transpose of Table 8.8, indicates that there are high barriers associated with investing to or from certain countries and the two tables provide two extreme cases.[4] Note, however, that these two tables do not necessarily provide bounds to the deadweight costs. Under the symmetry assumption (Table 8.9) we obtain somewhat less extreme results which could be closer to reality. The upper bound estimates of the deadweight costs (Table 8.10) are consistent with the results derived under specific assumptions to the extent that countries associated with higher deadweight cost estimates under the specific assumptions also have higher upper bounds.

A casual look at the data suggests that the barrier estimates are on the high side when compared with our estimates of the quantifiable costs and that there is a large difference between the barrier estimates of different countries. The average estimated level of barriers faced by the US investor investing in Canada and the Canadian investor investing in the US (2.2 per cent), though slightly on the high side, seems consistent with our expectation based on the quantifiable costs. On the other hand countries with similar barriers such as the UK and Germany are associated with costs of the order of 5–8 per cent which are substantially higher than our expectations; thus these estimates imply that in these cases the information costs or other non-quantifiable costs are higher than in the US/Canada case. Finally the high estimates associated with South Africa based on the assumption that the exchange controls are effective reflect the shadow price of these controls.

The high estimates for Singapore and Hong Kong are rather surprising since these two countries are free from all forms of exchange controls. Assuming that the high volatility estimates of the returns of the Hong Kong

Table 8.7. *Estimates of the barriers to foreign investment assuming that any barriers are due to investor's origin*

IO	US	CAN	UK	BEL	FRA	GER	ITA	NET	SWI	JAP	AUS	HK	SAF	SN	Average
CI:															
US	.0	3.9	5.0	4.7	7.1	2.7	22.4	4.0	2.3	3.4	6.1	23.4	32.2	16.7	10.3
CAN	.5	.0	4.2	5.2	7.5	3.2	20.3	4.8	2.6	3.7	4.7	21.8	31.3	16.8	9.7
UK	1.8	4.1	.0	3.5	7.0	1.6	18.3	3.1	1.2	2.2	6.0	21.0	33.8	16.6	9.2
BEL	1.7	5.8	3.4	.0	5.2	.6	20.0	2.0	.3	.5	6.5	23.7	31.9	16.4	9.1
FRA	1.1	5.0	4.3	2.4	.0	1.3	20.2	3.7	1.5	2.0	6.5	25.0	27.1	19.1	9.2
GER	1.3	5.1	3.7	3.1	6.3	.0	21.0	2.6	1.3	1.2	6.4	22.6	33.6	15.9	9.5
ITA	2.4	3.6	2.0	3.6	6.4	2.4	.0	1.9	2.1	1.5	3.6	18.3	29.6	15.8	7.2
NET	1.5	6.2	3.6	2.5	7.1	.7	18.1	.0	.9	1.0	6.7	20.6	35.9	14.2	9.1
SWI	1.3	5.0	3.3	2.6	6.5	1.3	21.0	2.6	.0	1.5	5.9	22.9	33.0	16.2	9.5
JAP	1.7	5.4	3.9	2.9	6.6	1.0	19.9	2.7	1.3	.0	5.7	21.6	32.1	15.9	9.3
AUS	1.2	3.2	4.5	4.7	7.5	2.9	18.8	4.2	2.1	2.5	.0	19.6	27.6	14.3	8.7
HK	2.4	4.0	3.2	5.4	9.2	2.9	16.7	2.6	2.7	2.0	3.1	.0	27.4	8.4	6.9
SAF	1.1	3.7	5.7	4.2	4.0	3.8	18.8	5.9	2.8	2.8	1.9	18.3	.0	21.6	7.3
SNG	1.4	4.8	4.6	4.3	8.8	2.0	20.6	2.5	2.0	2.3	4.0	15.4	37.5	.0	8.5
Average	1.5	4.6	4.0	3.8	6.9	2.0	19.7	3.3	1.8	2.0	5.2	21.1	31.8	16.0	

Note: IO = Investor's origin; *CI* = Country of investment.

Table 8.8. *Estimates of the barriers to foreign investment assuming that barriers are due to the country of investment*

IO:	US	CAN	UK	BEL	FRA	GER	ITA	NET	SWI	JAP	AUS	HK	SAF	SNG	Average
CI:															
US	.0	.3	1.8	3.1	2.5	2.9	4.3	2.1	2.1	3.8	1.9	3.1	3.5	2.3	2.6
CAN	4.1	.0	4.6	7.2	6.5	6.9	5.8	6.5	5.9	7.7	4.1	5.1	6.3	6.0	5.9
UK	5.0	3.8	.0	5.1	5.6	5.0	3.4	4.4	4.2	5.7	5.0	4.0	8.3	5.4	5.0
BEL	3.3	3.9	1.8	.0	2.2	2.4	3.6	1.7	1.8	2.5	3.9	5.0	4.9	3.6	3.1
FRA	5.7	6.0	5.7	5.4	.0	6.1	6.7	6.4	5.9	7.0	6.9	9.4	3.0	9.3	6.4
GER	1.2	1.4	.3	1.3	1.5	.0	2.8	.5	.9	1.4	2.0	2.2	4.8	1.3	1.7
ITA	20.5	18.1	16.9	20.0	19.9	20.6	.0	18.1	20.0	19.9	17.5	16.1	19.0	19.5	18.9
NET	3.4	4.5	2.2	2.7	4.4	2.7	1.9	.0	2.6	3.2	4.3	2.2	9.2	1.7	3.5
SWI	1.5	1.6	.3	1.2	2.1	1.6	3.1	.9	.0	2.0	1.8	2.8	4.6	2.0	2.0
JAP	1.4	1.4	.3	.9	1.7	.8	1.4	.4	.7	.0	1.1	1.0	3.1	1.1	1.2
AUS	5.5	3.9	5.5	7.3	7.1	7.3	4.9	6.5	6.1	7.1	.0	3.6	3.2	4.1	5.6
HK	22.7	20.7	20.2	24.0	24.8	23.3	18.9	20.9	22.7	22.6	19.1	.0	19.0	14.2	21.0
SAF	29.8	28.8	31.1	31.2	28.1	32.6	29.4	32.6	31.2	31.8	26.3	26.7	.0	35.8	30.4
SNG	15.8	15.6	15.7	17.1	18.6	16.6	16.9	15.0	16.2	17.0	14.2	9.5	23.2	.0	16.3
Average	9.2	8.5	8.2	9.7	9.6	9.9	7.9	8.9	9.3	10.1	8.3	7.0	8.6	8.2	

Note: IO = Investor's origin; *CI* = Country of investment.

229

Table 8.9. Estimates of the barriers to foreign investment assuming that barriers are due to both the country of investment and the investor's origin

IO:	US	CAN	UK	BEL	FRA	GER	ITA	NET	SWI	JAP	AUS	HK	SAF	SNG	Average
CI:															
US	.0	2.2	3.4	3.2	4.1	2.0	12.4	2.7	1.8	2.6	3.7	12.9	16.6	9.0	5.9
CAN	2.2	.0	4.2	5.5	6.3	4.2	12.0	5.5	3.8	4.5	4.0	12.9	17.5	10.8	7.2
UK	3.4	4.2	.0	3.4	5.6	2.7	10.2	3.3	2.3	3.0	5.3	12.1	19.7	10.6	6.6
BEL	3.2	5.5	3.4	.0	3.8	1.8	11.8	2.2	1.5	1.7	5.6	14.5	18.1	10.4	6.4
FRA	4.1	6.3	5.6	3.8	.0	3.8	13.3	5.4	4.0	4.3	7.0	17.1	15.6	14.0	8.0
GER	2.0	4.2	2.7	1.8	3.8	.0	11.7	1.6	1.3	1.1	4.7	12.8	18.7	8.9	5.8
ITA	12.4	12.0	10.2	11.8	13.3	11.7	.0	10.0	11.5	10.7	11.2	17.5	24.2	18.2	13.4
NET	2.7	5.5	3.3	2.2	5.4	1.6	10.0	.0	1.7	1.8	5.4	11.6	20.9	8.3	6.2
SWI	1.8	3.8	2.3	1.5	4.0	1.3	11.5	1.7	.0	1.4	4.0	12.8	17.9	9.1	5.6
JAP	2.6	4.5	3.0	1.7	4.3	1.1	10.7	1.8	1.4	.0	4.1	11.8	17.4	9.1	5.7
AUS	3.7	4.0	5.3	5.6	7.0	4.7	11.2	5.4	4.0	4.1	.0	11.3	14.8	9.1	6.9
HK	12.9	12.9	12.1	14.5	17.1	12.8	17.5	11.6	12.8	11.8	11.3	.0	22.8	11.9	14.0
SAF	16.6	17.5	19.7	18.1	15.6	18.7	24.2	20.9	17.9	17.4	14.8	22.8	.0	29.5	19.5
SNG	9.0	10.8	10.6	10.4	14.0	8.9	18.2	8.3	9.1	9.1	9.1	11.9	29.5	.0	12.2
Average	5.9	7.2	6.6	6.4	8.0	5.8	13.4	6.2	5.6	5.7	6.9	14.0	19.5	12.2	

Note: IO = Investor's origin; CI = Country of investment.

Table 8.10. *Upper bounds to the estimates of the barriers to foreign investment*

IO:	US	CAN	UK	BEL	FRA	GER	ITA	NET	SWI	JAP	AUS	HK	SAF	SNG
CI:														
US	.0	4.5	6.8	6.4	8.1	4.0	24.8	5.5	3.6	5.2	7.3	25.8	33.3	18.0
CAN	4.5	.0	8.3	11.0	12.5	8.3	23.9	11.0	7.6	9.1	7.9	25.9	35.1	21.6
UK	6.8	8.3	.0	6.9	11.3	5.4	20.3	6.7	4.6	6.1	10.5	24.2	39.5	21.1
BEL	6.4	11.0	6.9	.0	7.6	3.7	23.6	4.5	3.0	3.4	11.3	29.0	36.1	20.7
FRA	8.1	12.5	11.3	7.6	.0	7.6	26.6	10.8	8.0	8.6	14.0	34.2	31.1	27.9
GER	4.0	8.3	5.4	3.7	7.6	.0	23.4	3.3	2.5	2.2	9.4	25.5	37.4	17.9
ITA	24.8	23.9	20.3	23.6	26.6	23.4	.0	20.0	23.1	21.3	22.4	35.0	48.4	36.4
NET	5.5	11.0	6.7	4.5	10.8	3.3	20.0	.0	3.5	3.6	10.9	23.1	41.8	16.7
SWI	3.6	7.6	4.6	3.0	8.0	2.5	23.1	3.5	.0	2.8	7.9	25.5	35.8	18.2
JAP	5.2	9.1	6.1	3.4	8.6	2.2	21.3	3.6	2.8	.0	8.1	23.6	34.9	18.2
AUS	7.3	7.9	10.5	11.3	14.0	9.4	22.4	10.9	7.9	8.1	.0	22.7	29.5	18.3
HK	25.8	25.9	24.2	29.0	34.2	25.5	35.0	23.1	25.5	23.6	22.7	.0	45.7	23.8
SAF	33.3	35.1	39.5	36.1	31.1	37.4	48.4	41.8	35.8	34.9	29.5	45.7	.0	59.1
SNG	18.0	21.6	21.1	20.7	27.9	17.9	36.4	16.7	18.2	18.2	18.3	23.8	59.1	.0

Note: IO = Investor's origin; CI = Country of investment.

231

and Singapore markets are correct and that the price of risk is constant across countries one would expect

(i)   the marginal benefit to the residents of Hong Kong and Singapore of diversifying overseas to be very large

(ii) the marginal cost to foreign investors of investing part of their wealth in these countries to be small since a large part of the risk should be diversifiable.

The portfolio holdings for Hong Kong and Singapore residents used in the estimation of the barriers were based on data on investments by banks, which are not representative of the Hong Kong residents' portfolio holdings, since the majority of these banks are subsidiaries of international banks. Therefore, the magnitude of the cost estimates may be an artefact of our observations of portfolio holdings, which understate foreign holdings by Hong Kong residents, rather than any real underlying barriers in or out of Hong Kong.

On the other hand overestimates of the deadweight costs for Hong Kong and Singapore could be due to misestimation of the covariance matrix of returns. For instance if the difference between the variance estimates for Hong Kong or Singapore relative to the rest of the world is due to noise rather than true underlying differences, then the differences between the deadweight costs estimates would not be so large. The sensitivity of the deadweight cost estimates with respect to the portfolio holdings and covariance matrix of returns is discussed later in this section.

Our barrier estimates suggest that the shadow price of barriers due to information-gathering costs, withholding taxes and custody fees is about 4–6 per cent of the value of the net foreign investment if our input data for the portfolio holdings and the covariance matrix are correct. The shadow price of exchange controls could be as high as 30 per cent of the net foreign investment.

IV.3 Sensitivity analysis

(a) Sensitivity with respect to the covariance matrix

In our estimation we have used the sample covariance matrix of returns over the period 1978–82 as an estimate of the population covariance matrix. If, however, the noise in the sample covariance estimates is large we would obtain a better estimate for the covariance matrix by setting every covariance term equal to the average sample covariance and every variance term equal to the average sample variance.

Table 8.11 gives the average deadweight costs for each investor using the two alternative estimates of the covariance matrix of returns assuming that

Table 8.11. *Average deadweight cost estimates using the simple historic and average covariance matrices*

Investor's origin	Covariance matrix used	
	Simple historic	*Average*
US	5.9	8.6
Canada	7.2	8.7
UK	6.6	8.1
Belgium	6.4	7.2
France	8.0	7.3
Germany	5.8	8.6
Italy	13.4	8.9
Netherlands	6.2	7.0
Switzerland	5.6	7.4
Japan	5.7	8.9
Australia	6.9	8.7
Hong Kong	14.0	8.3
South Africa	19.5	9.2
Singapore	12.2	9.0

the costs depend both on investor's origin and country of investment. The conclusions from the comparisons of the estimates of the barriers under alternative covariance estimates are twofold. First the average magnitude of the barriers is approximately the same.[5] Secondly, estimated barrier differentials are mainly the result of covariance differentials rather than portfolio holding differentials.

The overall level of the estimates of the barriers is likely to be biased upwards due to errors in variables, since the returns are likely to be measured with error. The variance estimates would be biased upwards while the covariance estimates would be unbiased and as a result the estimated barriers would be biased upwards.

(b) Sensitivity with respect to the portfolio holdings

Table 8.12 presents the sensitivity of the deadweight cost estimates with respect to the portfolio holdings. We vary the portfolio holdings of one country at a time, leaving the portfolio holdings of the other countries unchanged. For example, if we assume that US investors do not hold any foreign assets, their average deadweight costs estimate is 0.001 per cent higher than the original estimate, while if they hold the world market portfolio their deadweight cost is reduced by 0.7 per cent. In other words, the average deadweight cost for a US investor would vary between 5.2 per

Table 8.12. *Results of the sensitivity analysis of the estimates of the barriers to foreign investment with respect to the portfolio holdings*

		US	CAN	UK	BEL	FRA	GER	ITA	NET	SWI	JAP	AUS	HK	SAF	SNG
		Average estimate of the barriers to foreign investment for each investor													
Estimates given in Table 8.9:		5.9	7.2	6.6	6.4	8.0	5.8	13.4	6.2	5.6	5.7	6.9	14.0	19.5	12.2
Investor:	Investor portfolio:														
US	DOM	5.9	7.2	6.6	6.4	8.0	5.8	13.4	6.2	5.6	5.7	6.9	14.0	19.5	12.2
	WRL	5.2	7.2	6.5	6.4	8.0	5.7	13.3	6.1	5.6	5.6	6.9	13.9	19.5	12.2
CAN	DOM	5.9	7.4	6.6	6.4	8.0	5.8	13.4	6.2	5.6	5.7	6.9	14.0	19.5	12.2
	WRL	5.7	4.9	6.4	6.2	7.8	5.6	13.3	6.0	5.4	5.5	6.8	13.8	19.4	12.0
UK	DOM	6.0	7.2	7.2	6.5	8.1	5.8	13.5	6.2	5.7	5.7	7.0	14.0	19.6	12.3
	WRL	5.7	7.0	4.6	6.3	7.9	5.6	13.4	6.1	5.5	5.5	6.8	13.9	19.3	12.0
BEL	DOM	6.0	7.3	6.7	7.7	8.1	5.9	13.5	6.3	5.7	5.7	7.1	14.1	19.6	12.3
	WRL	5.7	7.0	6.5	4.5	7.9	5.7	13.3	6.1	5.5	5.5	6.8	13.8	19.4	12.1
FRA	DOM	6.1	7.4	6.8	6.6	10.2	5.9	13.6	6.4	5.8	5.8	7.1	14.2	19.6	12.4
	WRL	5.6	6.9	6.3	6.2	4.6	5.5	13.2	5.9	5.4	5.4	6.6	13.6	19.4	11.9
GER	DOM	5.9	7.2	6.6	6.4	8.0	5.9	13.4	6.2	5.6	5.7	7.0	14.0	19.5	12.2
	WRL	5.8	7.1	6.5	6.4	8.0	4.8	13.3	6.2	5.6	5.6	6.8	13.9	19.4	12.1
ITA	DOM	6.0	7.2	6.7	6.5	8.1	5.9	14.2	6.3	5.7	5.7	7.0	14.0	19.6	12.3
	WRL	5.0	6.4	5.9	5.7	7.2	5.0	3.6	5.5	4.8	4.9	6.2	13.4	18.8	11.4
NET	DOM	6.0	7.3	6.7	6.5	8.1	5.9	13.5	7.5	5.7	5.7	7.1	14.1	19.7	12.3
	WRL	5.7	7.0	6.5	6.4	7.9	5.7	13.4	4.6	5.5	5.6	6.8	13.9	19.3	12.1

SWI	DOM	5.9	7.2	6.6	6.4	8.0	5.8	13.5	6.2	6.1	5.7	7.0	14.1	19.6	12.3
	WRL	5.8	7.1	6.6	6.4	8.0	5.7	13.4	6.2	4.7	5.6	6.9	13.9	19.4	12.1
JAP	DOM	5.9	7.2	6.6	6.4	8.0	5.8	13.4	6.2	5.6	5.7	6.9	14.0	19.5	12.2
	WRL	5.8	7.0	6.5	6.4	7.9	5.7	13.4	6.2	5.6	4.6	6.8	13.9	19.4	12.1
AUS	DOM	5.9	7.2	6.6	6.5	8.0	5.8	13.5	6.2	5.6	5.7	7.2	14.0	19.5	12.2
	WRL	5.7	7.0	6.4	6.2	7.8	5.5	13.3	5.9	5.4	5.4	4.3	13.9	19.5	12.1
HK	DOM	6.1	7.4	6.8	6.6	8.2	6.0	13.6	6.4	5.8	5.8	7.1	16.2	19.7	12.3
	WRL	5.0	6.3	5.8	5.5	7.1	4.9	12.7	5.4	4.7	4.8	6.2	3.5	18.8	11.6
SAF	DOM	5.9	7.2	6.6	6.4	8.0	5.8	13.4	6.2	5.6	5.7	6.9	14.0	19.5	12.2
	WRL	4.7	6.0	5.3	5.2	7.0	4.5	12.3	4.8	4.3	4.4	5.9	12.9	3.6	10.8
SNG	DOM	5.9	7.2	6.6	6.4	8.0	5.8	13.5	6.2	5.6	5.7	7.0	14.0	19.6	12.5
	WRL	5.3	6.5	6.0	5.8	7.3	5.2	12.8	5.7	5.0	5.0	6.4	13.7	18.7	4.2

Note: DOM = The portfolio held by the variable investor is 100% domestic; WRL = The portfolio held by the variable investor is the world market portfolio.

cent and 5.9 per cent depending on his foreign holdings. The results of Table 8.12 suggest that the deadweight cost estimates, especially for countries with low volatility, are not very sensitive to the portfolio input data for that specific country. Therefore, for accurate estimates of the deadweight costs greater accuracy for the covariance matrix rather than the portfolio holdings is required.

V Summary and conclusions

The aim of this paper was to develop an international capital market equilibrium model with barriers to crossborder investment to:

(i)   obtain unique solutions to the barriers under alternative assumptions
(ii)   obtain upper bounds to the barriers
(iii) provide empirical estimates for the barriers
(iv)   examine the sensitivity of the barrier estimates with respect to the covariance matrix and the portfolio holdings.

We employed a linear tax on net crossborder investment for each investor/foreign country pair to represent the barriers to crossborder investment. Then, using the capital market equilibrium relationships, we derived unique solutions for the deadweight costs, in terms of the portfolio holdings of the investors and the covariance matrix of returns on risky assets, under two alternative extreme assumptions. First, we assumed that costs are determined by the country in which the investor is investing. Secondly, we assumed that the costs are determined by the investor's origin. Then we derived unique solutions for the deadweight costs using the less extreme assumption that the cost of investor i investing in country j is equal to the cost of investor j investing in country i. The deadweight cost estimates under the latter assumption are equal to the average of the two extreme solutions.

Finally we attempted to obtain solutions for the deadweight costs by decomposing them into two elements, the one depending on the origin of the investor and the other on the country of investment. In this case, unique solutions for the costs related to each country could be obtained by treating the foreign portfolio holdings of any investor as unknown. In the absence of any short selling constraints however, the empirical estimates for these costs were unrealistic. Perhaps it would be an interesting topic for future research to attempt to estimate these costs with short selling constraints.

The empirical work in this paper has focussed on the estimation of the size of the barriers to crossborder investment for each investor/foreign country pair in a group of fourteen countries. We used observed portfolio behaviour and covariance matrix estimates of the returns on risky assets to estimate the effective deadweight costs in the model.

We found that high estimates of the deadweight costs were associated with countries with strict exchange controls. In other words, the exchange controls were reflected in the shadow price of the barriers to crossborder investment. Similarly, the shadow price of the barriers to investors with minimal or no exchange controls was on average 3–4 per cent which was higher than the estimated quantifiable costs which suggests that non-quantifiable costs such as information costs are fairly high. The high shadow prices obtained for Hong Kong and Singapore still remain unexplained since there are no obvious barriers that could give rise to such high estimates unless the variance of their returns has been overestimated or the foreign portfolio holdings for Hong Kong and Singapore residents are substantially higher.

Our results have normative implications for both the investment manager and the corporate treasurer. For example, Table 8.12 provides the investment manager with information on the optimal overseas diversification as a function of the level of costs. A UK investor should be prepared to invest some part of his assets overseas unless the costs of doing so exceeds 7.2 per cent per annum. At the other extreme, he should hold the world market portfolio only if the annual costs are less than 4.6 per cent. The average UK investor's international holdings imply a cost of 6.6 per cent a year.

Since UK investors *do* hold foreign investments, the expected return on these investments must provide the opportunity cost of capital for UK companies engaging in direct investments overseas. Thus Table 8.9 implies that the cost of capital for a UK company investing in the US is 3.4 per cent less than that for a comparable investment by a US company. As a final concluding remark it is worth noting that the deadweight cost estimates were found to be very sensitive to the covariance matrix estimate whilst fairly insensitive to the portfolio holdings input data.

APPENDICES

A An example illustrating the underidentification problem when estimating the deadweight costs

Suppose that there are three countries, of equal size, with zero covariance of asset returns, and variances equal to 0.4. The world minimum variance portfolio before costs consists of equal amounts of each.

Assuming that h is 2.5 and the variance of each market is 0.04, the portfolio holdings are

$$x_{11} = .53 \qquad x_{21} = .33 \qquad x_{31} = .13$$

$$x_{12} = .13 \qquad x_{22} = .53 \qquad x_{32} = .33$$

$$x_{13} = .33 \qquad x_{23} = .13 \qquad x_{33} = .53$$

The marginal deadweight costs in equilibrium are

$$c_{11} = 0 \qquad c_{21} = 2\% \qquad c_{31} = 4\%$$

$$c_{12} = 4\% \qquad c_{22} = 0 \qquad c_{32} = 2\%$$

$$c_{13} = 2\% \qquad c_{23} = 4\% \qquad c_{33} = 0$$

Some simple arithmetic shows that the same equilibrium could have been generated by the following deadweight cost structure:

$$c_{11} = 0 \qquad c_{21} = 1\% \qquad c_{31} = 2\%$$

$$c_{12} = 5\% \qquad c_{22} = 0 \qquad c_{32} = 1\%$$

$$c_{13} = 4\% \qquad c_{23} = 5\% \qquad c_{33} = 0$$

Therefore for a given set of portfolio holdings and a covariance matrix there exists more than one solution for the barriers to crossborder investment.

Although, in this second case, foreign investment looks less favourable to investor 1, foreigners find it more desirable to invest in his country, so returns on his domestic shares are bid down.

B An example illustrating the short selling problem when the barriers are decomposed

Suppose that there are four countries, US, Canada, UK and Japan, with the following covariance matrix of returns on risky assets:

	US	CAN	UK	JAP
US	0.0214			
CAN	0.0201	0.0388		
UK	0.0138	0.0182	0.0389	
JAP	0.0058	0.0057	0.0106	0.0115

Their market capitalization proportions are

US	62.45
CAN	5.68
UK	9.65
JAP	22.22

and the portfolio holdings held by investors in their domestic markets are

US	98.82
CAN	90.00
UK	80.00
JAP	96.50

Assume that the marginal deadweight cost of an investor i investing in country j, c_{ij}, can be decomposed into two elements, one depending on the origin of the investor, e_i, and the other in the country of investment, f_j. Solving the system of equations (20) and (21) we obtain unique solutions for $e_i + f_i$ for all i, and for the foreign portfolio holdings. In this particular case the estimates are as follows

	$e_i + f_i$ (per cent)
US	-21.82
CAN	-3.16
UK	-32.00
JAP	3.68

Foreign portfolio holdings (%) investor's origin.

IO:	US	CAN	UK	JAP
CO:				
US		-6000	-5800	-4614
CAN	-1419		2088	2788
UK	-1026	-730		1812
JAP	2446	$+6751$	3744	

Note: IO = Investor's origin; CO = Country of investment.

Investor's portfolios contain unrealistically large short positions and consequently the estimates of the barriers are meaningless.

NOTES

* We would like to thank Professor Richard Brealey for his helpful comments.
1 We will use the terms 'cost' and 'tax' interchangeably.
2 Like Black they assume that costs are symmetric on short positions.
3 The ratio of the annual market return and the variance of the market return in the US for the period 1926–81 was 2.4 (Ibbotson and Sinquefield (1982)).
4 Table 8.7 is exactly equal to the transpose of Table 8.8 if the beta relative to the 'active' portfolio holdings of investor i in country j is equal to the equivalent beta of investor j investing in country i, for all j. 'Active' is defined as the part of i's portfolio which represents deviations from the world market portfolio.
5 Note that the overall level of the barriers is a linear function of the variances and covariances. For instance, if the variances and covariances were 10 per cent lower, then the estimates of the barriers would be 10 per cent lower.

REFERENCES

Adler, M. and B. Dumas (1984). 'International Portfolio Choice and Corporation Finance: A Survey.' *Journal of Finance*, **38**.
Black, F. (1974). 'International Capital Market Equilibrium with Investment Barriers.' *Journal of Financial Economics*, **1**.
Brealey, R. A., I. A. Cooper and E. Kaplanis (1985). 'Exchange Controls and Asset Returns: The Case of the Dollar Premium.' Unpublished paper.
Cooper, I. A. and D. R. Lessard (1981). 'International Capital Market Equilibrium with Deadweight Costs to Foreign Investment.' Unpublished paper.
Grauer, G. W. J., R. H. Litzenberger and R. Stehle (1976). 'Sharing Rules and Equilibrium in an International Capital Market under Uncertainty.' *Journal of Financial Economics*, **3**.
Ibbotson, R. and R. Sinquefield (1982). 'Stocks, Bonds, Bills and Inflation: The Past and the Future.' The Financial Analysts Research Foundation.
Sercu, P. (1980). 'A Generalization of the International Asset Pricing Model.' *Review of the French Finance Association*, **1**.
Solnik, B. H. (1974). 'Equilibrium in an International Capital Market.' *Journal of Economic Theory*, **8**.
Stulz, R. M. (1981). 'On the Effects of Barriers to International Investment.' *Journal of Finance*, **36**.